WRITERS ON WRITING
Jay Parini, Series Editor

A good writer is first a good reader. Looking at craft from the inside, with an intimate knowledge of its range and possibilities, writers also make some of our most insightful critics. With this series we will bring together the work of some of our finest writers on the subject they know best, discussing their own work and that of others, as well as concentrating on craft and other aspects of the writer's world.

Poet, novelist, biographer, and critic, Jay Parini is the author of numerous books, including *The Apprentice Lover* and *One Matchless Time: A Life of William Faulkner.* Currently he is D. E. Axinn Professor of English & Creative Writing at Middlebury College.

TITLES IN THE SERIES

Michael Collier
Make Us Wave Back: Essays on Poetry and Influence

Nancy Willard
The Left-Handed Story: Writing and the Writer's Life

Christopher Benfey
American Audacity: Literary Essays North and South

Ilan Stavans
A Critic's Journey

A Critic's Journey

A Critic's Journey

Ilan Stavans

The University of Michigan Press

Ann Arbor

Published in the United States of America by
The University of Michigan Press
Manufactured in the United States of America
♾ Printed on acid-free paper

2013   2012   2011   2010   4   3   2   1

A CIP catalog record for this book is available from the British Library.

Library of Congress Cataloging-in-Publication Data

Stavans, Ilan.
    A critic's journey / Ilan Stavans.
       p.   cm. — (Writers on writing)
    ISBN 978-0-472-11706-2 (cloth : alk. paper) — ISBN 978-0-472-
03382-9 (pbk. : alk. paper)
       1. Authorship.   2. American literature—Hispanic American
authors—History and criticism.   3. Spanish American literature—
History and criticism.   4. Literature—History and criticism—
Theory, etc.   I. Title.
    PS3619.T385C75   2010
    864'.64—dc22   2009024925

Contents

Who Owns the English Language?

⁓⊗⁓

I MIGHT JUST AS WELL start with the simplest of answers. In general, language—"the whole body of words and of methods of combination of words used by a nation or race," as the *OED* announces—has neither owners nor servants. Its metabolism is the result of a slow process of decantation, an edging that happens as a group makes choices. And English in particular, after Chinese the second most frequently used language in the globe, with roughly 500,000,000 speakers, more than half of those in the United States alone, has been extraordinarily elastic in its odyssey. That elasticity, more than any other quality, is proof that Shakespeare's tongue has no ownership. (If it can be said of the language to have an owner, that owner is the Bard.)

Of course, the truth, as always, is more complicated. Languages don't exist in a vacuum. They are at the mercy of the elements: social upheaval, politics, scientific and technological advance, fashion . . . They are constantly engaged in power struggles, not only vis-à-vis other languages but in their own metabolism. English is the perfect example. Such has become the growth and dissemination of English, the *lingua franca* of diplomacy, business, and entertainment, that not to speak it today implies to exist outside the current, in the margins of modernization, just like to be unacquainted with Latin in the Middle Ages and French in the Enlightenment entailed parochialism, maybe even barbarism. However, the question isn't only "Who speaks English?" but, more suitably, "Who speaks what English?" For among those half billion users there are emphatic differences in parlance, differences defined by class, ethnicity, and geography.

It's a cliché to say that ours is a time when verbal transactions occur at a speed at once fast and furious. Still, clichés are usable snippets of knowledge, and it might be useful to reflect on this one for a bit. If modernity is said to be defined by a leitmotif, that leitmotif is migration. Over the last one hundred years, the massive movement of people from one corner of the globe to another has been nothing short of astonishing. According to the Census Bureau, in the United States alone more than 38 percent of the population was born elsewhere. The map of Europe is also being redrawn along the same lines. In Africa, Asia, Oceania, and the Americas, famine, military turmoil, economic instability, and political repression push people out of their homes, displacing them, forcing them to find a more suitable habitat. From west to east, from south to north, people are constantly on the go. If one were allowed to travel to outer space and out of chronological time, zooming in—*sub specie aeternitatis,* as Spinoza proposed—on human resettlements since the Napoleonic wars, the vision one would get might resemble a busy ant colony. This is an abstract vision, though. The story of each individual immigrant is far more poignant, and more emblematic too. Not only is there an exchange of a person's landscape, external and internal, but the journey often requires the abandonment of the native language and the acquisition of an adopted one. Arrival and departure: how to express their impact in a foreign tongue?

Needless to say, an itinerant life isn't something new. From Gilgamesh to the Bible, from the Icelandic sagas to *Beowulf* and the *Chilam Balam,* the chronicle of a hero driven from one confine to another is a recurrent theme. These books might be about a fictitious character, but they also draw light on the patterns of history. The Phoenicians, the Scythians, the Huns, the Babylonians, the Greeks, the Romans, the Berbers, the Almohads, the Ottomans all rose as civilizations eager to dominate others, not only militarily but culturally. The Hebrew letters of the alphabet owe much to their Phoenician counterparts. The impact of Latin in the Old Continent gave place to the Romance languages. As a civilization interacts, traces of its DNA are transferred onto its neighbors. Once it disappears from the face of the earth, only those traces survive.

In terms of mobility, the difference today isn't about quality—after all, a displaced people, unique as they are, go through the same register of emotions—but about quantity. There are more people alive right now than ever before. In a single minute, that number will already be preposterous, since five babies are born every second. These babies arrive into a universe of instantaneous encounter. Language gives the illusion of fluidity. Radio, TV, telephone, and the Internet disseminate images—and words—ceaselessly, allowing them to have a wider impact, to become ubiquitous. It's an illusion, obviously, for not everyone is hooked. Access is defined by education: the difference between the haves and have-nots today is less about money than about synchronicity. Are you tuned in? Do you know what I know? And do we both know it at the same time? Those that are connected share not only the medium but a common language too. Viewers of CNN in Jakarta and Buenos Aires share one thing: they speak English. There are global news channels in Spanish, French, German, Russian, and Portuguese too, yet English has unparalleled gravitas. Simply put, it is the language in which news happen. Those unfamiliar with Shakespeare's tongue aren't left "in the dark," to use a common image, but they often get their information from other sources.

Strictly speaking, English isn't a universal language, yet it's as close as humans might get to one in the foreseeable future. The biblical myth of the Tower of Babel, in which, as a result of human presumption, the use of a single unifying tongue allowing everyone to understand each other is canceled by the Almighty, replaced by a plurality of codes, is more current today than in the past, except that today there are "on codes" and "off codes." The imperial languages—French, Spanish, English, Portuguese, German—forced in the age of colonialism beyond their own confines from the fifteenth century onward, are part of modernity, and English among them reigns as king.

Again, who speaks what English? It's impoverishing to think of language only as a vehicle of communication. It is also data bank, a depository of memory. It is stated in the introduction to the *OED* that there are some 900,000 different words in the language. An average American—and I should say I don't know who that creature is—uses a vocabulary of roughly 2,000 different words a day. Since they aren't in vogue, are the 898,000 remaining words worthless? On the contrary, they are a reminder of what is left unsaid in a single day. More significantly, they are the reservoir uniting us to our ancestors, the Vikings, the Celts, the Saxons, the Normans, among others. Take the word *cross*. It has Germanic and Latin origins. Since it doesn't appear in Old English until the tenth century, it might have been brought by the Vikings. Some have also argued that it has Scandinavian roots. Whatever the answer—and evidently the word, in its religious connotation, might be closer to Latin—the compendium of clues signals an abundance of ancestry. When we say *cross,* the ghosts of our past appear at the crossroad. In his *Journal of a Tour to the Hebrides,* Samuel Johnson says to his biographer James Boswell: "There is no tracing the connection of ancient nations, but by language; and therefore I am always sorry when any language is lost, because languages are the pedigree of nations."

The pedigree of nations. Do English speakers have a pedigree? Isn't it miraculous that in nations as proud of their origins as England, as diverse as the United States, with immigrants from every point of departure imaginable and technology at the cutting edge, and in places as heterogeneous as Australia, Canada, India, and New Zealand, let alone Jamaica, the Philippines, and Belize, the English language manages to survive as healthily as it does? How come it doesn't deteriorate rapidly as a result of over-exposure to outside influences, to loans, to slang, Creole, and patois? Some purists believe English is in a state of decay, but they are not only few and of the intransigent kind. They would love to have stricter regulatory forms established, a more demanding language education, maybe even an institution in charge of legislating what could be called "usage and abusage." The effort behind Johnson's *Dictionary of the English Language,* published in 1755, arguably the most idiosyncratic of lexicons ever produced, was a cleansing of foreign influences. "Every language has its anomalies," Johnson writes in the preface, "which, though inconvenient, and in themselves once unnecessary, must be tolerated among the imperfections of human things, and which require only to be registered, that they may not be increased, and ascertained, that they may not be confounded: but every language has likewise its improprieties and absurdities, which it is the duty of the lexicographer to correct or proscribe." And in an earlier piece in *The Rambler,* Johnson states: "I have laboured to refine our language to grammatical purity, and to clear it from colloquial barbarisms, licentious idioms, and irregular combinations."

I don't want to give a false impression of Doctor Johnson, to whom I devoted an entire chapter in *Dictionary Days* and who is one of my idols. He was neither rigid nor dogmatic. His dream to purify English from excesses ought to be seen against the backdrop of eighteenth-century London, where the influence of Gallicisms needed to be addressed for national reasons. Interestingly, Johnson never requested the formation of a British equivalent to the Academie françoise. Others in his country have entertained such an idea, among them Daniel Defoe, thinking that, in spite—or perhaps because—of individual efforts of epic proportions such as Johnson's, it is simply too dangerous to leave the well-being of a language to a populace as entrepreneurial and moody as English speakers the world over. Defoe, the author of *The Life and Strange Surprising Adventures of Robinson Crusoe, of York, Mariner, as Related by Himself,* believes, as argued in an essay called "On Academies" of 1697, that "the Voice of this Society should be sufficient Authority for the Usage of Words, and sufficient also to expose the Innovations of other mens Fancies; they shou'd preside with a sort of Judicature over the Learning of the Age, and have liberty to Correct the Exorbitance of writers, especially the Translators." Amazing, isn't it? Defoe thought it useful to correct writers and translators. Would Joyce ever have come to existence? Henry Roth? Richard Wright? Defoe is clear-cut: "The reputation of this Society," he adds, "wou'd be enough to make them the allo'd judges of Stile and Language; and no Author wou'd have the imprudence to Coin without their Authority." As Yiddish speakers say: *oy, oy, oy* . . .

Jonathan Swift also thought English would go to the dogs. In a letter of 1712 to the Earl of Oxford, he states: "My Lord; I do here, in the

Name of all the Learned and Polite Persons in the Nation, complain to Your Lordship, as First Minister, that our Language is extremely imperfect; that its daily Improvements are by no means in proportion to its daily Corruptions; that the Pretenders to polish and refine it, have chiefly multiplied Abuses and Absurdities; and, that in many instances, it offends against every Part of Grammar." Swift would write to newspapers and members of Parliament asking them, as he did to Isaac Bickerstaff in *The Tatler,* to "Make Us of your Authority as Censor, and by an Annual *Index Expurgatorium* expunge all Words and Phrases that are offensive to good Sense, and condemn those barbarous Mutilations of vowels and syllables."

Honestly, I too puzzle about an academy. Spain has its own Real Academia de la Lengua, Italy the Accademia della Crusca, and modern Hebrew *ha-academia lelashon ha-ivrit,* among other examples. These institutions, funded at times by a monarchy, other times by taxpayers, are endowed with the responsibility of safeguarding the language. The one in Madrid was established in 1719, after the French model. Spain in the eighteenth century was in charge of colonies that extended from Idaho to La Plata and onward to the Pacific. Spanish was the unifier of a large mass of people, but it was clear there were linguistic differences: in Mexico, the influence of Nahuatl and other pre-Columbian sources impacted the way people used the language; in Puerto Rico it was Taino, in Paragua Guaraní. Already in 1492, the same year Columbus sailed the ocean blue, Antonio de Nebrija, the first Spanish grammarian, defined the language—the same one that originated in Castile and, with La Reconquista, became, along with Catholicism, a national unifier—as "compañera del imperio," language as a companion of empire.

To this day, the motto of the Real Academia de la Lengua is *limpia, fija y da esplendor*—clean, fix and give splendor. It sounds like a soap commercial. It isn't an accident that 1492 is also the year when Ferdinand of Aragón and Isabel of Castile, the Catholic king and queen, expelled the Jews from the Iberian Peninsula. Just as Spain was embarking in full on an age of exploration and colonization, it submerged itself in a process of defining its collective identity. That collective identity was as much about inclusion as about exclusion. The Jews and Arabs—the latter would also be expelled some years later—were unwelcome. After long and fruitful if also tense and bellicose centuries of what is known as La Convivencia–the cohabitation of the three religions Judaism, Islam, and Catholicism—splendor could only come by cleansing the nation of the first two. The Spanish Inquisition might have attempted to eliminate traces of *los indeseables,* but to this day the language retains their DNA. Just as there are numerous words *en español* of those fought by the conquistadors in the New World (*canoa, accumulate, malachite*), the catalog of Arabic, and to a lesser extent Hebrew, terms is substantial: *almohada, zanahoria, almacén,* even the ever-present *hola,* an invocation of Ala. Again, language as remembrance. Superficially, you might eliminate those you dislike, but their legacy is in your heart.

Presently the main project of the Real Academia de la Lengua is the republication, in revised, expanded editions, of its official dictionary. Employing the help of branches across the Americas, the matrix in Madrid collects words—called *voces*—and proceeds to deem them acceptable, e.g., correct. Nevertheless, it would be a mistake to approach the endeavor as democratic. Indeed, for centuries there have been accusations of racism, colonialism, and other misguided conceptions. The vast majority of *voces* in the dictionary come from the peninsula. For an Americanism to make it to the illustrious pages of the *DLE,* the acronym for the *Diccionario de la Lengua Española,* it might take a decade, sometimes more, to travel from say Managua, Nicaragua, to the royal offices across the Atlantic, be pondered and ultimately given the imprimatur of legitimacy, by which time it probably will have fallen into disuse in its place of origin. This explains the large amount of Americanisms not included in the *DLE.* Gabriel García Márquez, the author of *One Hundred Years of Solitude,* once counted the number of synonyms for *penis* used in Quito, Ecuador: more than one hundred. How many of these are registered in the *DLE:* two. And then there are the blunders. Recently, the *Diccionario Panhispánico de Dudas,* released under the auspices of the Real Academia de la Lengua, stated that the *gentilicio* for those dwellers living in Mexico City is *mexiqueño.* This came as a surprise to the more than twenty million *defeños, chilangos,* and *capitalinos,* myself included. Not a single one I know, not one, has ever used *mexiqueño* to describe him- or herself. Not *mexicano* but *mexiqueño,* like *oaxaqueño* and *acapulqueño.* I regret being the conveyor of bad news: according to the Madrid academy, we unfortunately have no clue who we are.

After you've wandered the metropolitan streets in the Spanish-speaking world, listened to rock bands like Café Tacuba, and read novels like *La guaracha del Macho Camacho,* you realize the Real Academia de la Lengua doesn't really matter. That is a false impression, though. In spite of its limited impact, it is unquestionable that the institution serves as a type of levee: it reminds people that a language, in order to survive, needs to retain a sense of propriety, a center of gravity. In other words, experimenting too much might push users into the abyss. And what is the abyss? Let me ponder this question in the context of Shakespeare's tongue, especially in the United States, a country with a surplus of "foreign" languages yet always nurturing delusive dreams of monolingualism. The issue of how English is spoken and by whom is a recurrent theme since the early days of the Republic. John Adams, in a letter to the president of Congress dated September 1780, alarmed by the deterioration of speech, recommended the creation of an institution like the Academie françoise. "This I should admire," Adams says. "England will never more have any honor, excepting now and then that of imitating the Americans. I assure you, Sir, I am not altogether in jest. I see a general inclination after English in France, Spain and Holland, and it may extend throughout Europe. The population and commerce of America will force their language into general use." Adams suggested that the role of the academy would be to nurse and police the language. He saw it as "refining, improving, and ascertaining." He and his son John Quincy eventually established the American Academy of Language and Belle Lettres in New York, expanding its horizon into the arts. Its president was John Quincy Adams, and its constitution stated its mission thus: "To collect, interchange, and diffuse literary intelligence; to promote the purity and uniformity of the English language; to invite a correspondence with distinguished scholars in other countries speaking this language in connection with ourselves; to cultivate throughout our extensive territory a friendly intercourse among those who feel an interest in the progress of American literature, and, as far as may depend on well meant endeavors, to aid the general course of learning in the United States."

The responsibility of preserving the language was echoed in 1828 by Noah Webster, a rigorous yet most innovative codifier. "Language is the expression of ideas," he declares in *American Dictionary of the English Language,* "and if the people of our country cannot preserve an identity of ideas, they cannot retain an identity of language." Nathaniel Hawthorne, in his *American Notebooks,* states his belief that language "after all is but little better than the croak and cackle of fowls, and other utterances of brute nature,—sometimes no so adequate." Happily, not everyone has been pessimistic. In the fourth edition, made in 1947, of *The American Language,* a sort of bible for English-language lovers, H. L. Mencken says: "The notion that anything is gained by fixing a language in a groove is cherished only by pedants." The making of a federally funded American Academy of the English Language is utterly unneeded. There is, sure, a Philological Society. There are also private institutions, from university centers devoted to the study of American English, to publishing houses in charge of updating Noah Webster's lexicon and other major dictionaries, such as Random House, Houghton Mifflin, Encarta, and the Oxford American. The one released by the Real Academia de la Lengua in Madrid is normative—i.e., its objective is to establish a norm. The ones I've just listed for English in the United States, and equally so their inspiration, the *OED*, aren't normative but descriptive: rather than telling people how to use the language, they explain how words are employed. Do they serve as an instrument of authority? No doubt they do. Yet this instrument finds its power not in handing down rules but in elucidating and enunciating popular patterns.

In the past decade, I've devoted a substantial portion of my attention to the study of Spanglish, the interface between the tongues of Shakespeare and Cervantes. My research has led me to numerous countries. However, for understandable reasons I've concentrated on this vernacular in the United States. There are more than forty-two million Latinos in this nation. Some have been American citizens forever, their roots traceable to the Treaty of Guadalupe Hidalgo, signed at the conclusion of the Mexican-American War, in 1848, selling a large portion of Mexico (almost the entire Southwest, as the territories are known today) to the United States. Others have been here a month, a week, a day, or maybe are just arriving. The language they speak is a *mishmash*—it's a Hebrew term: they engage in code-switching and code-mixing, in the reconfiguration of syntax, in daring grammatical propositions, in simultaneous and automatic translation, and in the coining of fresh terms, sometimes based on cognate relations, sometimes on phonetic appropriation, like *estresado, liquiar, sofacón, kennedito,* and *washatería.*

Spanglish isn't unique. Other immigrant groups to the United States have indulged in a similar effort. There have been such phenomena as Finglish, Yinglish, and Chinglish. All of them are natural responses to language contact. In the process of acquiring English, for a while newcomers might resort to juxtaposing their original language with the one welcoming them to these shores. After a couple of generations, this mechanism loses steam, allowing Shakespeare's tongue—a better image here might be Walt Whitman's tongue—to take over. The difference with Spanglish is that, after two, three, four, even five and six generations, this middle step in the acquisition of English doesn't disappear. Instead, in response to ceaseless immigration, the geographical closeness to the place immigrants once called home, and the explosive demographic growth of this minority group, the phenomenon is actually gaining strength. Corporations, media outlets, universities, even the military, have begun not only to endorse but to invest in Spanglish. In the arts, the manifestations of this new *mestizaje* are plentiful: novels are being written in it, movies and TV shows are made, and hip-hop, rap, salsa, *merengue,* and *regatón* musicians are embracing it. Even politicians are using it on the campaign trail and in office.

Even though there is a feeling of pride among Spanglish speakers, I often come across pejorative portraits of them. They are described as pollutants, illiterates, barbarians, and downright idiots. A few Spanglish speakers are bilingual (Spanish and Spanglish, English and Spanglish), others are monolingual (speaking only Spanglish), and a third entity is trilingual (Spanish, English, and Spanglish). Is their use of language a symptom of laziness? The idea is absurd. Its users are often concerned with sheer survival, having to juggle three, even four jobs to support their families. Are they guilty for not attending school? In the last few years, I've also come across thousands of Spanglish speakers whose use of the language isn't driven only by necessity but by choice. It has become cool to speak Spanglish!

My investigations in this realm have led me to ponder issues of marginality. To what extent is Spanglish affecting the way English is spoken? And what about Spanish? It strikes me that, when one looks at the history of the United States through the prism of language, the dialectics between inclusion and inclusion offer a syncopated rhythm across epochs. Even though there have often been cries of desperation, Whitman's tongue has never been at peril in our nation. Through legislative and pedagogical efforts, its status has always been uncontested. As long as Americans perceive themselves as a nation, this is as it should be. After all, English is our great equalizer. It is our responsibility as teachers to instruct our students as properly as possible. It falls on us to invite them to appreciate its beauty and magnificence as amply as our faculties allow. With a caveat . . . The language of Edgar Allan Poe and Elizabeth Bishop, Harriet Beecher Stowe and Edmund Wilson, William Carlos Williams and Zora Neale Hurston, Junot Díaz and Jhumpa Lahiri, is extraordinarily malleable. Every generation inherits the data bank. Its task is twofold: to digest it and also to reconfigure it. Each of us manipulates the language, deforms and reforms it. In so doing, we reclaim it as our own. Regardless of our ethnic background, Finglish, Yinglish, Chinglish, Spanglish are part of us, just as Ebonics, also known as Black English, isn't only black: it is American.

An Austrian-Jewish philosopher who lived in England, Ludwig Wittgenstein, in *Tractatus Logico-Philosophicus* of 1921, announces: "What can be said at all can be said clearly." I use this sentence as the epigraph to *Dictionary Days.* What I left out, and what I now reinstate, is that the sentence has two halves. The second half states: "whereof one cannot speak thereof one must be silent." In the privacy of my mind, I often find myself wrestling with Wittgenstein. I agree with him: we have at our disposal a set of grammatical rules and a rich vocabulary; it depends on us to use these clearly. The *OED* includes dozens of definitions of *clear,* related to light, the weather, morality, intelligence, skin color, etc. The one pertaining to words says—quite clearly, I should add—"easy to understand, fully intelligible, free from obscurity of sense, perspicuous." To speak and think clearly is to articulate ideas purely and convincingly, without obfuscation. It isn't an easy task: to state one's thoughts clearly one needs to learn to polish them. One also needs to trust oneself. Plus, one needs to make the language a full partner in our enterprise, not an enemy.

If a standard-English user can speak clearly, so can a Spanglish user. Elsewhere in the *Tractatus Logico-Philosophicus,* Wittgenstein categorically declares: "The limits of my language mean the limits of my world." Are the limits of my language the ones recorded exhaustively, and exhaustingly, in official dictionaries? In compiling lexicons—and I've done my fair share—their makers, I've come to conclude, inadvertently produce a double: on the reverse of the dictionary of available words is another one, nonexistent yet equally compelling, with all the words left out of it. Those exiled words belong to the unspeakable. And what is the unspeakable? In the last chapter of *Dictionary Days,* I reflect on it, arguing that there is a realm beyond all human language to which we don't have access, the realm beyond the limits of our world. That realm I call *the impossible.* But right now I'm not concerned with the impossible but with the shades of the possible. There isn't one English but many: youth English, immigrant English, ghetto English . . . Some of these possibilities diverge from the norm to such an extent as to become dialects. Yet clarity in them is still a quality. So is beauty.

Rebellion and consent: the health of a language is measured by the tension between its normative center and the extremes to which some of its speakers sometimes drift. In the case of English, there is no tyranny at the core. If you want to speak Spanglish, go ahead. No institution is in charge of cleaning, fixing, and giving splendor to our parlance. No one may draft an edict of expulsion, eliminating the polluters and other undesirables. Or might they? The spread of Spanish in the United States, and more recently the emergence of Spanglish as a legitimate form of communication, have incensed the conservative base. One response among others has been the formation of the English Only and English First movements. These, as I see them, are natural reactions to change. Xenophobia is a fixture of our environment since our inception as a nation. And again, the tension in language between the normative and the experimental serves as a thermometer. So long as neither side takes the approach of the Holy Office of the Inquisition, or the Balkanization of regions according to manner of speech, the country is in fine shape.

I now return to my original question. Who owns English? The answer is daunting: each and every one of us does. History proves that it is of the people, by the people, and for the people. Can a language have so many masters? It's too late to ask. There is, indeed, a tyranny of the many, a fact that infuriates those who feel territorial about it. In the end, it is an individual responsibility to protect it. It is also up to us, alone and together, to set it free, to keep it as elastic as ever, in a permanent state of fluidity. To put English in a glass box, away from the barbaric hordes, is to turn it into a fetish. It is the masses, precisely, who know best how to handle it. That, at least, is the lesson to be learned from the nation's past. The erudite and the non-native, the purist and the slang-dunker, have an equal stake in it.

English is our past and future. How we handle it defines us. Taste it, test it, claim your shared ownership of it!

The Translators of the *Quixote*

DON QUIXOTE IS A BOOK FOR ALL SEASONS: esteemed, even venerated by millions, but maddening in its length and contradictions, the constant target of attacks. The opinions it has generated throughout history are plentiful. Lord Byron believed Cervantes had "smiled Spain's chivalry away," while art critic John Ruskin perceived the novel as "a deadly work." The Czech writer Milan Kundera maintains that "Cervantes is the founder of the Modern Era" and that "the novelist need answer to no one but Cervantes." The German cultural critic Walter Benjamin infers that Don Quixote, "*the man with a single conviction . . .* , teaches us that in this, the best or worst of all conceivable worlds (except that this world is inconceivable), the conviction that stories of chivalry are true can make a whipped fool happy, if it is his only conviction."

Likewise, Lionel Trilling asserted that "it can be said that all prose is a variation on the theme of *Don Quixote*," yet Vladimir Nabokov squabbled that seldom has an author been as cruel to his character, although he also recommended that we "do our best to avoid the fatal error of looking for so-called 'real life' in novels." Nabokov added: "Let us not try and reconcile the fiction of facts with the facts of fiction. *Don Quixote* is a fairy tale, so is *Bleak House,* so is *Dead Souls. Madame Bovary* and *Anna Karenina* are supreme fairy tales. Without those fairy tales the world would not be real."

And if the story of the responses to *Don Quixote* isn't sufficiently fecund, its adventure in translation is proof of its vitality, but also of the acrimony it has left on its path. Of course, translating a classic, any classic, ends up generating enough rage for at least a fistfight, if not to mobilize an army. It is the equivalent of dressing up a traditional bride in a new wedding dress. Will it be appropriate? Does it make her look svelte? Is it fitting with her personality? Judging by the frequency with which translators actualize a centuries-old narrative and publishers reintroduce it through savvy marketing strategies to contemporary readers, the endeavor is rather attractive.

Take the Bible as an example. About a dozen full-fledged renditions have appeared since World War II, by, among other luminaries, Everett Fox and Robert Alter. The King James Version, released almost four hundred years ago, is still the runaway bestseller. The fact that it is still marketed as the "authorized" version (by no other than the Church of England, an institution with arguably little standing outside the United Kingdom today) doesn't appear to deter anyone. Without putting as much as a dent in the embrace the King James cadre of translators continues to receive, each of the fresh new versions sells thousands of copies, not bad at all, especially at a time when the act of reading is going through a disheartening crisis.

Surely I'm talking here about *the* book par excellence of Western Civilization. However, other less controversial recently translated classics also garnish a generous degree of enthusiasm. Anybody interested in delving into Tolstoy's *War and Peace* today has alternative means of entry, from the standard Aylmer Maude translation to the justly celebrated joint effort of Richard Pevear and Larissa Volokhonsky, which was published in 2007. While Russian readers have only one Tolstoy, we in English have a plethora. Which of the two languages is richer in its Tolstoyan tradition? The original is immovable: its words are set forever. Instead, all translations are guesses. But in the modern world translation is an unavoidable task, and when in the dark, most people are fine with a guess.

After all, we live in the age of relativism. There are no absolute truths. And while an original text has the advantage of being the source, the endless copies it generates are forms of interpretation, which is, in the end, what literature is about. No one would dare to tinker with the fixed Latin of the *Aeneid*. But compare the first sentence of Robert Fagles' and Sarah Ruden's performances and you'll realize the extent to which translators are creators. In fact, if anyone dares one day to embark on a retranslation of Virgil's epic in dactylic hexameter back from one of its English versions to the original Latin, I suspect the result would be utterly unrecognizable to Virgilian connoisseurs. And can a translation be better than the original? Well, when the original language isn't available to the reader, the translation is surely better. Actually not really better, but *the only way* to access a classic.

I am often at the receiving end of a litany from sophisticated readers who complain that the book industry in New York has little interest in translation of classic and commercial titles. Publishers say that translations of contemporary works into English are few and far between because English-language readers are a proud pod that doesn't like to read in translation, which explains why so few new translations are done every year. People, in turn, say that the limited sales of books in translation are a result of our provincial worldview (at its center, the empire is always parochial) and that if publishers made a legitimate effort to release more new translations, that provinciality would decrease. It's the chicken-or-egg conundrum. This, from a language with a long-standing obsession with translation. Think of the Homer translations by Alexander Pope, Edward FitzGerald, and Matthew Arnold, to name but a triptych of controversial practitioners. Still, when compared to other European-based tongues (French, Dutch, Spanish, and Portuguese), the English-language publishing industry is enviably vibrant. Shakespeare's language has been a global vehicle of communication for the better part of a millennium. What gets published in it today sets standards worldwide. There are several full-fledged renditions of *Madame Bovary* into Spanish, but, by my own estimation, not nearly as many as those available in English—to use conservative numbers, half a dozen, by translators like Stephen Heath, Mildred Marmur, Francis Steegmuler, and Eleanor Marx Aveling. Reading them in collated fashion, as I've done recently, is both a treat and a threat, an endless form of joy as well as a machine of displeasure. Is it really Flaubert who is behind them all?

I can't think of a more rancorous translation surfeit, a fiesta of larger possibilities, than the multiplications in English of *Don Quixote,* by far my favorite book. It is an inexhaustible study of human frailties, an open novel about friendship, love, liberty and censorship, about pursuing one's own dreams, about reading and mental illness, about class struggle, about the power of the imagination and the absurdities of old age, about choosing between a soldier's and a writer's life. It is, in my estimation, a secular Bible: everything about the so-called enlightened society is contained in it. I've reread the volume countless times and have reached the conclusion that the universe was created with *Don Quixote* as one of its fixtures. Without it, life would feel incomplete.

As the narrator repeatedly tells us, what we're reading isn't the original but a translation of a manuscript by an Arab historian, Cide Hamete Benengeli. In addition, Don Quixote, during a visit to a printer in Barcelona in chapter LXII of the second part, says to Sancho Panza that "translating from one language to another, unless it is from Greek to Latin, the queens of all languages, is like looking at Flemish tapestries from the wrong side, for although the figures are visible, they are covered by threads that obscure them, and cannot be seen with the smoothness and color of the right side." Then, also in the second part of Cervantes' novel, the protagonists, Don Quixote and his squire, react to villagers who have read the first part, and, similarly, are furious when they find out that an impostor—an author by the pseudonym of Alonso Fernández de Avellaneda, a mysterious Aragonese author who was an admirer of Lope de Vega, a famous playwright and rival of Cervantes— published, in 1614, an apocryphal second part that diminishes the quality of Cervantes' effort. In other words, the characters in the book are perfectly aware of their nature as literary creations available only—for better or worse—in translation.

I've counted eighteen different complete English versions, although some might exist under the radar. No other classic has been revamped as often into Shakespeare's tongue, and, yes, as atrociously. What a gang of divergent souls Cervantes' translators are: postmen, surgeons, linguists, painters, playwrights, poets, journalists, teachers, scholars, editors, collectors, naughty craftsmen, and downright plagiarists. There are rumors that at least one didn't even know Spanish.

James Fitzmaurice-Kelly, once a professor of Spanish language and literature at the University of Liverpool, and a prolific editor, translator, and biographer of Cervantes, persuasively showed that the British were the first in a "foreign country to mention *Don Quixote,* the first to translate the book [followed by the French, the Germans, and the Italians], the first . . . in Europe to present it decently garbed in its native tongue, the first to provide a biography of [its author], the first to publish a commentary on [the novel], and the first to issue a critical edition of the text."

The first of two parts of *Don Quixote,* published in Madrid in 1605, appeared in Shakespeare's tongue in 1612, translated as *The delightfull history of the wittie knight, Don Quiskote* by Thomas Shelton. (The complete title of the novel keeps on changing from one translation to another.) As a critic in 1613 put it, the "venerableness" of his style, "the rich and easy eloquence with which it steals on the soul, are such as no modern language can equal." It has been suggested that Shelton might have known Cervantes personally, since he traveled to Spain, but no proof has emerged. The second part, which, after an interval of a decade, Cervantes released in 1615, the year before his death, was completed by Shelton in 1616. In his dedication, Shelton, a personal-letter carrier from England to Dublin, explained that he had translated the novel for a friend who didn't know Spanish, in a period of forty days, no doubt an astonishing time, even by our fast-speed, impatient standards. He didn't use the original edition, but a 1607 version of *Don Quixote* issued in Brussels.

Fitzmaurice-Kelly is also right about the assiduity of quotations: unquestionably, references to the knight's odyssey have been ubiquitous in English from the eighteenth century on, showing up in the works of Ben Jonson, Henry Fielding, Samuel Johnson, Addison and Steele, Laurence Sterne, Washington Irving, Cotton Mather, Thomas Morton, Herman Melville, Mark Twain, William Faulkner, Ernest Hemingway, Graham Greene, V. S. Naipaul, and Salman Rushdie, to offer a succinct list. And then there is the inevitable question about the Bard: did Shakespeare read the novel, at least its first part? The answer is the subject of some polemics, for while Shakespeare knew little Spanish, Shelton's translation was released a few years before Shakespeare died, which was within days of Cervantes' own demise. All this to say that while it might seem preposterous to suggest that the fanciful adventures of *Don Quixote* are far richer in English than in Spanish, the proof is in the pudding. Some of Shelton's successors accused him of inaccuracy, especially when it came to rendering Sancho Panza's proclivity for using proverbs to convey his thoughts.

In 1687, John Phillips, one of John Milton's nephews and the author of an attack on Oliver Cromwell and Puritanism, translated Cervantes' novel. His critics—and they are plentiful—contend his work is barely an approximation. Phillips didn't use the Spanish original. He based it, as was his custom in general, on a French translation by Filleau de Saint-Martin. The effect is like drinking fresh water from a plastic bottle. Unsurprisingly, Samuel Putnam, himself a translator of the novel, who in my estimation has produced one of the best English-language renditions, called it the worst English translation ever made of a famous novel.

Among the most famous renditions is that of Peter Anthony (a.k.a. Pierre Antoine) Motteux, published in 1700. A native of Rouen, the birthplace of Flaubert, Motteux, who moved to England after the revocation of the Edict of Nantes and was editor of the *Gentleman's Journal,* believed in the spirit of the novel, if not in its body. In his own words, his translation of *Don Quixote* was done "from the original by many hands." Reading it against Shelton's version makes the reader think that Motteux was an inspired borrower of other people's talent. He tends to make subtle fun of the characters. And his English frequently sounds like French Cockney. John Ormsby, himself the author of the respectable 1885 translation, called Motteux's "worse than worthless." Still, it was reprinted several times before it entered the public domain, and on innumerable occasions since then. Eager to make a buck, publishers couldn't care less about its dubious quality.

Charles Jervas, an Irish painter and collector whose name was typographically misspelled as "Jarvis," and whose portrait of Swift is in London's National Portrait Gallery, enjoyed calling attention to Motteux's errors. His posthumous translation, released with what appears to be the first introduction about Cervantes and his work, is, in my opinion, more trustworthy, although Alexander Pope, a onetime friend, purportedly remarked, perfidiously, that Jarvis "translated *Don Quixote* without understanding Spanish."

Tobias Smollett, the author of the novels *Humphrey Clinker* and *Roderick Random,* translated the novel in 1755. Carlos Fuentes generously called this version "the homage of a novelist to a novelist." My opinion is far more radical: Smollett's translation is an abomination. Not only does he take liberties with Cervantes' text, but in several places the reader has the feeling—as Don Quixote himself says to Sancho about translation in chapter 62 of part two—of looking at a Flemish carpet from the back. Smollett hides his manipulation behind a facade of originality. In a translator's note, he claims his aim

> was to maintain that ludicrous solemnity and self-importance by
> which the inimitable Cervantes has distinguished the character of
> Don Quixote, without raising him to the insipid rank of a dry
> philosopher, or debasing him to the melancholy circumstances
> and unentertaining caprice of an ordinary madman; and to pre-
> serve the native humor of Sancho Panza, from degenerating into
> mere proverbial phlegm, or affected buffoonry. He has endeav-
> ored to retain the spirit and ideas, without servilely adhering to the
> literal expression, of the original; from which, however, he has not
> so far deviated, as to destroy the formality of idiom, so peculiar to
> the Spaniards, and so essential to the character of the work.

Smollett, expectedly, was accused of taking too many liberties. A revised version appeared in 1761.

The parade of renditions includes uneven efforts by John Stevens (1700), George Kelley (1769), T. T. Shore (1864), Henry Edward Watts (1888), and Robinson Smith (1910). Each has had the work of his predecessors at his disposal, for both inspiration and pillaging. At times a previous translation, perhaps in the public domain, was slightly edited and then reprinted under a new translator's name.

Released in 1961, the version by J. M. Cohen, an editor at Penguin Books in England and an authority on Spanish and Latin American letters, strikes me as lacking ambiguity. And what is ambiguity if not richness? In fact, Cohen replaces ambiguity with howlers, at one point describing someone as "a sow-gelder," which Shelton also does. Burton Raffel, a professor at the University of Southwestern Louisiana and also a prolific translator (his bibliography includes translations of *Beowulf* and works by Rabelais and Balzac), makes Cervantes' hero more industrious, less starkly opposed to the circumstances in which he lives. A dramatic change occurs between Motteux and Raffel: in the Renaissance, Don Quixote is laughed at as a loony; then the Romantic Movement turns him into a champion of individualism; finally, postindustrial capitalism strikes a balance by making the individual and society equally potent adversaries.

For a long time, the translation I liked the most was by Samuel Putnam, who was educated at the University of Chicago and at the Sorbonne, wrote among other books *Paris Was Our Mistress: Memoirs of a Lost and Found Generation* (what is it among *Don Quixote* translators into English that they are so close to the French?), and was the father of the American philosopher Hilary Whitehall Putnam. Penguin brought out Putnam's version in 1949. To my knowledge, the most serious—and suggestive—examination of it, by way of comparing its qualities with previous translations, was done by the British *homme de lettres* V. S. Pritchett. Pritchett's review, included in his *Complete Collected Essays,* released in 1991, is a bit capricious: he mentions Jarvis only in passing and altogether omits Phillips, and others. Still, it is worth quoting him at length:

> In the scene at the inn with Maritornes and the muleteer, and in the chapter following, Motteux, Jervas, and Cohen—to take only three—are superior in vigor to Mr. Putnam, whose colloquial phrases have a citified smoothness from easy over-use. To give an example: Don Quixote is about to reveal that the daughter of the supposed Castilian had come to him in the night, but stops to make Sancho swear that he will tell no one about this until after the Knight is dead, for he will not allow anyone's honour to be damaged. Sancho replies, without tact, that he swears, but hopes that he will be free to reveal the secret tomorrow, on the grounds that: "It's just that I'm opposed to keeping things too long—I don't like them to spoil on my hands."

> Both Motteux and Cohen stick closer to the more vigorous original image. The Spanish word is "go mouldy" or even "rot," and not "spoil." Literally "go mouldy on me." In [an] earlier chapter one can catch Motteux adding direct, eighteenth-century animal coarseness when Cervantes is not coarse at all; in fact, *Don Quixote* is unique in picaresque literature in its virtual freedom from obscenity, except in some of the oaths. When Maritornes rushes to Sancho's bed to hide there from her angry master, Motteux writes: "The wench . . . fled for shelter to Sancho's sty, where he lay snoring to some tune; there she pigged in and lay snug as an egg."

> This is picturesque, but it has arisen from the mistranslation of two words in the text. Possibly it is an improvement on Cervantes

who wrote merely that "she went to Sancho's bed and curled up in a ball." Mr. Putnam's pedantry spoils his accuracy here for, instead of "ball," he writes, "ball of yarn." The objection to Motteux is that in making Cervantes picturesque and giving him Saxon robustness, he endangers the elegance and the finely drawn out subtleties of the original. Motteux was half-way to Smollet [*sic*], which is a long way from Cervantes.

By the end of the twentieth century and the beginning of the twenty-first, the quality standards of translation were notably higher. The work of John Rutherford (2000), Edith Grossman (2003), and Tom Lathrop (2005) is proof of it. Given the multiplicity of interpretations, it isn't advisable to suggest that a single English translation of *Don Quixote* is the best. I prefer to compare them—that is, to keep them *all* at my side. I believe the true spirit of Cervantes' novel is to be found not by subtraction but by addition. Still, in the last few years I've fallen in love with Grossman's version (she is the only woman in the bunch), which I reviewed for the *Los Angeles Times* when it was first published.

Grossman's mission is inspiring: to leave aside the idea that Cervantes is a relic and, instead, to make him our contemporary. "[Cervantes'] writing is a marvel," she writes in a translator's note. "It gives off sparks and flows like honey. Cervantes' style is so artful it seems absolutely natural and inevitable; his irony is sweet-natured, his sensibility sophisticated, compassionate, and humorous. If my translation works at all, the reader should keep turning the pages, smiling a good deal, periodically bursting into laughter, and impatiently waiting for the next synonym (Cervantes delighted in accumulating synonyms, especially descriptive ones, within the same phrase), the next mind-bending coincidence, the next variation on the structure of Don Quixote's adventures, the next incomparable conversations between the knight and the squire." I disagree with Grossman that Cervantes is such an accomplished stylist. In fact, he's careless and repetitive (and would have benefited from a tightening editor). Among other things, the name of Sancho's wife keeps on changing: Juana Panza, Mari Gutierrez, Juana Gutierrez, Teresa Cascajo, and Teresa Panza. And Sancho's donkey (*el rucio*) disappears at one point without a trace only to reappear later on without explanation. Cervantes himself makes fun of these inconsistencies (one of the most astonishing aspects of *Don Quixote,* in my eyes, is the way in which it incorporates literary criticism—softly, engagingly—into the story), but that doesn't altogether streamline the bumps in the narrative.

Needless to say, the word *masterpiece* isn't a synonym of perfect.

There are numerous flips, malapropisms, detours, and infelicities in them. What makes the translations superior is the symmetry between form and content. More than anything else, what makes them an endless source of curiosity is the way they connect with readers across time. Grossman makes Cervantes look good. What else can an author wish for from a translator?

It is logical, at this point, to embark on an exercise of comparison of available translations. Herein a quotation in the original followed by four translations, listed chronologically, of a handful of lines in part 1, chapter 38, in which Don Quixote discusses the pen and the sword, e.g., the difference between military and literary affairs:

CERVANTES:
Estoy por decir que en el alma me pesa de haber tomado este ejercicio de caballero andante en edad tan detestable como es esta en que ahora vivimos; porque a mí ningún peligro me pone miedo, todavía me pone recelo pensar si la pólvora y el estaño me han de quitar la ocasión de hacerme famoso y conocido por el valor de mi brazo y filos de mi espada, por todo lo descubierto de la tierra. Pero haga el cielo lo que fuese servido.

MOTTEUX:
I could almost say I am sorry at my Heart for having taken upon me this profession of a Knight-Errant, in so detestable an Age; for tho' no Danger daunts me, yet it affects me to think, whether Powder or Lead may not deprive me of the Opportunity of Becoming Famous, and making myself known throughout the World by the Strength of my Arm and Dint of my Sword. But let Heaven order Matters as it Pleases.

JARVIS:
I could almost say I repent of having undertaken this profession of knight-errantry, in so detestable an age as this in which we live; for though no danger can daunt me, still it gives me some concern, to think that powder and lead may chance to deprive me of the opportunity of becoming famous and renowned, by the valor of my arm and edge of my sword, over the face of the whole earth. But Heaven's will be done.

COHEN:
It grieves me to the heart to have adopted this profession of knight errantry in such a detestable age as we now live in. For although no danger frightens me, still it causes me misgivings to

think that powder and lead may deprive me of the chance of winning fame and renown by the strength of my arm and the edge of my sword, over all the known earth. But let Heaven do what it will.

GROSSMAN:
When I consider this, I am prepared to say that it grieves my very soul that I have taken up the profession of knight errant in an age as despicable as the one we live in now, for although no danger can cause me to fear, it still fills me with misgivings to think that powder and tin may deprive me of the opportunity to become famous and renowned throughout the known world for the valor of my arm and the sharp edge of my sword. But God's will be done, for I shall be more highly esteemed, if I succeed in my purpose, for having confronted greater dangers and any faced by the knights errant of old.

Not only does each translator insert another degree of subjectivity. They also improvise within the parameters of Cervantes' prose. It pleases me to think that these renditioners, as conduits of the sensibility of their respective age, have turned Don Quixote into an excuse. Whereas Motteux and Jarvis are British Romantics, Cohen is down to earth, and Grossman makes him a deliciously postmodern American hodgepodge.

A classic, Mark Twain once argued, is "a book which people praise and don't read." Except for its translators, of course, who not only read but revise it imaginatively, at times dreaming of supplanting the author himself. Proof of this is the throng of Quixote innovators.

Teaching Spanish

SPANISH RANKS TODAY as the most fashionable foreign language on American campuses. It is the most widely taught, with enrollments often surpassing, in certain institutions, the combined number of students of Russian, German, Italian, Portuguese, French, Greek, and Latin. This uncontestable popularity didn't materialize from out of the blue. It became visible in the 1990s as the result of a number of factors, including immigration, free-trade agreements, and an exponential demographic growth of Hispanics in the United States.

Unfortunately, Spanish departments have been ill-equipped to respond to the increasing demand. The faculty, to a large extent, is poorly trained in pedagogical matters. It also seems unaware of the impact the ethnic changes are having in all walks of American life: it resists recognizing the linguistic challenge Cervantes' tongue faces north of the Rio Grande, and it rejects Latino culture north of the Rio Grande as a legitimate branch of Hispanic civilization.

Administrators, too, also curtail the growth possibilities, often by simply being unaware of what transpires inside the Spanish departments, the interstice struggles that end up wasting enormous amounts of energy. This disconnection isn't casual, though. It is based on an institutional racism whose roots date back to the late nineteenth century, when Hispanic civilization was incorporated, willy-nilly, into the curriculum.

The ones paying the bill are, of course, the students, and they surely aren't getting their money's worth.

Interest in foreign languages in the American academy started as the humanities became a legitimate field of study. Already in the seventeenth century, after Harvard University was founded, instruction in Greek and Latin became worthy disciplines. An enlightened individual versed in the pillars of Western Civilization needed to approach Sophocles, Thucydides, and Homer in the original. At the time of the Civil War, scientific treatises were in German, and sophisticated poetry came in French. Interestingly, Spanish was nowhere on the map.

The defeat of the Spanish Armada brought embarrassment to the once-mighty Iberian empire. Its decline prolonged itself until the Spanish-American War in 1898, which, as countless intellectuals put it, sealed the coffin's last nail. Soon thereafter Spanish popped up in the halls of academia as an unworthy tongue used by awkward, primitive people. The atrocities committed by Spanish soldiers in Cuba, monitored by the media that followed Teddy Roosevelt's Rough Riders, had a lasting impact on the American imagination. The result was an understanding of Spaniards as cruel and barbaric. This perception contributed to making the study of Iberian culture a not-quite-genuine field of intellectual inquiry in comparison with Italian, French, and German, whose literary traditions, from Dante to Diderot and Goethe, were considered far more sophisticated.

As a language of instruction, Spanish crept back into consciousness after World War II, part of the package of "Romance languages," whose semantic pedigree dates back to Hellenistic times. Teaching Cervantes' tongue as part of this philological group emphasized its philological origins. In other words, it stressed the past of Spanish, not its present. Indirectly, this period laid the foundation for what was to come: the language as "the great equalizer" of millions of people on both sides of the Atlantic, from Andalusia to the Pampas.

The 1960s were years of upheaval. Revolutionary movements by disenfranchised *campesinos* spread south of the border while a struggle for civil rights took place on campuses and beyond on the opposite side. The Chicano Movement made Spanish the recognizable code of the indigent, especially the farm workers in the Southwest. But the quest was for political pride, not for verbal competency. And so, when programs focusing on Mexicans and Puerto Ricans were established on campus, Spanish wasn't part of the package. This resulted in a rivalry between new ethnic courses and Spanish departments, which felt alienated. They expressed their alienation by looking down at Chicano activism as an activity of the low-brow.

The current popularity of Spanish as a language, as well as the civilization it expounds, dates back to the mid-1980s. During the Cold War, Russian, German, and the Slavic languages were magnets for students interested in international relations. But the fall of the Berlin Wall and the collapse of Communism in the Soviet Union radically changed the *zeitgeist*. The literatures of these regions of the globe ceased to hypnotize people. Shortly after, the White House began to look at Latin America as a potential business partner in the new world order. Treaties such as NAFTA, signed between Canada, Mexico, and the United States, were also encouraged in the Southern Cone. Plus, the Hispanic minority north of the Rio Grande began a period of astronomical enlargement. Transnational corporations looking for cheaper manufacturing products sought Spanish-speaking countries in which to relocate their facilities.

Yes, the late 1990s gave way to "la vida loca," a mercantile bonanza that placed things Hispanic at the forefront of American culture. Latin American nations embraced democracy. They also endorsed neo-liberal policies. On this side of the divide, Latinos, long seen as the "sleeper" in the nation's ethnic mosaic, saw their idiosyncrasy embraced by the mainstream: music, gastronomy, dance, radio, and TV—Spanish was *en todas partes*, just everywhere.

By the year 2000, the U.S. Census Bureau declared Hispanics in the United States to be the largest minority, surpassing blacks. A couple of years later, the size of the minority reached forty million, which constitutes approximately 10 percent of the whole Spanish-speaking world.

The overall transformation of Cervantes' tongue from peripheral player to protagonist in the post–World War II curriculum happened too fast for Spanish departments. Were they caught off-guard? Why were they unable to adjust? The answer is multifaceted. It points to vicious internal fights, which in turn are a reflection of colonial fractures.

It was only in the 1950s that Spanish departments started devoting sufficient attention not only to teaching the language but to showcasing the cultural manifestations of the Iberian Peninsula and its American satellites. The focus was on continuity. In what way were the leitmotifs of Spanish culture in Europe replicated, and then transformed, on this side of the Atlantic Ocean? To establish connections, faculty taught fiction, essays, theater, poetry, and folklore. Areas of concentration included the misnomered Spanish Golden Age (Lope de Vega, Luis de Góngora, Francisco de Quevedo, et al.); the work of Miguel de Cervantes, especially *Don Quixote of La Mancha;* the literary generation of '98 (Ramón del Valle Inclán, Miguel de Unamuno, et al.); the Charles Dickens of Spain: Benito Pérez Galdós; and the Spanish Civil War, especially the oeuvre of Federico García Lorca. From the former colonies, courses were offered on the Modernista movement (José Martí, Rubén Darío, et al.) and the indigenous novels of the nineteenth century, followed by the novels of the Mexican Revolution. From the late 1960s and up until the late 1980s, the work of authors like Julio Cortázar, Gabriel García Márquez, and Mario Vargas Llosa, known collectively as the generation of "El Boom," was added to the canon.

By the 1980s, two opposing sides emerged: the *peninsularistas,* as the faculty known for teaching topics exclusive to Spain were called, and their nemesis, the *latinoamericanistas,* those devoted to material from the former colonies. The tension was, in truth, a matter of pride. Had the Americas usurped Iberian cultural prestige by producing far more appealing cultural artifacts, which the world celebrated without regard to its peninsular ancestry? In other words, was Europe no longer the center of the world? Time and again, the apprehension saw itself manifested in tenure cases. Who are the true keepers of Spanish civilization? Should one group be outnumbered by the other?

It should be argued, for sure, that the confrontation was nothing but a smoke screen. When other impending issues needed attention, internal strife kept people distracted. Similarly, it is important to state that at the heart of Hispanic civilization, especially when studied vis-à-vis the Anglo-Saxon tradition, is an inferiority complex whose source is traceable to the defeat of the Spanish Armada. Intellectuals keep themselves busy battling one another for a morsel of pride rather than interact on a larger cosmopolitan stage.

Proof of sluggishness is the type of Spanish taught in courses until the late 1980s. Traditionally, the Castilian variety, i.e., the syntactical form used in central Spain—Madrid—was considered to be the standard, adequate way to learn the language. This meant that Americans used *vosotros,* a second-person plural conjugation, even though in four fifths of the Spanish-speaking orbit this modality was never employed. Some teachers quietly dismissed the approach, but in general the idea of correctness was related to the Iberian Peninsula, where the Royal Academy of the Spanish Language is based.

In any case, Spanish departments were asleep at the wheel when the wake-up call of the 1990s came about. They reacted by simply ignoring it. Their refusal to accept the refreshingly new gravitas of Hispanic civilization denounced nearsightedness. For these departments, the democratic changes in Latin America were not necessarily good news. They suggested an Americanization that eclipsed local authenticity. Likewise, Hispanics in the United States, in the eyes of faculty members, were *not* full-fledged Latin Americans. They were "ethnics." Their language was bastardized, and their literature and culture was second-rate.

This morose response was neither unexpected nor surprising. After World War II and up until the 1970s, a cadre of philologists trained in Europe was the most visible group of professors in Spanish departments. They were first supported by refugees from the Spanish Civil War. In the aftermath of the Cuban Revolution, they were joined by exiles from Latin American dictatorships whose view of the world was formed by the French and German intelligentsia. Ironically, for the latter the United States was the enemy, an imperial force often meddling in other nation's issues south of the border. The comfort of a tenured job quieted their animosity. Or better, they transferred it to Latinos born in this country, whom those exiled saw as ugly ducklings, the internal byproduct of the same imperialism they detested overseas. The fact that countless of these students made it to campus with a scholarship only exacerbated their status, for, in the eyes of the old faculty, they were not scholarship kids but affirmative action tokens.

For years the wealth of students enrolling in Spanish departments were Anglos. But in the late 1980s and early 1990s, the ugly ducklings increasingly began knocking at the door. And, as a result of the multicultural climate, blacks and Asians also showed up in large numbers. This student body was interested in Spain, Latin America, and Hispanic life in the United States in equal measure. It was antsy, skeptical, and ideologically uncommitted, a brainchild of MTV and the Internet, approaching the planet in a versatile, borderless fashion.

This, hence, is the dysfunctional picture, one that recalls Rip Van Winkle.

Things are beginning to change, I'm happy to report. As a result of the pressure from the diverse student body, courses on Latinos north of the Rio Grande have trickled into the catalogue. Interest in a post–magical realist Latin America is also showing up in classes devoted to drugs, rock, and urban life today. This material is at times taught in Spanish, at others in English. There is also a slow overhaul of faculty styles. The exiled guard is retiring and dying out, and an army of U.S.-trained professors, scores of them Latinos from Florida, California, Texas, and New York, whose kaleidoscopic interest in Hispanic civilization is approached from the ethnic perspective, is replacing it.

By far the most visible change, as far as I'm concerned, is in language instruction. In the 1990s an array a fresh textbooks was published under the editorship of scholars less dependent on the Iberian Peninsula. The recognition of other varieties of Spanish aside from Castilian is tangible. These resources value the so-called *autonomías* in Spain, suggesting that Catalan, Galician, Vasque, and other regional tongues are worthy of attention. Likewise, there is an assessment of non-Spanish forms of culture in Latin America, including those produced by the Nahuátl, Otomí, Taíno, Mapuche, and Quechua people. Obviously, the textbooks still endorse the "standard" form of Cervantes' language, but that standard is more flexible, less suffocating than it ever was before.

Curiously, some textbooks are also endorsing Spanglish, the hybrid vehicle of communication mixing English and Spanish, as an object of study—or, at least, of worthy debate. I've come across a rising number of examples of Spanish course material that makes reference to verbal expressions only heard in East Los Angeles and on the Lower East Side.

Language instruction is no longer the domain of faculty wives. Nor is it an improvised activity. Conferences and seminars devoted to pedagogical strategies, and concentrating especially on teaching Spanish for native speakers, have become fashionable. It is recognized today that Latinos are an essential group in Spanish departments. The fact that they come from homes where the language is used mostly orally, and often in haphazard ways, need not be seen as a handicap. Instead, this linguistic skill is an asset upon which faculty ought to build.

All these are welcome changes. Regrettably, they aren't backed by any rationale announcing a novel look at the entire state of affairs. What is needed is a complete reevaluation, internal as well as institutional, of the sum total of expectations for these departments. The transformation of the United States into a multi-ethnic society has pushed Spanish departments to the forefront. They are in charge of educating young people about the ins and outs of a diverse, heterogeneous civilization born with the demise of the Roman Empire. The faculty needs to reevaluate its view of the curriculum. For how long should the division between *peninsularistas* and *latinoamericanistas* project itself on the way texts are taught? A more dynamic approach is needed, one allowing the different geographical and chronological periods to relate to each other in an agile, ongoing manner.

If the classroom isn't the place where the depth and complexity of the Spanish language and the culture it has fostered are dissected, why should we await from the graduating class a less stilted, more energetic view of Hispanics in tune with our demanding times?

In order for Spanish departments to live up to the expectations set before them, it is crucial for all parties involved—administrators high and low, core full-time faculty, linguistic pedagogues, and graduate students—to engage in strategic planning. A foundation for a new way of understanding the world of Sor Juana Inés de la Cruz and Pedro Almódovar, Borges and Rigoberta Menchú, is urgently needed. *Adiós* to the centuries-old inferiority complex. Hispanics north of the border are already redefining what it means to be American. Their assimilation is a two-way street: as they integrate to the American ways, they also modify those ways. In other words, as Latinos are becoming *gringos,* Americans are also being Hispanisized. Similarly, globalization is making the Americas, from Tijuana to Buenos Aires, more like the rest of the hemisphere, with Taco Bell as the signature.

Administrators need to go beyond the stereotype of Hispanics as awkward and primitive people. This stereotype casts a pernicious shadow in the academy in its entirety. It is crucial for them to acknowledge, for instance, that the rules of the game applying to other language programs don't concern Spanish departments. I don't mean this as a false invitation of exceptionalism. There aren't forty million Germans,

Italians, or Russians in the United States. Plus, these tongues are not spoken just across the border from El Paso. In truth, these languages are indeed foreign to the vast majority of us—but not Spanish, not anymore. Any way you look at it, *el español* is already part and parcel of the American psyche.

Despierta América—it is time for Rip Van Winkle to wake up.

How Richard Rodríguez Became Brown

⚮

"AMERICAN HISTORY BOOKS I READ AS A BOY were all about winning and losing," Richard Rodríguez states in "Peter's Avocado," the last of the nine essays that make up his latest book, *Brown*. "One side won; the other side lost. . . . [But] the stories that interested me were stories that seemed to lead off the page: A South Carolina farmer married one of his slaves. The farmer died. The ex-slave inherited her husband's chairs, horses, rug, slaves. And *then* what happened? Did it, in fact, happen?"

Off the page and into the imagination—what happened *then,* in the 1960s, when Rodríguez was in his teens (he was born in 1947), is that an alternative narrative was established as a response to the one-sided, triumphalist vision accepted at face value. Their elders had falsified history, they had turned it into yet another chapter in the chronicle of Manifest Destiny. The young wanted change: a vision less polarized, fleshed out by marginal tales of vanquished people. Rodríguez was never a hippie, at least not to the best of my knowledge. He was too preoccupied with his own quest for redemption, too driven by the need to overcome his ethnic handicap. He had been born a Mexican but wanted desperately to whiten his path. While rich kids abandoned their wealthy environs to embrace the culture of the slums, he moved in the opposite direction. Therein a counter-narrative: to insert in history books the anecdote of an Indian raped by an explorer on the banks of the Mississippi River. Would he one day?

In the last thirty years or so, Rodríguez has offered a gamut of similar anecdotes, mostly about himself in action in an environment not always attuned to his inner life. These anecdotes take the form of a trilogy that started in 1982 with the classic *Hunger of Memory* and concludes now. This isn't a trilogy about history. It isn't about sociology or politics either. Instead, it is a sustained meditation on Latino life in the United States, filled with labyrinthine reflections on philosophy and morality. Apparently, the trilogy came along, especially *Brown,* its latest installment, after Rodríguez's agent, as the author himself puts it in "Hispanic," the fifth chapter in the book, "encouraged from me a book that answers a simple question: *What do Hispanics mean to the life of America?* He asked me that question several years ago in a French restaurant on East Fifty-seventh Street, as I watched a waiter approach our table holding before him a shimmering *îles flottantes.*" The image of the *îles flottantes* is a fitting one, I believe, for the Latino mosaic on this side of the border—Rodríguez often prefers to use the term *Hispanic* in his pages—might be seen as nothing if not an archipelago of self-sufficient subcultures: Cuban, Puerto Rican, Mexican, Salvadoran, Nicaraguan, Dominican . . . and the whole Bolivarian range of possibilities. Are these islands of identity interconnected? How do they relate to one another? To what extent are a Brazilian in Tallahassee, Florida, and a *mexicano* in Portland, Oregon, kindred spirits?

Judging by his answer, Rodríguez might have been asked the wrong question. Or else, he might have chosen to respond unpractically. For the question that runs through the three installments is: *How did Hispanics become brown?* His belief is that brown, as a color, is the *sine qua non* of Latinos. He sees brown as a metaphor of mixture. "Brown is impurity," he reasons. "I write of a color that is not a singular color, not a strict recipe, not an expected result, but a color produced by careless desire, even by accident." It is the color of *mestizaje,* i.e., the miscegenation that shaped the Americas from 1492 onward, as it was forced, in spite of itself, into modern times. It is the juxtaposition of white European and dark aboriginal, of Hernán Cortés and his mistress and translator La Malinche. And it is also the so-called *raza cósmica* that Mexican philosopher José Vasconcelos talked about in the early twentieth century, a master race that, capitalizing on its own impurity, would rise to conquer the entire hemisphere, if not the globe itself. But have Hispanics really become brown in the Technicolor screen of America? Not quite, I answer.

Rodriguez is mistaken, I'm afraid. The gestation of race in the Caribbean, from Venezuela to Mexico and the Dominican Republic, has a different tint, since African slaves were brought in to replace Indians for the hard labor in mines and fields, and their arrival gave birth to other racial mixtures, among them the mulattos and *zambos.* Argentina, on the other hand, had a minuscule aboriginal population when the Spanish viceroys and missionaries arrived. The *gauchos,* a sort of cowboy, are at the core of its national mythology, in works like those of Domingo Faustino Sarmiento, José Hernández, and Borges. Brown, in Rodríguez's conception, might be the color of Mexicans in East L.A., but surely not of Cubans in Miami.

Some Latinos might have become brown, but not all. And then again, what does brown really mean? Rodríguez embraces it as a metaphor of impurity. *Mestizos* are crossbreeds, they are impure, and impurity is beautiful. But the term *brown* has specific political connotations. It is, to a large extent, a byproduct of the Civil Rights Era, the era of César Chávez and the Young Lords, coined in reaction to the black-

and-white polarity played out in Washington, D.C., and the media: brown is between white and black, a third option in the kaleidoscope of race. A preferred term in the Southwest was *La Raza,* but brown also found its route to manifestos, political speeches, legal documents, and newspaper reports.

Rodríguez isn't into the Chicano Movement. My gut feeling is that he feels little empathy toward the 1960s in general, let alone toward the Mexican-American upheaval. Still, his views on *la hispanicidad* in America are defined by his Mexican ancestry and by his residence in San Francisco, where for years he has made his home. He is disconnected from the Caribbean component of Latinos, and, from the reaction I see in readers on the East Coast, these Caribbean Latinos are also disconnected from him. They aren't brown, nor do they have a deep connection to the color. All this to say that Rodríguez's response to *What do Hispanics mean to the life of America* is partial at best, not to say subjective. That subjectivity he embraces wholeheartedly.

His tool, his astonishing device, is the essay—not, thank God, the academic essay, obtuse in content, obscure in language, meant for a minuscule audience of five colleagues; not the reportage either, turned into kitsch by our complacent *New Yorker* culture. His model, I believe, is Montaigne, the father of the mother personal essay, a genius in taking even a mosquito tempted, like the Phoenix, by a candle flame, as an excuse to meditate on the meaning of life, death, and everything in between. Not that Montaigne is Rodríguez's only source. In *Brown* he chants to Alexis de Tocqueville and James Baldwin. And in the previous two installments of the trilogy he has also emerged as a successor of Octavio Paz.

The anti-model in this genealogical tree I'm shaping is perhaps V. S. Naipaul, or at least he appears so to me, a counterpoint, as I reread Rodríguez's oeuvre. They have much in common: they explore a culture through its nuances and not, as it were, though its high-profile iconography; they are meticulous *littérateurs,* intelligent, incessantly curious; and, more important, everywhere they go they retain, to their honor, a position of outsiders looking in. Rodríguez, in particular, has been a Mexican-American but not a Chicano—that is, he has rejected the invitation to be a full part of the community that shaped him. Instead, he uses himself as a looking glass to reflect, from the outside, on who Mexicans are, in and beyond politics.

This, predictably, has resulted in large bastions of animosity against him. I don't know of any other Latino author who generates so much anger. Chicanos love to hate him as much as they hate to love him. Why this is so isn't difficult to understand: he is customarily critical of programs and policies that are seen as benefactors to the community, for example, bilingual education and affirmative action, which, in his eyes, have only balkanized families, neighborhoods, and cities. In *Hunger of Memory* he portrayed himself as a Scholarship Boy who benefited from racial profiling. This generated an unending feeling of reproach in him. He reached a succinct conclusion: not race but individual talent should be considered in a person's application for school or work—not one's skin color, last name, and country of origin, only aptitude. Naipaul too is the devil's advocate: his journeys through India and the Arab world, even the lands of El Dorado, might be unsettling when one considers his rabid opinions on the uncivilized natives.

But Naipaul delivers these opinions with admirable grace. He forces his readers to rethink the colonial galaxy, to revisit old ideas. In that sense, Naipaul and Rodríguez are authors who force upon us the necessity to sharpen our own ideas. We read them, we agree and disagree with them, so as to fine-tune our own conception of who we are. They are the kind of writers who infuriate, who unsettle us. What they never do is leave the reader unchanged. For that alone, one ought to be grateful.

How exciting it would be, I found myself thinking while reading *Brown,* if Rodríguez would one day offer us a travelogue on the Sudan. Of if he would dare to take a transcontinental rail from Alaska to the Patagonia and beyond. How much he would learn about America from the rest of the Americas! And how enriched his readers would be as a result of his experiences elsewhere on earth! For an aspect Naipaul has that Rodríguez doesn't is his restless nature: relentless, maddening travel, and not a sedentary life, is what his odyssey is about. The trilogy by Rodríguez shows a mind engaged too, but its subject is almost unmovable. *Hunger of Memory* was an autobiographical meditation set in the United States as the country was about to enter the Reagan era. It denounced a stagnant society, interested in the politics of compassion more than in the politics of equality, a society with little patience for Mexicans. *Days of Obligation* was also about los Estados Unidos, as the first Bush presidency was approaching its end. By then the Reagan mirage was officially over. We were about to enter another house of mirrors under the tutelage of Bill Clinton.

And this third installment of the trilogy arrives in bookstores at a time when the Melting Pot, *la sopa de culturas,* is boiling again, with xenophobia against Arabs at a height, and Latinos, already the largest minority according to the latest U.S. census data—35.3 million strong by late 2000, if one counts only those officially registered—still in the fringes, fragmented, compartmentalized, more a sum of parts than a whole.

These changes are and aren't in the trilogy. Rodríguez seldom makes use of political facts. He lives in a dreamlike zone, a universe of ideas and sensations. Somewhere in *Brown* he announces: "A few weeks ago, in the newspaper (another day in the multicultural nation), a small item: Riot in a Southern California high school. Hispanic students protest, then smash windows, because African-American students get four weeks for Black History month, whereas Hispanics get one. The more interesting protest would be for Hispanic students to demand to be included in Black History month. The more interesting remedy would be for Hispanic History week to include African history." This sums up Rodríguez's approach: a micro-management of identity delivered periodically from the exact same viewpoint.

Or has the viewpoint changed? It is possible to see how Rodríguez has matured by reading the trilogy chronologically. He started as an anti-segregationist, a man interested in assimilation of Mexicans to the larger landscape of America. His feelings toward Mexico and toward his homosexuality were tortured at the time. These became clear, or at least clearer, in the second installment, in which a picture of a San Francisco desolated by AIDS, an argument with the author's own *mexicanidad* personified by his own father, among other changes, were evident. Assimilation was still a priority, but by the 1990s Rodríguez had ceased to be interested in larger issues and was more attracted to his own condition as a public Latino gay.

This third book is again about assimilation, but from a different perspective. The key word now is *miscegenation*. The issue isn't so much that Hispanics need to assimilate. Instead, it is the changing nature of America, a country shaped by layers of ethnicity, where nothing is pure anymore. At one point, he describes the conversation of a couple of girls one afternoon on Fillmore Street. He describes them and their dialogue thus: "Two girls. Perhaps sixteen. White. Anglo, whatever. Tottering on their silly shoes. Talking of boys. The one girl saying to the other: . . . His complexion is so cool, this sort of light—well, not that light . . ." And Rodríguez ends: "I realized my book will never be equal to the play of the young." This need to capture what surrounds him, to shape a book that is at once a mirror and a tape recorder, is always evident, although it isn't entirely successful in the pen of Rodíiguez because he is an intellectual obsessed with his own stream of consciousness, not in catching the pulse of the nation.

I've tried to explain the continuity of themes in Rodríguez's three volumes only tangentially. There is another take, summed up in three catch words: *class, ethnicity,* and *race*. He himself appears to endorse this take. The first installment is about a low-income family whose child moves up in the hierarchy; the second about the awakening to his across-the-border roots; and the third about "a tragic noun, a synonym for conflict and isolation": race. But Rodriguez adds: "race is not a terrible word for me. Maybe because I'm skeptical by nature. Maybe because my nature is already mixed. The word race encourages me to remember the influence of eroticism on history. For that is what race memorializes. Within any discussion of race, there lurks the possibility of romance."

So is this what the trilogy is about? I'm not sure yet. The endeavor strikes me as mercurial. It is likely to change with time because Rodríguez loves metaphor and hyperbole. Each future generation will read into these what it pleases, depending on the context. I still like *Hunger of Memory* the best. *Days of Obligation* strikes me as a collection of disparate essays without a true core. And *Brown* I felt is a book that is not fully embracing. For one thing, it refuses to recognize the complexity of Latinos in the United States. In it Rodríguez describes his namesake, Richard Nixon, as "the dark father of hispanicity." "Surviving Chicanos (one still meets them) scorn the term Hispanic," Rodriguez argues, "in part because it was Richard Nixon who drafted the noun and who made the adjective uniform."

A similar reference was invoked in an op-ed piece by him in the *New York Times,* in which he declared George W. Bush the first Hispanic president of the United States, the way Bill Clinton was the first black president. Is this true? The argument developed is not always clear-cut: it twists and turns, mimicking Rodríguez's own labyrinthine mind. This mind I've learned to respect and admire.

Years ago, when I was a newly arrived immigrant in New York City, I stumbled upon an essay of his, and then read his first book. I was mesmerized by the prose but found myself in strong disagreement. Then, in the mid-1990s, I sent him a personal letter, to which he kindly replied. I was about to fly to the West Coast and wondered if we might have breakfast together. In the last section of my memoir *On Borrowed Words* I re-created that encounter. A correspondence ensued, and then an ongoing connection. It is a connection based on mutual disagreement but also on respect. In *Brown,* for instance, Rodríguez embraces miscegenation, but only at the racial level. What about promiscuity in language? Promiscuity might be a strong word, but it surely carries the right message. Rodríguez's English is still the Queen's English: overpolished, uncorrupted, stainless. How is it that he embraces *mestizaje* but has little to say about Spanglish, that disgustingly gorgeous mix of Spanish and English that is neither one nor the other? Isn't that in-betweenness what America is about today?

On the issue of language, I have another thought: I find it embarrassing, appalling even, that none of Rodríguez's volumes is available in Spanish to Mexicans and other Latinos. Years ago, an Iberian academic press released *Hambre de memoria,* a stilted, unapologetically Castilian translation. Those, clearly, were the wrong chords to touch in a box of resonance that is closer to San Antonio than to San Sebastián. How much longer need Mexicans wait to read the work *en español mexicano* of a canonical figure, whose lifelong quest has been to understand Mexicans beyond the pale? This question brings to mind Octavio Paz's "The *Pachuco* and Other Extremes," the first chapter in his masterpiece *The Labyrinth of Solitude,* released in 1950. It has angered Chicanos for decades, and with good reason: this is a chapter that distorts Mexican life north of the border.

In his work, Richard Rodríguez established a colloquy with Paz, especially with his views on the Pachucos, a social type alive in Los Angeles in the 1940s. It is an unpredictable, enlightening colloquy, filled with detours. But only English speakers know about it, unfortunately— a fact, as far as I am concerned, that amounts to censorship. For while Mexicans might not like to hear what Rodríguez has to say about them and about himself (he has talked of "hating Mexico"), at least they will be acquainted with his opinions. Acquaintance is already a step toward understanding, is it not? I wonder, though: how does one translate the term *brown* into Spanish? The dictionary option, *café,* simply doesn't work: it brings back images of coffee and sugar, syncopated opposites in the Caribbean, but brown is about mainland Mexico, about Central America, about the Southwest. So, is there an alternative?

At any rate, where will Rodríguez go from here now that the trilogy is finished? I have no idea. Might he finally take a long journey overseas? Is his vision of America finally complete? Not quite, I say, for the country is changing rapidly. *Mestizaje,* he argues, is no longer the domain of Latinos. We are all brown: dirty and impure. "This is not the same as saying 'the poor shall inherit the earth' but is possibly related," Rodríguez states. "The poor shall overrun the earth. Or the brown shall." This is a statement for the history books. Is the Melting Pot a mechanism to eliminate ethnic identity? No, it only fuses it so as to turn primary colors into a miscellany that is not quite the Rainbow Coalition dreamed by Jesse Jackson but a dirty mishmash that invokes eroticism but also "dense concentrations of melanin." In his view, America is about to become América—everyone in it a Hispanic, if not physically, at least metaphorically.

Death, Drugs, and Narcocorridos

❧

Rosalino "Chalino" Sánchez isn't someone you are likely to know about. Yet his legendary role as the revitalizer of the corrido—as the Mexican border folk song is known—is unquestionable among the twenty-five million people who inhabit the territories that unite or separate Mexico and the United States. In fact, his reputation reaches far beyond, from his native state of Sinaloa to the nearby Coahuila and Durango, and, emphatically, in the Mexican "suburbs" of Los Angeles, where Chalino spent his most artistically fruitful years. Songs of his like "El crimen de Culiacán" are listened to religiously on the radio in cantinas, at birthday parties, malls, and mechanic shops. His cassettes and CDs are astonishingly popular. By all accounts a mediocre singer with little stage charisma, he is nevertheless to Mexicans a folk hero of epic proportions. Soon after his mysterious death in Culiacán in 1992, more than 150 corridos about his plight were recorded.

This, in the opinion of ethnomusicologists, makes him the most written about corrido subject ever. That the Anglo music radar refuses to acknowledge Chalino's durability is, to my ears, proof of abysmal distrust. He is a bestseller in a tradition whose luminaries often make it to the Billboard Latin chart, one that not only easily outsells tropical rhythms—salsa, merengue, cumbia–but also accounts for approximately a third of the overall Latin record sales in the United States. But the explanation for Chalino's anonymity among nonbelievers is more complex: together with scores of other solo corridistas and troupes, like Jenny Rivera and Los Hermanos Jiménez, like Los Pajaritos del Sur and Grupo Exterminador, he eulogized in his lyrics a symbol regularly satanized in the English-language media: the narcotrafficker.

The protagonists of Chalino's songs and those by his peers are immigrants to the United States. They address head-on urgent political and social issues: poverty, drug traffic, injustice, discrimination, and the disillusionment of a life built through the ever-evasive dollar bill. (The term *corrido* comes from *correr*, "to run.") In one ballad a couple of girls disguise themselves as nuns and drive a van full of cocaine, which they claim is powdered milk for an orphanage in Phoenix. In another two brothers, Carlos and Raúl, are the owners of a circus that uses unfair strategies to push other circuses out of business. The circus, of course, is an allegory for the Mexico of the late 1980s and early 1990s: Carlos is an obvious reference to former Mexican president Carlos Salinas de Gortrai, and Raúl is his drug-convict brother. These and other similar lyrics insert themselves in one of the oldest rural musical traditions of the New World. They deliver a rough-and-tumble plot succinctly and without circumvolutions, offering a recognizable startup that leads to a denouement, and following a rhymed metric that is simple and straightforward. In that sense they are structurally similar to the British broadside, the cowboy songs of the Southwest, and gangsta rap. Instrumentally, though, they use accordion and guitar, although acoustics and percussion might also be on display.

The corrido spread its influence in the nineteenth century but reached its apex in the Mexican revolution that started in 1910, when political figures like Pancho Villa and Emiliano Zapata, as well as prototypes like the female soldier La Soldadera, were the stuff of corridos. I've personally heard corridos about bandit Tiburcio Vázquez and activist César Chávez, about *tejana* singer Selena and revolutionary Subcomandante Marcos, even about scholar and folklorist Américo Paredes. These figures are extolled in a way that allows people to spill out their emotion. There are also corridos that address historical events. In fact, the vitality of the form lies in the fact that no sooner does an important incident take place, than a song is already available to reflect on it.

This immediacy is crucial: it grants it the quality of a news report. For instance, there is a corrido about the troublesome racial affair of police brutality in Los Angeles against Rodney King in 1992. More recently, I've listened to a corrido that recounts the tragedy of September 11, 2001, in New York City. I'm also familiar with a handful of movies based on corridos, including the highbrow *The Ballad of Gregorio Cortés,* directed by Robert Young. The narcocorrido is a slightly different item, though: once a subgenre of the tradition, it has emerged since the 1970s as the principal instrument to chronicle the odyssey of Mexicans across the Rio Grande in a drug-infested universe.

In the last few months a couple of American journalists have published insightful books on the narcocorrido that are useful as a compass to navigate critically the cultural scene. Perhaps this is a sign that the American radar is finally becoming less dogmatic, more flexible to subtleties in the catalog of Latin musical variations. Elijah Wald, a Bostonian whose father was a Nobel Prize honoree, is a nomadic guitarist responsible for the biography *Josh White: Society Blues.* Wald was for a time the music critic of the *Boston Globe.* His book on the narcocorrido offers an enlightening rendezvous: rather than dwell on the origin and varieties of this sort of ballad in a scholarly mode, he delivers a travelogue. For almost eight months he hitchhiked, with a guitar on his back, across the Southwest, northern and central Mexico, and down to Chiapas. He talks to truck drivers, impresarios, vocalists, and fans. The reader at times stumbles upon anecdotes that might add little to the overall context of the topic. Yet these detours, approached with patience, are a midrash to understand the overall context that nurtures this kind of transnational phenomenon. (Wald's volume is also available in a Spanish-language version; also, selections of the ballads discussed in its pages are featured on the CD entitled *Corridos y Narcocorridos,* released by Fonovisa.)

Sam Quinones, a freelancer whose attention has focused on Mexico since 1994, has a literary manner that oscillates toward a succinct, almost telegraphic narrative; this brevity I find appealing and easier to empathize with. He also is less patient than Wald, which results in an eagle-like overview of the ballads themselves that left me hungry for examples. Actually, his *True Tales from Another Mexico* is only marginally about narcotics; instead, it is a collection of profiles of various personalities and a survey of popular themes that pertain to what Quinones describes as "the other side of Mexico." In his introduction, he argues that "the press [abroad], other governments, and tourists are most aware of the official, elite, corrupt Mexico; the Mexico that won't allow a poor man a chance; the Mexico behind the sunglasses." He then adds: "I've even been told by people, including Mexicans, that this *is* Mexican culture. But I know that's not true." In response, Quinones follows the unlikely life of soap-opera diva Verónica Castro, as well as the unascertained path of the discoverers of the popsicle—*la paleta*—in Tocumbo, Michoacán, and the rise of their business empire: La Michoacana.

But the chapters in Quinones' book I was mostly drawn into are about Chalino and about the so-called "Angel of the Poor": Jesús Malverde. These two figures strike me as veritable paradigms of complex popular sentiment. Malverde, for instance, is the type of magnet of collective faith that allows people to sustain themselves through violence and loss. Did he ever exist? How to explain that thousands of people stop regularly at his shrine in Culiacán to ask for a miracle, from a recovery from an illness to protection against the federal police and the narcotraffickers? Scholars of various persuasions claim he is a fusion of Catholic iconography and the biographical leftovers of Sinaloan outlaw Heraclio Bernal, another representative of the oppressed, executed in 1909 by a mean-spirited governor and hung for weeks on a tree. But Eligio González, a composer and self-made entrepreneur devoted to the construction and administration of La Capilla, a chapel dedicated to honor Malverde, believes that the bandit's name was Jesús Juárez Maso, and that Malverde became his appellative, as

González put it to Wald, "because of the green (*verde*) pants in which he use to hide himself from the *rurales,* the rural police." In any case, Malverde, he explains, was a self-righteous bandit who, according to the legend, was one day severely wounded. His condition was desperate; he was almost dying. Suddenly, he decided to immolate himself by requesting that a friend of his turn him in so as to collect a reward posted on his name. Malverde then asked the friend to distribute the money among the dispossessed. He especially cared for those involved in the drug trade, thus his nickname "El Narcosantón," an unofficial narcosaint.

González is known in Sinaloa for handing out wheelchairs and coffins, and for officiating at funerals. In La Capilla he has placed various narcocorridos about Malverde on sale. Also available are human-size busts of him, and Wald includes a photograph of one. He describes how these sculptures came about: at the request of González, of course, to satisfy a devout folk in need of a tangible object of worship. Given that no material evidence of the bandit has ever been available, González commissioned a local sculptor to make the figurines. He tells Wald: "Since at that time Pedro Infante and Jorge Negrete were popular [Mexican movie stars], I said to him, 'Look, [Malverde] was a good-looking boy, white, and so that people will identify with him, make him somewhere in between Pedro Infante and Jorge Negrete."

González also describes Malverde's miracles. For instance, the Sinaloan government decided to build a state office building in the land where people congregated to pay tribute to El Narcosantón. A huge protest ensued, lasting two years. In that time stones jumped like popcorn on the ground, machinery frequently broke down, and other mishaps occurred. In the end, the building was finished, but the aggregated faith among the people was by then undefeatable. A portion of the illustrious "Corrido a Jesús Malverde" follows:

> Voy a cantar un corrido de una historia verdadera,
> De un bandido generoso que robaba dondequiera.
> Jesús Malverde era un hombre que a los pobres ayudaba,
> Por eso lo defendían cuando la ley lo buscaba.
>
> [I am going to sing a corrido of a true story,
> Of a generous bandit who robbed wherever he went.
> Jesús Malverde was a man who helped the poor,
> Because of that, they protected him when the law was after
> him.]

Truth, generosity, and bravado . . . Most of the narcocorridos I'm acquainted with are similar in tone: they celebrate the semi-fictitious adventures of a righteous person, usually a male, who dared to fight against the establishment. It is as if the best of Mexico, its source of endurance, was built against the current. The lyrics by composers like Paulino Vargas, Julián Garza, and Jesse Armenta are fatalistic in nature: they recount fateful, bloody encounters, in which individuals avenge themselves in order to leave their dignity intact. *Dignidad,* indeed, is what the narcocorridos are about: the supremacy of honor.

In what he described as "a journey into the music of drugs, guns, and guerrillas," Wald patiently explores the half-accomplished modernity that colors northern Mexico, where the drug business has radically transformed people's daily routine, yet has left untouched the sense of morality. The people he comes across are never appalled by the consumption of narcotics. Why should they be? As a bystander tells him, that is someone else's problem. The immigrant's sole concern is with survival: *la sobrevivencia.* In *The Labyrinth of Solitude,* Octavio Paz once described Mexicans as unafraid of death. The narcocorrido is proof of this. Malverde, for instance, is anything but a submissive figure. He is eager to subvert the official rule, although he knows his subversion will ultimately be ineffectual. In no way does he follow the pattern of a Stallone/Rocky archetype, who is able to overcome, with charisma and stamina, every obstacle to emerge in front of him. In the end, Rocky is the underdog who becomes an undisputed bellwether.

No such emblem exists in the Spanish-language drug culture: in this ballad, as in "The Wetback's Tomb," "The Circus," and countless others, the concept of the underdog is alien to such a degree that the Spanish language doesn't even have an approximate translation of it. Malverde is a source of endurance; in the end, though, the establishment prevails—the gringos, the corrupt politicos. Still, confrontation is embraced by corridistas: for them, better a dignified death than a life lived on one's knees. Sooner or later, society figures out a way to pay tribute to the martyr. In the case of Malverde, his timelessness is to be found not only in La Capilla and the handsome busts on sale but also in the Denny's-like cafeterias called Coco's Malverde and Chic's Malverde, as well as in businesses like Malverde Clutch & Brakes. And, according to Quinones, the timelessness extends to a corporate connection Eligio González has established with Pepsi-Cola. As it happens, local distributors give the saint's caretaker discounts so he can sell soda at concerts and dances (of narcocorridistas), allowing him to keep the profits for El Narcosantón. Once during a large encampment of campesinos outside the state building that lasted two months, González is said to have sold four thousand cases of Pepsi.

Of the myriad of troubadours that parade in the volumes under review, probably the most emblematic is Chalino. Thus, I'm delighted to see his travels hereby delineated for the first time for an English-language audience. His impact among youths is so fertile, the reader is exposed to a trend of Chalino sound-alikes that, demographically and in ambition, eclipses even the Elvis Presley mania. Wald recalls how in ten minutes a record store owner showed him cassettes and CDs of twenty-five different so-called "chalinitos." Why there is such a craze is to me difficult to fathom. I own three of his records: his voice in them is rough, uninspiring. His lyrics are appealing, but my predilections, as far as narcocorridos go, are to be found elsewhere. (I'm a long-standing admirer of Los Tigres del Norte.) As in Malverde's case, it is no doubt the myth, the way people inject their own dreams into Chalino's life, that holds the clue to his celebrity. For he was a warrior, and that is how every immigrant, no matter the background, wants to see himself: as a fearless combatant. He was killed in a shootout at the age of thirty-one.

This isn't at all unexpected, of course: almost to the end of his days he carried with himself a pistol, and he made sure everyone noticed it. His was a distinctive outfit, even for an "antistar" like him: a cowboy hat, white or striped shirt, dark slacks, and boots, accompanied by ostentatious jewelry (rings, necklaces, watches) that is *de rigeur* among narcotraffickers. He spoke with a distinctive Sinaloan rancho accent: for instance, he said *te fuites* for "you left," rather than *te fuiste*. "[Chalino] looked straight out of the mountains," a devotee assures us, "one more of the shy, fierce men drinking in the cantinas and carrying drugs across the border in suitcases, ready to do the jail time with quiet fatalism, or to kill someone over a woman or a thoughtless remark."

From Sinaloa he moved north not only in search of work, but because he needed to run away from the law. Apparently, Chalino at the age of fifteen had gone to a party where he found the man who raped his sister Juana four years earlier and killed him on the spot. He followed the harvests up through California to Oregon, finally settling in Inglewood, a Mexican-immigrant satellite town around Los Angeles. For a series of small crimes he was sent to prison in Tijuala, and it was there that he came across contraband smugglers with guitars. With them he began to write corridos. It was his first exposure to composition. Back in LA, he traded in marijuana and cocaine, but stopped the moment his musical career—which lasted only a total of four years—took off. He asked a *norteño* band to record his lyrics, but was unhappy with the result, so he tried his own luck in front of the microphone at the studio. Soon his cassettes were selling like hotcakes. *True Tales from Another Mexico* reconstructs Chalino's roving path, reflecting on his success in packed clubs, cantinas, and *quinceañera* parties. Soon everyone, from *coyotes* to wetbacks, was endlessly replaying his albums, in which he collected songs made to order on *narcotraficantes* of any stature. Eventually, after a performance in Coachella, twenty miles east of Palm Springs, in which he took requests, a drunk unemployed thirty-three-year-old jumped on stage and fired a 25-mm pistol into Chalino's side, injuring him. The incident made it to *ABC News Tonight,* another case of Anglos paying attention, obviously not because of the artistic quality of the performance but as a result of the gunshots.

Chalino's reputation as a *valiente,* a brave macho, was bolstered by the incident. But his reputation as a daredevil and a singer of revenge followed him, and sooner rather than later it caught up with him. Probably filled with regret, he gave up his gun collection shortly after, and he also sold the rights to his music for the lump sum of $115,000. These were the last acts of a singer whose themes often got him in trouble. In May, after a packed performance back in Culiacán, he and some relatives were stopped by armed men driving Chevrolet Suburbans. An hour later, a couple of campesinos found his body, dumped by an irrigation canal near a highway. The mystery of his death remains unsolved. In a lawless landscape such as the one Chalino inhabited, it is likely to remain unsolved. A stanza in his homage reads:

> Para cantar estos versos voy a quitarme el sombrero,
> Para contar la tragedia de un amigo y compañero.
> Chalino Sánchez ha muerto, que Dios lo tenga en el cielo.

> [To sing these verses I will take off my hat,
> To recount the tragedy of a friend and companion.
> Chalino Sánchez has died, may God have him in heaven.]

News of his death spread far and wide through technology—radio, TV, even email. But in the migrant communities it was through narcocorridos that the tragedy was widely disseminated. It had been through these ballads that Chalino had become famous, and it was in them that he was immortalized. This to me adds another crucial aspect, one which Quinones discusses in some detail: "In the Mexican badlands," he argues, "where the barrel of a gun makes the law, for generations dating back to the mid-1800s the corrido recounted the worst, best, and bloodiest exploits of men." Indeed, the corridos are the newspaper of an illiterate people. And they are something else: for migrants weary of corrupt politicians, this is a literary form that is alive orally for those unexposed to the written word. This is a form, needless to say, that is authentically democratic, one in which people express themselves in full.

Democracy isn't a system immigrants have been exposed to. They run away from a dictatorial regime, looking for a better future elsewhere. They often don't find it, though. Still, the corrido allows them a sense of freedom. What has kept the tradition alive in the border region is the fact that workers with scarcely a cent to spare are eager to unpocket what to them is handsome pay to a composer to create a customized ballad about their own journey. Chalino's career flourished in large measure thanks to the endless commissions he satisfied from his avid customers. In the melodic tales he told about them, their anonymity was suddenly unlocked.

This wasn't anything but liberating. Through the corrido the laborer, pushed to oblivion by History (with a capital "H"), was allowed the key to a room of his own: *un donnadie,* a nobody, unexpectedly got the chance to become *un alguien,* a somebody, at least for the few minutes that Chalino's stanzas lasted. And in taped form, replayed time and again, they could last forever. Producer Abel Orozco put Chalino's contribution in perspective for Quinones: "Before, they'd only do corridos about legendary figures. Now people want to hear about themselves while they're alive. Although they may be nobodies, they want to make themselves known. Corridos have become, over the last several years, a little less news and a little more publicity for common people. They're fifteen minutes of fame that they pay for themselves."

Chalino the Mexican immigrant: Isn't he an American hero too?

Betraying Latino Students

THIS YEAR'S FRESHMAN CLASS at Amherst College, where I teach, has twenty-four Latino students, or 5.5 percent of the total enrollment. There are almost twice as many Asian-American students, forty-five, and there are forty-one black students. Plus, there are thirty-one students who identify themselves as mixed-race.

You might infer from those figures that Latinos are a small minority group in the general population. Yet according to the U.S. Census Bureau, there were more than 41.3 million Latinos in the United States as of 2004—about 14 percent of the population. Now our largest minority group, the Latino population is also projected to grow faster than other groups for the foreseeable future.

In other words, twenty-four is an embarrassing number.

It gets worse. Our admissions office classifies as Latino anyone who has a Latino background—not just students from underserved, predominantly underprivileged American Latino families, but also, for example, wealthy students from South America who reside in the United States and are U.S. passport carriers.

It is no secret that the number of applications from "diversity" students fluctuates from year to year. Ironically, for the 2005 class Amherst received more applications from Latino candidates than at any point in its history: 325. The number of accepted students was also a record: 115. But after endless maneuverings by admission officers and others, only 24 enrolled.

I'm focusing on Amherst because I know it best. But I've spent hours talking to admissions officers and colleagues at other private colleges in the Northeast, and give or take a few numbers, the picture is equally bleak at most of them. The class of 2009 at Harvard University, for example, is roughly 7 percent Latino. I suspect the same is true at many, perhaps the majority, of the nation's prestigious institutions.

As elite colleges constantly tell us, what they do matters: from creating the next generation of leaders for a multicultural society, to opening doors to the talented of all backgrounds, to sustaining a functioning democracy. From where I sit, it's clear they're not doing a very good job.

To some extent, the problem is systemic. While institutions in regions like the Southwest, where Latinos already make up a significant part of the population, are doing a slightly better job of recruitment, nationwide higher education continues to fail Latinos. In 2002, according to the most recent figures available, Latinos represented about 17 percent of the college-age population, but accounted for just 10 percent of all college students, and just 7 percent of students at four-year colleges. With the mission they set for themselves—the gateway to the American Dream—and the resources they have available, it is inexcusable for elite institutions to do so miserably. Why have they failed?

It's not so much a lack of interest. I've been part of countless events on and off campus where admissions officers entertain prospective "students of color"—usually with a generic program catering to a vague "otherness" that is supposed to appeal to a wide range of minority students.

Unfortunately what elite colleges have in goodwill they lack in knowledge. Like most of our nation, they have little awareness of the intricacies of Hispanic civilization north, south, and east of the Rio Grande beyond a vague association with an unethnic Jennifer Lopez and an asexual Ricky Martin. Latinos are a multifaceted minority with a labyrinthine history. A segment of the population has been in United States since before the *Mayflower*. Others came in successive waves of immigration from Mexico, Central and South America, and the Caribbean, as well as from Europe. Issues of race and class among Latinos are divisive. A mestizo laborer in Oregon, whose original home was in Guadalajara, has little in common with an upper-class Caucasian student from Monterey, although both are from Mexico. Afro-Cubans, Puerto Rican *jíbaros,* and numerous other subgroups complicate the matter.

Then there is the issue of language. Latinos are embracing English as speedily as any previous immigrant wave, but they are not renouncing their allegiance to Spanish. The duality results in a heightened sense of cultural loyalty. Add to it a shared yet amorphous connection with similar historical motifs and cuisines, and a passion for musical rhythms, and the result is a sum of parts more than a homogenized whole. We haven't even begun to think about how to make our campuses welcoming to such a mixture.

Like other minority students, Latinos are also burdened with being asked to "represent" their group on campus. The complexity of the Latino minority worsens the challenge. For instance, a Nuyorican student of mine from New York was asked to orchestrate an evening about the Day of the Dead, a traditional Tejano festival, to which she has absolutely no connection. Refusing to do it made her feel like a traitor. That kind of insensitivity is palpable everywhere.

Another reason that elite colleges fail in recruiting Latino students is that, often, they rely on a short list of qualified students—determined by SAT scores—from the College Board. Competing with other elite institutions for the names on that list, they torpedo prospective candidates with letters, invitations to campus, and more. That means that, roughly, the same 325 Latino students applying to Amherst also apply to similar institutions. The results are predictable. Amherst has sought alternate strategies, like going through organizations in California and Texas, states with large Latino populations, to identify appealing "diversity" students. Success, however, has been minimal.

One handicap is that admissions officers, at least in the Northeast, are hardly ever Latino. That isn't a small point. Without someone in the office fully immersed in Latino life, the possibility of understanding its complexities is lessened.

Another predicament is that most presidents and deans of elite colleges aren't Latino either. Nor are trustees. For the first time in 1999, Amherst had a Latino on its board. It took the institution almost two hundred years to enlist one. His term ended last year. And then there's the faculty. Elite colleges in the Northeast are still lagging far behind in hiring Latino professors. Most teach in the humanities, not in fields like chemistry, geology, or neuroscience. All that makes our institutions appear unwelcoming to Latino students: certainly not a part of the fabric of the college.

The lack of Latino representation is also felt in the development office. Latinos are slowly moving into the middle class, but overall they are far from affluent. In elite colleges like Amherst, money doesn't shape policy, but it ratifies influence. Without major Latino donors, the priority of recruiting this minority is likely to remain low for the time to come.

Furthermore, it is vital to comprehend what happens beyond the freshman year. The retention level at Amherst is superb: enrolled Latino students tend to graduate at the same speed as everyone else. Still, there is a recognizable feeling of alienation. The consensus among faculty members is that Latino advisees seek their advisers less frequently than other students, maybe because it is harder to build teacher-student trust with them. Student organizations dealing with Latino culture are less active than other organizations—partly because of the small number of Latino students, partly because of the divisions among Latinos. The problem, therefore, becomes circular. The fewer Latinos there are, the fewer ways to make the campus attractive in recruiting them.

I'm aware that by focusing on ethnicity, I run the risk of being perceived as a throwback to the 1990s, when there was more support for affirmative action and promoting a multicultural climate than I think there is today. Now, increasingly, the topic is class. I know some institutions are hoping that, by focusing on class, they can also attract more minority students. And I know they are eager to address the social disparities affecting the United States at the dawn of the twenty-first century. But I have serious doubts that class will prove to be adequate. There is no single, homogeneous working class in America. Ethnicity is a major factor in the way people perceive themselves. A white family in Wyoming with an income of $38,000, whose roots in America date back to the nineteenth century, isn't the same as a recently arrived mestizo family from El Salvador that makes annually the same amount of money. True, poverty makes no distinctions, but racism does.

Too often, the fact that our elite institutions do such a poor job recruiting Latino students is swept under the rug. If you lump every student from a non-white, European background together, the overall numbers might look impressive. But why should people of such diverse backgrounds as Cambodians, Nigerians, and Dominicans be put together, other than to inflate a misconstrued sense of political correctness? How would Americans react if a foreigner confused them with a French person, an Italian, or even a Briton? Beyond their shared humanity, they are all defined by cultural differences. Only by embracing, and not erasing, those differences can the United States be stronger. It takes time and energy to recognize that every face on a graduating-class photo has its own history and that history had an emphatic impact on the student's education.

To bring this issue into the light, and to finally do something about it, we need a starting place. I'd suggest that we set up a task force to go beyond the efforts of individual institutions. We could begin here in the Northeast, where the problem is so serious. Let's ask why we have so few Latino students enrolled in some of the nation's top colleges. If the system is the problem, the system is also the solution.

A few months ago I participated in a panel discussion at Amherst for prospective students of color. There were four professors seated in a large, elegant room filled with almost one hundred high school seniors looking to make a choice. The conversation was about how Amherst is a terrific place to study, where resources are plentiful, and the facilities state of the art, where intellectual rigor prevails, and faculty members and students interact on a regular basis. By all accounts it sounded like a magnificent buy.

At one point, during the Q&A, a shrewd, black Latino young man asked: Why aren't there any nonwhite professors in the room? I told him Amherst is changing. I stressed the fact that knowledge isn't ethnicized: You don't have to be Greek to teach the classics. Still, the number twenty-four kept popping up in my mind.

Jimmy Santiago Baca

From Bondage

⚬∞⚬

"WHEN I WRITE, I BID FAREWELL TO MYSELF," Jimmy Santiago Baca said in 1992. "I leave most of what I know behind and wander through the landscape of language." This is a memorable quote from a poet whose voice, brutal yet tender, is unique in America. The landscape of language is what redeemed Baca at twenty-one, when, still illiterate in a maximum-security prison on charges of selling drugs, he discovered the power of words. And then he let himself loose, reading anything and everything that touched his hands, writing frantically, even magically, a set of autobiographical poems that speak of injustice and alienation. His characters are young males handcuffed by poverty, with "nothing to do, nowhere to go." Denise Levertov once talked of them as fully formed people, with engaged imaginations, of the type who witness brutality and degradation yet retain "an innocent eye—a wild creature's eye—and deep and loving respect for the earth."

Baca made his name in the late 1970s, when *Immigrants in Our Own Land* was released in Baton Rouge. For a decade he steadily produced an oeuvre endorsed by small presses about the tortured experience of Chicanos. In it the reader senses a poet ready to denounce, and to do so angrily, but careful not to turn his poetry into an organ of propaganda: "I am with Those / Whose blood has spilled the streets too often, / Surprising bystanders in hushed fear," he wrote in one poem. "I am dangerous. I am a fool to you all. / Yes, but I stand as I am, / I am food for the future."

These poems came in the aftermath of the Chicano Movement, as the country moved away from activism. Change had been fought for by César Chávez and Dolores Huerta and by the Crusade for Justice, but it remained intangible. Baca's anger spoke to the unredeemed and non-affiliated in the fringes and also to a mainstream audience aware of the social limitations inherited after the Civil Rights Era. He refused to give up denunciation, exposing the tension between whites and Mexicans in the Southwest. Then came an age in which complacency was accentuated. Activism was institutionalized. Poetry left the trenches to enter the classroom: It wasn't what you'd done, but the expository strategies you'd used, that mattered. The Chicano middle class saw this as an occasion to reject outspokenness and endorse consent. Even the term *Chicano* came under fire and was replaced by *Mexican-American*. Baca's pathos was acquired by Hollywood. He left the stage and moved into screenplays, one of which, about three friends in California's prisons, became *Blood In, Blood Out,* an epic directed in 1993 by Taylor Hackford, with Benjamin Bratt, Damián Chapa, and Jesse Borrego. On occasion he would surface temporarily with a pugnacious reflection, and soon he assembled these reflections into a volume with a symbolic title: *Working in the Dark.* But it was silence that impregnated his journey, silence and detachment. That at least was the view of his readership. Was Baca the poet still active or had he turned mute?

The evidence, happily, points to hibernation. *Black Mesa Poems,* published more than a decade after, already shifted his concerns from the roughness of crime and conflict to depictions of barrio and rustic life. There were some existential poems in that collection, but a significant amount dealt with community, in particular with his second home on a New Mexico *rancho:* about the redemptive power of love, about birth and death, about motherhood, and about rivers and *piñón* trees. The move from the individual to family, from confrontation to introspection, is, apparently, what has occupied Baca all these years, and his resurfacing comes with a vengeance in the form of two interrelated books: a hefty series of lyrical poems billed by the publisher as a love story; and a poignant memoir that is at once brave and heartbreaking. One feels a gravitas in the poet's voice absent before. Impetuousness apparently has given way to fortitude. He seems more patient, attentive to the passing of seasons, in tune with the smile of children and the wisdom of elders.

The style of *Healing Earthquakes* is at times flat, even repetitive, and the plot insinuates itself by accumulation of insights. But the overall work is stunning, the product of a poet in control of his craft, one worth paying attention to. Divided into five solid, symmetrical sections that range from adulthood to rebirth and back, Baca shapes the series as a quest—again, semi-autobiographical—for balance in an eminently unbalance universe. But this is no redraft of the *Pilgrim's Progress,* though, from earth to hell and up to heaven. Instead, it is a downpour of passion. That passion leads the narrator astray as he lusts for women, tangible and chimerical, and explores myths and archetypes that come from Mesoamerican civilization. He reflects on his imperfections, runs into trouble with others, and wonders: where to find dignity? Not in religion but in morality. It is through others, through their vision, turning that vision into a model, that one might find a sense of self. This reminds me of the late Pablo Neruda, ready to turn himself into a

Boswell of the heart's disasters: burning with life, agitated by the confusion around, yet eager to turn poetry into his metronome. The series includes an explanation of silence that readers should welcome. It uses the emphatic "I" that is a sine qua non of minority letters and that is ubiquitous in Baca's poetry, a device that is used as an affirmation of the self in spite of all odds. "Here I am," it announces. "You better pay attention to me, because I will not go away." But the later Baca has become philosophical with age, and his "I" is now more contemplative:

> I used to party a lot, but now I study landscapes
> and wonder a lot,
> > listen to people and wonder a lot,
> > take a sip of good wine and wonder more,
> > until my wondering has filled five or six years
> > and literary critics and fans
> > > and fellow writers ask
> > why haven't you written anything in six years?
> and I wonder about that—
> > I don't reveal to them
> > that I have boxes of unpublished poems
> and that I rise at six-thirty each morning
> > and read books, jot down notes,
> > compose a poem,
> > > throwing what I've written or wondered
> > > on notepads in a stack in a box
> > > > in a closet.

In hindsight, to my mind Baca's most concentrated, lucid effort is *Martín,* a forty-five-page-long exploration about a young Chicano abandoned by his parents, whose itinerary from Santa Fé and Albuquerque and across states forces him to confront his own limitations. After it appeared in 1987, Baca ran into trouble with Chicano critics for his portrait of Mexican adolescents, a portrait that didn't shy away from negative attributes such as alcoholism, violence, and narcotic escapes. They accused him of pushing down his people by stressing the ugly and not the beautiful. His reaction, in an essay entitled "Q-Vo," was a welcome respite in an atmosphere of cheap ethnic pride. (The title is a phonetic redrawing of *¿Qué hubo?* Was'up?)

> [In the critics' view] Chicanos have never betrayed each other, we never have fought each other, never sold out; nor have we ever experienced poverty or suffering, wept, made mistakes. I never responded to these absurdities. Such narrowness and stupidity is

its own curse. . . . Because I am a Chicano, it doesn't mean that I am immune from the flaws and the suffering that make all us human.

The incident recalls a comment I once heard from a Chicano aspiring critic, whose teachers reiterated to him that to write a bad review of a fellow Chicano author is to become an Uncle Tom: *un traidor.* "Why add to the stereotypes?" he was told. Baca responded to the nearsightedness with courage. And it is that type of unremitting courage that colors *A Place to Stand,* his memoir subtitled "The Making of a Poet."

It is, once again, a thunderous artifact. Readers of *Martín* especially will find it a box of resonance. It follows a straightforward, chronological pattern with an occasional detour into the realm of the fantastic, in which the author offers dreams and imaginary visions of the past. This fantastic element isn't atypical. For instance, in a chapbook of 1981 that includes the poem "Walking Down to Town and Back," about rural New Mexico, a widow sets her adobe house on fire after she believes it has been taken over by snakes. From the flames emerges the image of the Virgin Mary. The tale is delivered in a voice that once belonged to a child. The voice makes use of what Freud called "the uncanny": real incidents twisted by memory into supernatural anecdotes. "Miracle, miracle," the town's people announce. Is it all in the widow's mind? Figuratively speaking, Baca's memoir only partially takes place in his mind, as he ponders the loss of his father, mother, and brother. A few passages, injected with the macabre, push the narration to a more surreal level, but these are far between. The bulk is not about miracles but about the summons of a life on the verge:

> I was born [in 1952], and it was about this time that Father's drinking and his absences first became an issue. . . . The whites looked down on Mexicans. Mother's frustration began to show. La Casita, with its two tar-papered cardboard rooms, one bed where we all slept, woodstove, and cold water spigot, wasn't the white picket-fenced house in the tree-lined city suburb she'd dream of.

Indeed, most of *A Place to Stand* deals with Baca as his Indian father leaves and his Chicano mother has a romance with a man who persuades her to leave her children behind, mask her Mexican ancestry, and begin a WASP family in California. Baca went to his grandparents first, then to an orphanage. He soon found himself destitute on the street, afraid of the deceitful manners of adults. By then he was already a school dropout. His race, obviously, accelerated his status as pariah.

Mexican was synonymous with slime. Perennially harassed by the police, he was adrift, disoriented, a stranger in his own land, incarcerated on murder charges. Upon his release, he sought to find his center, to turn himself into an honorable man. But he stumbled, and in flight he sold drugs, rambling without direction from San Diego to Arizona. Arraigned again, he ended up in solitary confinement, after defying the system that purposely sought to reform him ("prison did not rehabilitate me. Love for people did"), and learned to read. From that moment on he read, and read, and read . . . and then turned ink to paper, at which point he surprised himself a poet—and he surprised others too: his gifts were pristine, unadulterated from the start.

I was often overwhelmed by the sorrow and commiseration conveyed in Baca's memoir. It is a luminous book, honest to a fault. Every so often the author indulges in epiphanies that sound like clichés: for instance, "I didn't know what I'd done to deserve my life, but I'd done the best I could with what I had." But it is those platitudes that people less interested in literature and more in the rough-and-tumbleness of life are likely to respond to fully. *A Place to Stand* is about place in the largest, most flexible sense of the term: as home but also as the soil of one's roots and as the literary pantheon in which one fits. In that sense it belongs to the subgenre of prison tales, for which the twentieth century was fertile ground. From *The Autobiography of Malcolm X* to Vaclav Havel's diaries, the central paradigm doesn't change: involuntary confinement as a ticket to enlightenment and even messianic revelation. In the Americas, this subgenre is obviously substantial, filled with names like Graciliano Ramos and Reinaldo Arenas; north of the Río Grande, figures like Piri Thomas, Miguel Piñero, and Luis J. Rodríguez have also heard the sound of their voices behind bars. Baca too enters jail as a lost soul and leaves it empowered; in the early fragments of the book he is a *vato loco,* a crazy dude, but after the imprisonment he is an unapologetic, ideologically defined Chicano. The epilogue is especially moving: in it Baca's mother returns to her Mexican identity, but her second husband stops her short with five bullets in her face with a .45—a mesmerizing image of defeat, which Baca successfully turns around.

Maturity . . . For years I've been looking for an accurate definition of the word. What does it really mean? "Fullness or perfection of development or growth," announces, tentatively, the *Oxford English Dictionary,* but this is unsatisfactory explication. The purpose of any artist who takes himself seriously is to make the best of his talents fit the condition in which he finds himself. Is maturity the capacity to change and still remain loyal to one's own vision? Earlier on in this review I referred to Baca's work as an oeuvre, which isn't the same as work. *Oeuvre* entails mutation, the desire to change from one mode to another, the willing-ness to comprehend nature and society from contrasted stands. His poetry is monochromatic, but the same might be said of any poet of stature: a set of motifs and anecdotes reappear under different facades. But every time they do, the reader reaches a depth unlike the previous one. Baca's latest books are about anger, but he seems to be less angry than before. Time has allowed him to zoom in on his mission: to travel outward and inward as a Chicano in America, with all the complications that the identity entails; and to use language to bid farewell to his many selves. In *Healing Earthquakes* he describes his search as "leading me back across the wasteland of my life / to marvel at my own experience and those around me / whose own humbled lives graced me with assur-ance / that if I stayed on the path of love, of seeking the good in people, / of trying to be an honorable man, / that I too would one day have the love of family and friends / and be part of life as it spun like a star in the dark / radiating light on its journey—." This search, it is clear now, is a towering legacy.

A *rebozo* for Sandra Cisneros

GENEALOGY RULES LATINO LITERATURE TYRANNICALLY. Is this as it should be? Among its authors, fiction is a device used to explore roots. There are exceptions to the rule, of course, but a battalion of novels published within the last decade is about . . . what else if not multigenerational sagas where ancestry becomes the clue to the mystery. You find it in the narratives of Victor Villaseñor and Cristina García, in Rosario Ferré and in the Chilean-cum-Latina Isabel Allende, and in scores of others too. This is not only a trend but perhaps also, at this point in the game, a dead end. How many more Buendía-like trees are readers capable of handling? Gabriel García Márquez, by the way, turns seventy-five next year, and the thirty-five-year birthday of his masterpiece, *One Hundred Years of Solitude,* is taking place as I write. The Colombian has switched to autobiography to tell the tale, or, as someone stated it ignominiously, to trail the tail. Memory loss has forced the colonel to retirement now, and a flaccid physique has put his clairvoyant prostitutes out of business.

Not north of the border, though. Mnemonic clinics and plastic surgery have allowed the colonel and the prostitute to find other jobs there. Genealogical odysseys among Latinos are often called "magical realist" for lack of a better term. People, out of laziness, simply attach the exotic and the supernatural to the Hispanic imagination. Lewis Carroll had more magic than anything likely to appear in Juan Carlos Onetti's mythical Santa María, but I'm afraid that doesn't matter. Uruguay is a land of enchantment, isn't it? In contrast and by virtue of their mongrel self, minorities—ethnic, racial, linguistic—in the United States are propelled to constantly rethink their status. Who am I? How do I fit into this context, being infused, as I am, by another set of cultural motifs? And where on earth—literally and metaphorically—is home? Latinos are attuned to these questions, obviously. *El hogar,* how might I define it?

The answer, in fiction, comes in the form of transgenerational adventures: *una, dos, tres* . . . sagas in every shape and form. Their purpose is different from the Macondo model, though. The Buendías are not, for the most part, migrants. They are born and bred in the exact same coastal corner of the world. In other words, the land was theirs before they were the land's. In the literature of Latinos, the soil is not ours, at least not fully—or better, only *fooly*. Ours is a drive to make it our own, a quest to prove that the land is worthy of us and we are worthy of the land.

Think of Elena Poniatowska, the famed Mexican journalist of Polish ancestry whose masterpiece on the Tlatelolco student massacre of 1968 is a classic. She has also produced a superb novel about a female *criada, Here's to You, Jesus,* as well as a multi-layered novel about Italian photographer Tina Modotti, active in the age of Leon Trotsky and Diego Rivera. Poniatowska's work is always political. Her characters exemplify the gender and class struggle that enwraps them, and their actions are at the crossroads where power and consent collide. A few years ago, Poniatowska explained to me the difference between a Chicana author and a female Mexican one: "The first one, Ilan, introduces herself thus: '*Hola, mi nombre es Soila Fulanita. Soy chicana y lesbiana.*' The second one, instead, is rather naive. '*Hola, me llamo Dulce de Gracia.*' No national reference is given, no gender, no ideology."* The difference, Poniatowska insinuated, pertains to more than a mere how-do-you-do. It colors life in the United States altogether in grades of green, white and red. Thus, it also outlines the branches of the genealogical crusade.

Poniatowska's *norteña* friend Sandra Cisneros just published a long-awaited novel. It is a lavish, multifarious, richly textured meditation on family and culture as perceived shrewdly by a Celaya "Lala" Reyes, the rebellious and verbose daughter of a middle-class Mexican clan in a condition—mental, physical—of constant mutation. Over the past decade, since Vintage reprinted her simplistic coming-of-age novella *The House on Mango Street,* Cisneros has become the favorite *Latina* author of her generation. Her lifestyle, her color preferences, and her Frida Kahlo manners are the subject of legends, and also of heated debates. I've italicized the word *Latina.* Should I have used *Chicana,* instead? She is of a generation that struggled to break the semantic abyss between the two: Chicana (i.e., Mexican-American, but with a political twist) by origin, Latina by the proximity to others whose ancestry is from the Caribbean, Mexico, Central and South America. *Caramelo* emphasizes the universal by pinpointing the particular.

The book is dedicated, as its last sentence states, *"a la Virgen de Guadalupe, a mis antepasados.* May these stories honor you all." There are scores of *vírgenes* in the Hispanic world, each with its mood and preferences. It doesn't matter, for all of them are the same: La Vírgen, the metaphor of metaphors—a vigilant Mother whose eyes never stop

---

*See Elena Poniatowska, "Tender Gender," in *Conversations with Ilan Stavans* (Tucson: The University of Arizona Press, 2005): 160.

watching over her children. Likewise, the plot of *Caramelo* might be about a single Mexican clan, but Cisneros evidently aims it to be about the millions who "leave their homes and cross borders illegally" all over the world.

The structure of the novel isn't innovative. It begins on Route 66, on a family trip to Acapulco, and it ends in another trip: the trip of reminiscence. Transitions, transitions . . . Lala's conscience is explored through pop cultural references. Chapters are inundated with references to and quotations from songs, movies, and stars famous and infamous; *telenovelas;* and, less frequently, historical events and figures. Marlon Brando, Pedro Infante, Libertad Lamarque, Emilio "El Indio" Fernández . . . All inspire a passing comment, an insight into esthetic and historical trends. Raquel Welch, for instance, parades through the pages; she, as it happens, was Raquel Tejeda, "and she's Latina." Cisneros argues: "We would've cheered if we'd known this back then, except no one knew it except Raquel Tejeda. Maybe not even Raquel Welch." Lala takes pride in commenting on this galaxy of gods and goddesses. Their abundance might feel obsessive, but therein, I think, is the point.

The protagonists are alive in that ethereal homeland that is the consumerism of ethnic culture. Where else might one be at home, *en casa,* if not in these referents? As *Caramelo* progresses, the reader is brought into the awareness not only of Lala but also of her forefathers and foremothers, and the door is open for us to witness domestic feuds. At times it feels as if we're with a contemporary, upwardly mobile version of Steinbeck's Joads. Whereas they start on a farm near Sallisaw, Oklahoma, and end up outside of Tulare, in the center of California, about two hundred miles north of Los Angeles, the Reyes are more peripatetic: Chicago to San Antonio to Mexico City (described by one, in an affront to Buenos Aires, as "the Paris of the new World") . . . Their journey covers far more miles, for they aren't transient, but are, instead, veritable migrant souls. This is not, as in *The Grapes of Wrath,* a struggle between destiny and conviction. Cisneros isn't interested in large philosophical questions. Still, the Reyes are equally at the heart of the American Dream, a dream deferred, no doubt, a different dream, which, in our day and age, might occasionally feel like a poor replica of yesteryear.

Curiously, the pages of *Caramelo* are deprived of literary references. No connection is drawn between Lala, ever an iconoclast, and the universe of intellectuals. Instead, it is music and the silver and small screens that become the fountainhead of imagery. Garrison Keillor, the map of his *Prairie Home Companion* a response, once said that the generation that matured in the 1970s and 1980s replaced personal memories with TV notes. Lala is sublime proof. Also the scenes that build up the storyline have a fabricated feel to them. They are deliberately contrived. This is because, as in the case of Ana Castillo, Cisneros' principal source of influence—and her paragon—is the soaps, the ubiquitous *telenovelas.* In a footnote, she argues that "a famous chronicle of Mexico City stated Mexicans have modeled their storytelling after the melodrama of a TV soap opera":

> I would argue that the *telenovela* has emulated Mexican life. Only societies that have undergone the tragedy of a revolution and a near century of inept political leadership could love with such passion the *telenovela,* storytelling at its very best since it has the power of a true Scheherazade—it keeps you coming back for more. In my opinion, it's not the storytelling in *telenovelas* that's so bad, but the insufferable acting.
>
> The Mexicans and Russians love *telenovelas* with a passion, perhaps because their twin histories confirm la Divina Providencia the greatest *telenovela* screenwriter of all, with more plot twists and somersaults than anyone would ever think believable. However, if our lives were actually recorded as *telenovelas,* the stories would appear so ridiculous, so naively unbelievable, so preposterous, ill-conceived, and ludicrous that only the elderly, who have witnessed a lifetime of astonishments, would ever accept it as true.

Unquestionably, Lala sees herself as a present-day Scheherazade, and *Caramelo* is her *Thousand and One Nights.* The plot is rather unremarkable: a father's extramarital affairs; his accidental conscription of a relative— the novel is dedicated to Cisnero's father: "*Para ti, Papá*"; a mother's endless rages; the arts of upholstery and, more important, of *rebozo-*making; food and vacations and more food. . . . The *rebozo,* by the way, is the typical shawl made traditionally in Mexico in a custom that harks back Andalucía. (*Caramelo,* in Spanish, means caramel. It is also a striped type of *rebozo.*) Is it symptomatic that shawls make leading and at times cameo appearances in stories and novels by Cynthia Ozick, Alice Walker, and Amy Tan? In Cisneros it is a leitmotif across generations and an object-cum-allegory that pushes toward the conclusion of the narrative.

Her talent for succinct, impressionistic imagery is well recognized. The stories in the collection *Woman Hollering Creek,* let alone *The House of Mango Street,* which is barely one hundred pages, are all brief. They are also intense, but their intensity is deceiving. I've never been a fan of the novella, and I've stated my views publicly. It strikes me as prepubescent and reductive. In any case, briefness has become Cisneros' signature. To read a 440-page volume by her, thus, is a shocker. Somehow, in the sweeping chronicle that covers more than a century of history, she manages to remain brief. *Caramelo* is composed of chapters so condensed, so meteoric, they read like snapshots in a family album. Symptomatically, the book concludes with an eccentric chronology that starts with Hernán Cortés and Moctezuma and ends with the canonization of Juan Diego in Mexico City by Pope John Paul II, followed by the death of silver-screen goddess María Félix and a reference to the fact that her funeral cortege caused pandemonium. As Lala struggles to understand herself and her family tree through profiles of her parents and grandparents, it is evident that what she is after—and what Cisneros is driving toward, it appears—is a need to find the foundation of her culture. The Spanglish term *rootas* is attractive: it is at once *roots* and *routes.*

Frequently, *Caramelo* includes italicized footnotes, which I mentioned before—not at the bottom of the referenced page but on the next one. I'm not altogether sure why this device was left in. Toward the middle point of the story, as Lala looks back into her family past to offer the tale of her grandparents, one of her grandmothers, impatient with the tone of the tale, attempts to take control of the material. Lala negotiates with her but ultimately prevails. Are the footnotes a way to show that the author, Sandra Cisneros, is also a usurping power? In the end, the reader might ask whose story this is: Is it Lala's, her grandmother's, or the family's? Or is it the author's and hers alone? The answer, of course, is all of the above. The novel is a semi-autobiographical *crónica:* like Sandra, Lala is her father's *favorita,* she lives in Chicago and San Antonio, she travels to Mexico City, etc. . . . In the end, of course, who cares who is the one in control? Still, this and other narrative devices seem gratuitous in the book. The reader is not always convinced the author knows what to do with them.

But the blah-blah-blah isn't. The subtitle used is *Puro Cuento,* an expression in south-of-the–Río Grande Spanish that means simultaneously "only stories" and "untruthful tales." Just as we read the conclusion, we come to the realization that Lala's journey–her identity–is made of pure blah-blah-blah. Everyone around her talks, talks, talks, and she does too. Talking (in Yiddish, or perhaps Yinglish: *schmoozing*) is at once their *joie de vivre* and their *raison d'être.* These French terms might seem cliché, but *Caramelo* is about clichés, about the art and act of turning clichés into truth. Lala herself reaches that conclusion:

> And I realize with all the noise called "talking" in my house, that talking that is nothing but talking, that is so much a part of my house and my past and myself you can't hear it as several conversations, but as one roar inside a shell. I realize then that this is my

life, with its dragon arabesques of voices and lives intertwined, rushing like a Ganges, irrevocable and wild, carrying away everything in reach, whole villages, pigs, shoes, coffeepots, and that little basket inside the coffeepot that Mother always loses each morning and has to run to the kitchen upside down looking for until someone thinks to look in the garbage. Names, dates, a person, a spoon, the wing tips my father buys at Maxwell street and before that in Mexico City, the voice that gasped from that hole in the chest of the Little Grandmother, the great-grandfather who stank like a shipyard from dyeing *rebozos* black all day, the car trips to Mexico and Acapulco, *refresco* Lulú soda pop, *taquitos de canasta* hot and searing from a basket, your name on a grain of rice . . . All, all, all of this, and me shouting the noise out with my brain as if it's a film and the sound has gone off, their mouths moving like snails against the glass of an aquarium.

It is at this level that *Caramelo* is most memorable. If nothing else, its inventive, irreverent use of the English language is a lesson to reckon with. The Reyes go back and forth from Spanish to English. They also live in translation, so to speak. Hear them talk, and you'll be mesmerized by the way they think in one language but use another:

> The old proverb was true. Spanish was the language to speak to God and English the language to talk to dogs. But father worked for the dogs, and if they barked he had to know how to bark back. Father sent away for the Inglés Sin Street home course in English. He practiced, when speaking to his boss,—*Gud mórning, ser.* Or meeting a woman,—*Jáu du iú du?* If asked how he was coming along with his English lessons,—*veri uel, zanc iú.*

In her delivery of the English style, Cisneros infuses the language with a flair that is enlightening. "Vamos al Más-güel," a character states when announcing a trip to church on Maxwell Street. Or, "May I trouble you to ask for what time is?" states one character, marked by the Spanish, *¿Puedo molestarlo con preguntar qué hora es?* These automatic translations mark the entire volume. They made me think of the best portions in Jonathan Safran Foer's ingenious yet unsatisfying *Everything Is Illuminated:* loose renditions, in neither Spanish nor English and yet both at the same time. Throughout *Caramelo,* Cisneros also invents a system of dialogue that borrows from the Spanish: rather than use the customary quotations, she uses dashes. The strategy is confusing, even clumsy at first, but it ultimately enables her to frame the Reyes family in a linguistic context that stands on its own. This is an achievement, for more than anything else, *son lo quer dicen y cómo es que lo dice:* they are what they say and how they say it.

This, in short, is a mature work. Whereas *The House of Mango Street* was more about form than content,* *Caramelo* is brave, kaleidoscopic, and ambitious. Its length allows Cisneros to move in different directions at once, and to bring life to her creatures. These creatures "do not always feel well-rounded, nor are they invariably interesting. But the effort that has gone into modeling is a leap from *The House of Mango Street.* An earlier class of Chicano authors was Faulknerian in tone. (García Márquez once defined Faulkner as a Latin American master.) The oeuvres of Tomás Rivera, Rolando Hinojosa, and Rudolfo Anaya have an attachment to the soil that is decisive. The genealogical saga in them is telluric, and also marked by a type of folklore, in the case of Anaya, that is found in religious rites and legends. Rivera's . . . *And the Earth Did Not Part* is a series of interrelated vignettes about migrant life in Texas. This class was succeeded by a generation defined by the Civil Rights Era, particularly by the Chicano Movement. Their tone was belligerent. Theirs was a journey of self-definition in political terms—equality, justice, and affirmation—and the literature they produced, at an earlier stage, was in the form of protest. A few of these authors moved on to a more introspective mood, but their activism still defines them. Cisneros inherited from them her confrontational ethos, but her connections to los Unaited Estaits are more abstract.

In *Caramelo* her explorations of the labyrinthine dialogue between the U.S. and Mexico are sophisticated. They champion an erasing of borders, even as the border, in and of itself, becomes a more totemic barrier between them. Cisneros, like Poniatowska, is always ideological. Politics per se are relatively absent in her previous work, and in *Caramelo* they are displayed in the form of reflections on America and, even more instructively, in comments on the treacherousness of intra-ethnic relations. She sprinkles her narrative with sharp, arresting comments on Mexicans north and Chicanos south of *la frontera:* "something happened when they crossed the border," Cisneros writes. "Instead of being treated like the royalty they were, they were after all Mexican, they were treated like Mexicans. . . . In the neighborhoods [in Chicago] she could afford, [Lala's grandmother] couldn't stand being associated with these low-class Mexicans, but in the neighborhoods she couldn't, her neighbors couldn't stand being associated with her." Elsewhere, her father, always ranting and raving about Chicanos, described them as "*exagera-*

---

*See "Sandra Cisneros: Form over Content," in *The Essential Ilan Stavans* (New York: Routledge, 2000): 41–46.

dos, vulgarones, zoot-suiting, wild-talking, *mota*-smoking, forgot-they-were-Mexican Mexicans . . ."

What does a single novel teach? Everything and nothing. *Caramelo* will not cure us of the genealogical tyranny that has become endemic in Latino letters. It is occasionally self-indulgent, and structurally speaking, it doesn't appear to come to us in a fully developed stage. Also, it investigates archetypes not always under a refreshingly new light. It does, however, present an opportunity to rethink the marriages of literature and society and of language and the novel in Latino letters. Why are we, ethnic authors, so prone to family sagas? To what extent does pop culture replace individual memory? And what is the fate of English in our hands? Cisneros, by surfing on the obsessions that define her own generation, challenges us to go beyond. Through verbal ingenuity, through the unrepentant border-crossing of her imagination, her novel is as much Mexican as it is American.

Sepharad Is Nowhere

~~~⸎~~~

THERE IS SOMETHING UTTERLY ANNOYING, even infuriating, about this novel, the second by Antonio Muñoz Molina, a Spaniard born in 1956, to be translated into English. (The first one was *Winter in Lisbon* [1999].) Originally written in Madrid in 2000, *Sepharad* is subtitled in Spanish "una novela de novelas"—a novel of novels. The statement is accurate: it is a lyrical meditation not only on other people's books but on other people's memories. Its centrifugal structure reminds me of the oeuvre of W. G. Sebald, in particular *The Emigrants.*

Sebald, who died in 1998, showered us with a phantasmagorical prose juxtaposed with strange, at times macabre photographs he found in antique stores. A German who came of age after World War II, his quest was to explore the interstices of silence and abjuration in his native country after the Holocaust. Less than a decade younger than Sebald, Muñoz Molina comes from an altogether different landscape. He was only twenty years old when Generalísimo Francisco Franco died and *la España dogmática* finally embarked on a journey that made it one of the liveliest, most dynamic partners in the European Union today: *la España democrática.* Yet *Sepharad* is also about loss, although a less tangible, more metaphorical one. Actually, the engine that moves the narrative is loss but also memory and exile.

Divided into seventeen sections thematically interconnected, *Sepharad* explores the dilemmas of *desplazados,* i.e., artists and thinkers on the verge of an abyss. The Holocaust is one of Muñoz Molina's concerns, as are Stalinism and Franquismo itself. One chapter places Kafka and his mistress Milena Jesenka in a protagonist role. Another one deals with the purported plot by Jewish physicians to murder Stalin. Other chapters discuss the plight of suffering creatures like Primo Levi, Willi Münzenberg, and Jean Améry (née Hans Mayer), who, by the way, was also eulogized by Sebald in *On the Natural History of Destruction.* The location shifts from Moscow to Madrid, from Copenhagen to New York. Margaret Sayers' English-language translation is superb, although it ought to be striking to any curious reader to find out that the original version published under the aegis of Alfaguara has 599 pages while its American counterpart only has 384. I trust it's all in the font, though; a superficial check doesn't acknowledge any editorial casualties.

So what makes *Sepharad* exasperating? The title, of course, is a reference to the eviction in 1492 by King Ferdinand and Isabella of approximately two hundred thousand Jews from Spanish soil. But the novel is only marginally about the Sephardim, who by my own estimate appear in some 5 percent of the overall content. Instead, Muñoz Molina creates a multinational, ahistorical gallery of refugees, mostly twentieth-century dwellers, whose plight, in his eyes, resembles that of the Sephardim. Yes, each and every one of these *desplazados* is for him *un sefardí*—an evicted soul, itinerant, homeless, permanently on the run. "To be Jewish was unpardonable, to stop being Jewish was impossible," the author quotes an interlocutor, Emile Roman, a *desplazado* himself who discusses with Muñoz Molina the infamous Edict of Expulsion, then points in the direction of Levi and Améry. Jewishness, Roman states, is simultaneously "an illness and a strangeness." He recounts how the Nazis forced the yellow Star of David on him and his family: "And if for an instant I forgot I was a Jew and couldn't be anything but, the looks of people I met in the street or on a streetcar platform . . . reminded me of it."

An illness and a strangeness—that, exactly, is how Muñoz Molina approaches his circus of anguished Jews and other literary freaks. He turns the term *Sepharad* into an allegory. Needless to say, Sephardic culture isn't about victimhood any more than it is about fortitude. To focus on loneliness and banishment and not on stamina and reconstruction is foolish. A number of the approximately two hundred thousand Jews who left Spain moved first to Portugal and from there to the Netherlands, Italy, Turkey, the Balkans, and other geographies that became part of the Ottoman Empire. Departure gave place to arrival, and arrival to renewal.

More than half a millennium after 1492, Spain is still in denial. Of the canon of Iberian novels, I could count while standing on a single foot, like the Talmudic sage Hillel, and in less than a minute also, the total number of works eager to discuss Jewish themes without bias. Miguel de Unamuno's poem on Ladino, Federico García Lorca's eulogy to a Jewish cemetery in New York, Jorge Semprún's memoir *The Long Voyage* . . . Of course, to recite the plethora of anti-Semitic texts from Spain, I'll need the strong support of my two feet and at least an hour.

Why a non-Jewish Spaniard like Muñoz Molina would choose to write a novel about Jews, call it *Sepharad,* and almost refuse to address the topic in a balanced, convincing fashion escapes me. Ironically, the same week I got my set of uncorrected proofs I also received as a gift a copy of Noah Gordon's *The Last Jew,* published in 2000, about the life of the *converses* from 1489 onward. A quick surf-ride through Amazon.com shows a total of twenty-four readers' responses, most of them enthusiastic. But more important is the fact that *The Last Jew* has become a huge bestseller in Spain, where it has sold millions of copies. To compare Gordon's fluffy style with that of Muñoz Molina might be seen as an insult: the former is an entertainer, the latter a *litterateur*. Still, it strikes me as symptomatic that an exploration—a recrimination, really—of the Iberian expulsion should be left to an American Jew. Apparently, no Spaniard, no matter how talented, is ready to discuss the issue frontally.

All of which makes me think of *Sepharad* not only as an affront but as a dangerous waste, too. Who needs yet another book about exile and memory, especially after W. G. Sebald perfected the genre? No, Muñoz Molina doesn't need to meditate on why Jews have become transient when his own country is in desperate need of a soul-searching voyage to recognize the trauma of the past. Why not give us *una novela de novelas* on why and how *la España católica* became amnesiac?

The Holocaust in Latin America

❦

NOT LONG AGO, I WAS SENT A slim volume published recently in Buenos Aires, barely a hundred pages long, called *Barbarie y memoria*. It is a compilation of international authors, edited by Manuela Fingueret and meant for a general Spanish-language audience. Its subtitle indicates that it includes reflections on both the Holocaust and the military dictatorship in Argentina from 1976 to 1983. That intrigued me.

The number of anthologies about the Nazi atrocities has multiplied in the United States in the last twenty-five years, after a period of silence immediately following World War II; today, the Holocaust is a permanent fixture in American-Jewish life, explored in documentaries, films, memoirs, museum exhibits, and more. Nothing like the Shoah business exists, even remotely, south of the Rio Grande.

I thus browsed Fingueret's volume with enormous excitement. At first, I was disappointed by some of the selections: poems, nonfiction, testimonials, and stories by figures like Anne Frank, Elie Wiesel, Primo Levi, Simon Wiesenthal, and Nelly Sachs. Those seemed predictable choices, although, I realized, probably not for the Hispanic public in the Southern Hemisphere, where the names might be recognizable, but nowhere near the heart of the region's intellectual debate. As I read on, however, what made my exposure to *Barbarie y memoria* far more satisfying was the way that the obvious sat side by side with the unanticipated.

Among the prominent figures from the Spanish-language world (not only from Latin America but from the Iberian Peninsula as well) were Jorge Semprún, Spain's former minister of culture, whose 1964 account of an agonizing truck ride to Buchenwald after he was captured working with the French resistance (translated as *The Long Voyage*) is one of the few works on the Holocaust in Spanish. But there was also the poetry of León Felipe, Héctor Yánover, and Mónica Sifrim, and the prose of Simja Sneh, León Rozitchner, and Santiago Kovadloff. Some of the selections deal directly with the effects of the Nazi genocide in Spanish-speaking countries, barely known within the writers' linguistic boundaries, almost never beyond them; others concern the impact of the Argentine dictatorship, far more a subject that people around the globe have come to expect from Latin American authors. A few selections even relate, compare, and contrast the two events.

Ultimately, the juxtaposition of the Holocaust and Argentina's tyranny during its "Dirty War" is nothing if not provocative. It is an invitation to open up the discussion of the role of anti-Semitism in Hispanic America. Yes, I reflected, Fingueret's effort might seem minuscule to those exposed to the overwhelming amount of Holocaust literature in English, French, German, and other European languages. But "minuscule" carries the wrong connotation in reference to a book on the Holocaust published in Argentina—a book that is limited, perhaps, by the region's circumstances, but not unimportant.

At first glance, it may seem strange that the Nazi genocide has played such a slight role, to date, in the Latin American imagination. According to the World Jewish Congress, about half a million Jews live in Latin America, mainly in Argentina, Brazil, and Mexico, but also in countries like Guatemala, Peru, Costa Rica, and Colombia. This, in fact, is the fifth-largest concentration of Jewish population on the globe, after the United States, Israel, Russia and Central and Eastern Europe together, and France. Argentina alone has 250,000 Jews—eighth in the congress's listing of national populations.

A large percentage of the Jews in the region arrived from the 1880s to the 1960s, a substantial number of them Yiddish speakers from *shtetlach* and urban centers of the Old Continent, and another considerable portion from what was once the Ottoman Empire. Before that influx came the immigration of Marranos, or "crypto-Jews," who had first converted and then fled Spain, desperately trying to escape the mighty fist of the Inquisition.

There is little doubt that the Holocaust itself played a significant role in increasing Jewish immigration to Latin America—and in the history of the Jewish communities there. Eager to flee increasingly vehement persecution in their homelands, many German-speaking Jewish refugees from Nazi-dominated Central Europe found havens in the Southern Hemisphere in the 1930s. Numerous others—survivors of concentration camps and displaced persons from Eastern Europe, Greece, and Turkey—immigrated to Latin America in the aftermath of World War II.

Yet the Jewish presence has remained peripheral in Latin America. In my youth in Mexico, Jews were approached not just with curiosity, but also with suspicion. In the early 1970s, when I was an adolescent, my sixth-grade teacher took us to a school screening of Alain Resnais' *Night and Fog*. To better illustrate the Holocaust, an Auschwitz survivor was invited to the classroom. I vividly remember the moment he raised his sweater sleeve and showed us his tattooed number. But mine was a small, insular, Yiddish-language day school, so discussion of the Holocaust was not so surprising. Few non-Jews in Mexico at the time (or, for that matter, until recently) were introduced to the Holocaust through more than, at best, a smattering of popular culture—television mini-series like *Holocaust,* with Meryl Streep, and movies like Steven Spielberg's *Schindler's List,* imported from the United States. As a result, knowledge of the Jews and their history has remained fractured, incomplete. Just how incomplete was brought home to me in 1981, when, by then a college student, I was confronted in a public bathroom by acquaintances who wanted to see what a circumcised Jew looked like.

It has long been a puzzle to me that Octavio Paz, a Renaissance man whom I admire wholeheartedly, whose work fills my library shelves, reflected on just about anything, from Buddhism and T. S. Eliot to Sor Juana Inés de la Cruz and Surrealism. But not on the Jewish presence in his homeland. The more than a dozen hefty tomes of his *Obras Completas* are a veritable map that links Mexico to the rest of the globe. But absent in those reflections is any serious consideration of Jewishness. So ubiquitous in Western Civilization, Jews seem to have been nonexistent in Paz's eyes.

The indifference is not always as blunt. Mario Vargas Llosa's *The Storyteller* is about a Jew in Lima, Peru, who is described as "strange," and the writer's essays tackle controversial issues, including the entangled Middle East conflict. The novels of Carlos Fuentes, from *A Change of Skin* to *Terra Nostra,* analyze Jewish-Hispanic relations since the Middle Ages. But even in the oeuvres of those authors, Jews, although mentioned, are usually dealt with superficially, not as a significant part of Hispanic culture.

The opposite should be said about Jorge Luis Borges, whose reaction to Nazism was uncompromised by his environment, and whose interest in Judaism ran deep: ranging from Hebrew and Hasidism to kabbalah and the birth of the state of Israel. Borges was arguably the most important twentieth-century intellectual in Latin America. But was he truly Latin American? I don't want to enter into meaningless debates about authenticity. Nevertheless, the fact is that the Argentine writer was superb precisely because he turned Argentine letters upside down, because he proved that cosmopolitanism was a legacy not only of Europe, but also of the globe. His preoccupations weren't those of his continent, by even the most generous stretch of the imagination.

It ought to be noted that Latin America is not alone among Hispanic cultures in holding an ambiguous relation to the Jews in its midst. Spain gave us Rafael Cansinos-Assens and Ramón Gómez de la Serna, both of whom wrote sympathetically about Jews, as well as Angel Pulido, whose dream it was, at the dawn of the twentieth century, to create an atmosphere that would facilitate the return of Jews to the peninsula. Federico García Lorca was inspired by a Jewish cemetery in his *Poeta en Nueva York,* and Miguel de Unamuno wrote an obscure poem, "Canción del sefardita," about nostalgia for Sepharad, which is the word used by Levantine Jews to refer to Spain. Iberian theater includes references to the Nazis and the Old Testament and to some claims that Christopher Columbus was Jewish. But the amount of anti-Semitic literature—which includes works by Francisco de Quevedo, the poet, and Benito Pérez Galdós, the novelist—is far more substantial. Significantly, debate or dismay about it is conversely small.

In Latin America, not even the topic of Marranos and Jews in colonial times—so important a part of the history of the area's settlement—elicits much attention. Indeed, the silence is almost palpable. Figures like Luis de Carvajal the Younger—whose autobiography, drafted in Spanish prison in 1589, named other crypto-Jews and ignited so much fear among his compatriots that many left Spain—remain little known. Carvajal's writings, including his letters, are long out of print and unavailable today to Latin American readers. Scholars know about him, but most other readers know at best only a problematic biography of the Carvajal family, filled with ambiguous feelings toward Jews by the author, Alfonso Toro. More than thirty years ago, Seymour B. Liebman produced a bibliography of Inquisition cases and sources about Marranos in the New World; he and Martin Cohen also studied Carvajal. At least such a resource is available in English. But only a small portion of that research has been translated into Spanish, and it is mostly unobtainable today. Anthologies about Sephardic civilization have appeared, but their circulation is limited.

Again, the question is why. Peter Novick's *The Holocaust in American Life* (1999) attempts to explain how remembering the Nazi genocide became such an industry—even a religion—in the United States. For years after the war, Novick argues, a combination of factors, from Cold War politics to the reluctance of American Jews to be considered victims, silenced discussion of the Holocaust; then, events like the trial of Adolf Eichmann and the Six-Day War in the Middle East opened up the topic. That hasn't happened in Latin America. For one thing, the region's Jews themselves have yet to "go public" about who they are and how they are perceived. More often than not, they still prefer silence to open debate about their status in society. Fear of anti-Semitism, fear of being stigmatized as a minority, still runs high.

Of course, Jewish immigrants to new lands have always struggled to assimilate and become full citizens. But those who fled to Hispanic America faced a particular kind of anti-Semitism. For the overall structure of Hispanic society since the Middle Ages has been colored by the concept of *pureza de sangre,* "purity of blood," used by Old Christians to vilify half-hearted converts—mainly former Jews. That has made a world of difference. The anti-Semitic bias has deep roots; even in territories where Jews were not actively persecuted, the xenophobia against those who are not genealogically Roman Catholic is still ubiquitous. To complicate matters more, the concept of purity of blood also pervaded the subjugation of the New World, echoed by conquerors, explorers, and missionaries, who saw aboriginal people as impure. For the conquered, the concept carried with it the sound of doom.

It must also be remembered that many Jewish immigrants who survived the Holocaust and came to Latin America faced a sad irony: they found themselves living with often-visible Nazi fugitives who had also found their way there, aided by "rat lines" and sympathetic officials who, fascinated by the militarism of the Nazis and fed by anti-Semitism, made the region a haven for Nazis. Adolf Eichmann, Josef Mengele, and Klaus Barbie were only the best known of the German escapees to the region.

Then too, for many people in Latin America, the Holocaust took place far away and out of sight. If, at the time, it was reported scantily in North America, south of the border it was covered nothing short of abysmally. Part of the reason is that tragedy is always local, and the history of the Hispanic Americas, especially as they were forcibly introduced to modernity, has more than its own share of genocide to occupy its people.

The arrival of the Spanish conquistadors gave rise to a devastation of human life just as unimaginable as that of the Holocaust. How many Indians in the Hispanic world died in wars or as the result of plagues and famine is up for grabs, but the numbers historians debate are in the millions. The collective memory of such devastation persists to the present day. Add to those memories the wreckage of the battles for independence, and of the chain of oppressive regimes that followed, and the effect is a chilling museum of human atrocities in which anti-Semitism, for many people, seems to play only a small, often tangential role.

Terror has played a part. No one should minimize the effect of living in fear: for a long period, neither the survivors of the Holocaust in Latin America nor anyone else living in the shadow of the dictatorial regimes there dared draw attention to themselves by speaking about their own experience with fear.

And yet, and yet . . . Fingueret's anthology is the product of a slightly more open atmosphere that dates to the late 1980s and the end of the very visible dictatorship in Argentina. Jews seem more comfortable talking about themselves, and others seem a bit more willing to listen. There's a refreshing new sense of self-consciousness about the Nazi period in Latin America, and about the role of Jews in Hispanic society. The openness is more evident in some Latin American countries than in others, but it is safe to say that the pattern is beginning to span the region. The presence of sustained, if fragile, democracy is probably part of it. So, too, is a kind of envy with which some Hispanic Jews regard their seemingly more comfortable and more open coreligionists to the north. Many children and grandchildren of survivors are scattered throughout Argentina's capital, as well as in urban centers in Brazil, and want more information about the emotional troubles faced by Jewish immigrants. And perhaps third- and fourth-generation Jews in Latin America are finally beginning to feel more at ease than their forebears.

That is not to say that full acceptance of Jews is at hand. Much of the new feeling is still unspoken, unexplored. But the silence, at least in my view, is not as emphatic as it once was.

Jewish authors, for example, seem to have more presence in the Southern Hemisphere. From Argentina, there is Ricardo Feierstein, Marcos Aguinis, Jorge Goldenberg, and Fingueret herself; from Mexico, Rosa Nissán; from Uruguay, Mauricio Rosencof. Many of those authors began their careers decades ago, but now the collective impact of their work is beginning to be felt. Some are even achieving popular success. And while few take the genocide in Europe as their central focus, many do offer it as backdrop. Editorial Milá and the Acervo Cultural in Argentina publish Holocaust survivors' accounts, like that of Charles Papiernik, originally a French citizen, who endured four years in Auschwitz. And a recent fiction contest, organized by Feierstein, brought a handful of Holocaust-related narratives, including *El último día,* by Mina Weil, about a Jewish girl growing up in Mussolini's Italy. I've also seen some nonfiction articles, like one about relationships among Holocaust victims by Diana Wang, a psychologist in Buenos Aires, who found out she was Jewish as she was about to take first Communion.

Films, too, are part of the trend. I'm acquainted with fewer than half a dozen movies made in Latin America that address the Holocaust directly, but several others deal with the topic at least tangentially. Those include Luis Mandoki's 1987 *Gaby,* a true story about a handicapped Mexican woman whose parents were refugees from Nazi Europe, and a 1993 adaptation of Nissán's novel *Novia que te vea* ("Like a Bride").

Of course, time continues to add to the emotional traumas faced by

Jewish refugees. Like Simja Sneh (1914–99), a Yiddish- and Polish-speaking intellectual in Argentina, they fled fascism only to live through the Dirty War, often run by hoodlums who had been trained by Nazis or the children of Nazis. Then they witnessed the *atentados*—terrorist attacks–on the Israeli Embassy and the Asociación Mutual Israelita Argentina in Buenos Aires in the early 1990s. Today, they still often confront the presence of the children of escaped Nazis—a presence obvious in areas like Bariloche, Argentina, where the heirs of the Nazis are known in popular lore as "Swiss Germans," as well as in Asunción, Paraguay, where the German population divides itself into "good" and "bad" Germans.

However, the Holocaust survivors and their children are freer to discuss their mounting burden publicly. Take an example, again from Argentina: Daniel Feierstein, a son of the novelist Ricardo Feierstein, leads a group of young Holocaust scholars—Marcela Bartoló, Guillermo Levy, Damián Montero—at the University of Buenos Aires, where they have produced a body of essays about Nazi methods in the ghettos and camps of Europe. Recently, the university's press published Feierstein's revised *Seis estudios sobre genocidio,* first available in 1997. Feierstein is also one of the first to examine Argentine-government archives containing secret correspondence with the Axis powers during World War II, and he has now edited those documents and published them on a CD-ROM.

I want to reiterate a word of caution: the emerging consciousness that grapples with the Holocaust in Latin America has probably reached only a tiny fraction of the population; it may also be more evident to a viewer looking to Latin America from the United States than in Latin America itself. For most of the Hispanic Americas, the Holocaust is still little acknowledged.

Indeed, it is to the north that the real impact of new discussions about the role of the Holocaust in Latin America is being felt most strongly. A number of intellectuals and scholars of Jewish-Hispanic descent—I include myself here—have moved to the United States in search of a more open atmosphere to explore our Jewishness. As a group, we are forcing American Jews to see the Holocaust not only from a U.S. viewpoint, but from a more pluralist perspective. The evidence is growing: museum exhibits, films, drama, fiction, and poetry on the impact of the Holocaust in Latin America (some written or produced in English, some translated from the Spanish or Portuguese); relatively recent scholarship like *Jews of the Latin American Republics,* by Judith Laikin Elkin, *Hotel Bolivia: The Culture of Memory in a Refuge From Nazism,* by Leo Spitzer, and *Welcoming the Undesirables: Brazil and the Jew-*

ish Questions, by Jeffrey Lesser; personal essays by the Cuban-American anthropologist Ruth Behar. Sadly, such work tends mainly to be ignored in Latin America.

So I see *Barbarie y memoria* as testimony to a moment of intriguing change. It is a moment when Jews in Latin America are beginning to be more open about their Jewishness, and when scholars in the United States are creating a field to study them. Nothing like the Shoah business north of the Rio Grande exists to the south. But it is a start.

Forverts & I

cᐟ❦ᐠ

MY RELATIONSHIP WITH *FORVERTS* started in adolescence, when one of my teachers at the Yiddishe Schule in Mexico, a refugee from the war and an old-fashioned intellectual with a Sisyphus complex (his fanciful, life-long mission was to bring Mexican Jewish youngsters to Yiddish), talked to me about its importance. I had never heard of it before. In class, we had been reading Israel Joshua Singer's novel *The Family Carnovski* in the original. I was impressed by the author's epic view of Polish life and told him. He not only reacted sympathetically; he promised to lend me other books in Yiddish, which he did, officiously, the next day: a volume of Peretz's writings as well as *Yoshe Kalb*. (I remember him talking nastily of I.J.'s younger sibling, Isaac Bashevis, an opinion my grandmother, also a reader of literature, shared: he was a pornographer.) Plus, the teacher gave me a recent issue of *Forverts*, describing it as a newspaper "where both the writers and readers are of high quality."

I took an immediate interest. Soon I began to write—in Yiddish. My first literary pieces, a detective story among them, were inspired by what my teacher gave me and other wonderful stuff I stumbled upon in general libraries: Edgar Allan Poe, Jorge Luis Borges, Fyodr Dostoievski. In my senior year in high school, I wrote a play, again in Yiddish, inspired by the work of Antoine de Saint-Exupéry.

When I moved to New York in 1985, the fact that I would buy my weekly copy in newsstands was, in my eyes, a huge cultural leap, since access to it in Mexico was restricted. (My grandmother subscribed to a local Yiddish publication of suspicious quality. The sole copy of *Forverts* I remember was at the library of Centro Deportivo Israelita.) I still have a vivid memory of a Sunday-morning pilgrimage to the historic building in the Lower East Side, from which the editorial offices moved in 1974. It happened a few weeks after my arrival. I made it with an Italian roommate with Communist sympathies. We shared an apartment on Broadway and 121st Street. The two of us were still novices in the art of navigating the Manhattan map, and we spent almost six hours finding the place. Since we were fans of *Call It Sleep*, the trip also had the purpose of visualizing the scenario where Henry Roth's protagonist child undergoes his epiphanies. Exhausted yet exhilarated, I remember writing my mother a letter in Yiddish that night about the outing. I told her that more than ever I wanted to become a Jewish writer and that I wanted to write for *Forverts*.

Less than a hundred years after its foundation, the first issue of the English-language edition, called *The Forward,* came out on May 22, 1990. I remember the date because I lived at the time almost on the corner of Amsterdam and 110th Street. Although it cost seventy-five cents, free copies were in abundance in banks, pastry shops, even pizzerias of the Upper West Side. I grabbed one right away, thrilled about its new life. To me its existence announced that American Jews were ready to look at themselves through a different prism. Yiddish was in the background, but English was now in the present. Furthermore, that English wasn't anymore a gentile language; it was a Jewish language, showcasing their verbal cadence, their psychological traits.

I got a subscription. What I would frequently feel while reading it still isn't easy to explain, and in many ways puts me at odds with members of my literary generation. Already then I knew, without a reasonable doubt, that I wanted to make my life in the United States. But I was still a correspondent for newspapers and magazines in Spain, Mexico, and Venezuela. Virtually all of my work was done in the Spanish language. Reading *The Forward* made me want to become an American writer—to add a different perspective to Jewish life north of the Rio Grande. My Hispanic heritage was seldom taken into account in Jewish circles, which were defined by a Eurocentric (non-Sephardic) appreciation. There were other diasporas worth paying attention to. If in Yiddish *Forverts* had helped Jewish immigrants become Americans, the English version could make them be less parochial, more cosmopolitan, a feat only achievable by adding another perspective, by helping them look at themselves under other lenses.

Of course, in doing so I myself became an American Jew. I found a copy of Irving Howe's *World of Our Fathers.* I reread Isaac Bashevis Singer, now away from the tutelage of teachers and grandmothers. And I became convinced about the social side of literature: to write isn't exclusively an esthetic effort, but a historical one, too. I convinced myself that the only responsibility a writer has is to make full use of his talent as witness and participant of the time into which he was accidentally placed, to discern the major issues that define it, to use the imagination as mirror to better understand our place in history.

My debut in *The Forward,* if memory serves me well, occurred in 1994. It was a long paragraph accompanying an excerpt from "Camacho's Wedding Feast." It belongs to *The Jewish Gauchos of the Pampas,* by Alberto Gerchunoff. I had selected the story for my anthology *Tropical Synagogues: Short-Stories by Jewish-Latin American Writers,* the first book I

74

ever sold to a New York publisher. I worked with Philip Gourevitch. Since then, I've been blessed by a string of superb editors, with whom I've developed strong friendships: Jonathan Rosen, Robin Cimbalest, Blake Eskin, and Alana Newhouse. They've taught me how to be more succinct, less flamboyant with my style. Over the years I've had sustained discussions with them (over lunch, on the phone, at panels, in trips overseas) about the function of criticism in the age of the Internet.

It's no euphemism to say that with their help I learned how to write in English, how to appraise and reflect on culture in the broadest sense of the term: local and global, private and public. Other writers of my age seem allergic to the ethnic press, perceiving it as at once parochial and passé. Mine is the opposite view. The readers of *El Diario/La Prensa* (where I've had a weekly column) are neither sophisticated nor affluent, but they have the pulse of America, a nation mapped across racial lines, where Latinos are already a country within a country.

The syncopated pages of *The Forward,* whose influence in political, social, and cultural terms has only grown in almost two decades, represent, in my view, a return to ethnicity by American Jews. They serve as a digest of the community, reawakening to the excesses of assimilation, a register of the dreams, emotions, and ideas we have, about ourselves and the world at large. What I enjoy in them is precisely what I can't find the *New Yorker:* the feeling that I belong to a small group, and that the group has a purpose, a *raison d'être.* In many ways, this feeling is a reverse of the mission of the Enlightenment, when European Jews were invited to be equals at the banquet of Western Civilization. Their acceptance was about erasing difference, about giving up an awkward, primitive religion (in their opinion) while becoming citizens, with all the rights and privileges thereof. Today Jews are indeed equals—perhaps a little too much. Our role in the shaping of world secular culture is unquestionable since the French Revolution; and in the United States, that role, nowadays more than ever, is central. But there's nostalgia for what was lost along the way and perhaps even the awareness of a betrayal that took place. With equality Jews might have lost a cherished quality: uniqueness. Is there a way to recover it?

Ironically, almost every time I file a contribution to *The Forward* (first by mail and fax, now by email), the image comes to mind of Edmund Wilson, the dean of American literary critics in the twentieth century, whose oeuvre to me is the most distilled example of calibrated wisdom and accessible, esthetically pleasing style. When I started writing in English, I had him as my model—and still do. As Wilson, who attended Princeton, attempted to reflect, in one lucid essay after another, the value of novels by Ernest Hemingway, F. Scott Fitzgerald,

John Dos Passos, and William Faulkner, he also became infatuated with his country's past (he wrote *Patriotic Gore,* a book on the Civil War) and on the Iroquois Indians. The tension between the particular and the universal defines his thought. That tension intrigues me as well. The editors I've worked with at *The Forward* have always been open to it. Jewishness, they would all agree, is a mode of being. The more as Jews we erase our differences, the more we emphasize them.

My Yiddish teacher in Mexico died years ago. Sometimes I wish we could sit together again and schmooze about his gift to me.

Hispanic Anti-Semitism

c⊗ɔ

In Caracas last summer, as Venezuelan President Hugo Chávez, the most vocal anti-American leader since Fidel Castro, delivered a speech against the Israeli incursion into Lebanon, anti-Semitic graffiti were scribbled on the central Sephardic synagogue. One of them read: "Zionism = Terrorism." Another stated: "Jews Assassins." The periodicals *Diario Vea* and *Temas Venezuela,* loyal to the regime, included cartoons with swastikas, Stars of David, and American flags juxtaposed. Unfortunately, such messages aren't uncommon in Venezuela, where the Socialist-leaning leader is building strong ties with Iranian president Mahmoud Ahmadinejad in a proud axis to counter-balance American weight worldwide. Every time the Middle East is embroiled in another explosive episode, the effect on the streets in Chávez's country is foreseeable.

It would be a mistake to see these as disparate incidents. In fact, while Venezuela represents the most fertile soil today for this type of hatred, Latin America as a whole has a history of anti-Semitism that is little known yet increasingly worrisome. In 2005, Jewish tombstones were sprayed with Nazi slogans in Cochabamba, Bolivia. Similarly, swastikas were drawn on the outside of the Hebraica Club in Montevideo, Uruguay. Other attacks have taken place in recent years, not only in cities where an active Jewish community lives but in towns without Jews as well. At times, neo-Nazi groups are blamed, but aggressions are also committed by Communist groups. In Valparaiso, Chile, after a documentary on neo-Nazi activities made by the country's TV network was shown, the network's office was vandalized. In Argentina, arguably the Latin American country where anti-Semitism is most vocal, the list of occurrences is longer than anywhere else in the hemisphere.

It's time to conceptualize Hispanic anti-Semitism on its own terms. Seeing it in the global context, and using external tools and categories to understand it, doesn't offer a full picture of its reach. It is a phenomenon with a complex, multifaceted history. But before I go any further, a word ought to be said about the term *anti-Semitism* per se. A few months ago, I delivered a lecture on the topic at the U.S. Holocaust Museum in Washington, D.C. Prior to my visit, I received several emails from potential attendees complaining about the use of "anti-Semitism" in the event's title. A couple of them suggested that the term refers to aggression against people of Semitic background. Jews are among them, but so are Arabs. They suggested *anti-Judaism* as an alternative. But anti-Judaism is abhorrence against the Jewish religion. So how about *anti-Jewishness*? It is equally loose, since Jewishness is generally understood as the secular culture of Jews in Western Civilization, most of it beyond politics. My response was two-fold: first, that the word *anti-Semitism* is to such an extent ubiquitous at the global level, that while its semantics might be vague, the public always understands its focus on Jews; and second, that my interest in anti-Semitism isn't limited to the detestation of a single group, but to xenophobia in general, its target being Jews, Arabs, and anyone else whose mere presence is deemed to be a threat.

Approximately a dozen representatives of the United Nations from different parts of the Hispanic world had been invited to my lecture. These diplomats were all educated, middle and upper middle class, with an average age of fifty, and none of them (to the best of my knowledge) Jewish. I was struck by some of their comments during the Q&A section. A couple of them said they had never witnessed any anti-Semitic remark directed at people in the Hispanic world or, for that matter, anything more physical stemming from such hatred. My impression was that as official representatives of their respective nations, they were eager to condemn, at least on paper, any form of discrimination. Given a bit more time and upon further reflection, though, those offering comments suggested that misconceptions about Jews did indeed exist in their countries of origin but remained skeptical that they amounted to any orchestrated phenomenon.

Their skepticism isn't surprising. The Hispanic world, constituted by Spain, Latin America, the Spanish-speaking Caribbean, Equatorial Guinea in Africa, and Latinos in the United States, has a population of almost 475 million. With the exclusion of the United States, the estimated number of Jews in those places, which varies from one source to another, is not larger than 350 thousand. Most Hispanics never see a single Jew in their life. Of course, this doesn't mean they don't have preconceptions about them.

The Latino minority north of the Rio Grande is a fascinating case study. Made of some forty-three million people, its attitudes toward Jews have undergone changes in the last few decades as the process of assimilation has unraveled. A survey conducted by the Anti-Defamation League in 2002 showed that 35 percent of Hispanics in the United States harbored anti-Semitic views, a substantially higher number than among average Americans, which, according to the same source, were at 17 percent. Interestingly, the survey suggested that among Latinos, the percentage was higher among the foreign-born, at 44 percent, whereas Hispanic Americans born in the U.S. were at 20 percent. When it was released, the survey was at once enlightening and controversial. No similar analysis is available for the Hispanic world in general. And the sample of respondents might not have been representative of the diversity within the Latino community. Still, the high percentage of anti-Semitic views among Hispanics, and the discrepancy between newcomers and the native U.S.-born, are symptomatic. Among other things, it announces that the northbound immigrant journey that millions of people from places like El Salvador, Peru, and Colombia undertake, and their exposure to American values through the educational system as well as the media, cut the recurrence of those views in more than half.

Let me offer a definition: Hispanic anti-Semitism is the animosity—verbal and physical—targeted toward Jews in Spain, Latin America, the Spanish-speaking Caribbean, and among Latinos in the United States, which stems from concrete historical, religious, and political forces pertaining to that civilization, although it is also, and frequently, influenced by global events. (For the sake of this definition, and of this essay, I'm not including Brazil.) Each of these regions that constitute the Hispanic world, and each of the nations, has its own idiosyncrasies, and consequently, anti-Semitic sentiments tend to be different from place to place. For example, anti-Semitism in Argentina, where about two thirds of Hispanic Jews reside, needs to be understood on its own terms. Yet there's enough continuity among nations to suggest that broader, more comprehensive tools should be applied to recognize pan-Hispanic patterns. And those patterns, starting in the Middle Ages, point at the Jew as interloper, hypocrite, and agent of dissent.

There are three distinctive modalities of Hispanic anti-Semitism. These are often interconnected, to the point that unscrambling them might seem like a hopeless endeavor. Yet each displays unique characteristics, and, as such, ought to be considered on its own terms. The three modalities are a Church-connected and sponsored type; an ideologically driven and thus secular one; and a third modality that relates to the Middle Eastern conflict. The first two are usually perpetrated by the locals, although outside pressure is a major factor. The last modality, obviously, springs from Zionism as a nationalist movement that emerged in the second half of the nineteenth century. It presented itself in teleological terms with the creation of the state of Israel in 1948 as its climax, and has evolved as Israel and its Arab neighbors have gone through arduous times. While anti-Zionist feelings are harbored by the locals, extreme attacks of the terrorist kind have been carried out by fundamentalists from the Islamic world.

The origins of Hispanic anti-Semitism and the source of the first modality is the period known as La Reconquista in the Iberian Peninsula, i.e., the quest to homogenize the territory under one religion, Christianity. To achieve the objective, two of three faiths that coexisted in Spain during the period called La Convivencia, Judaism and Islam, needed to be extricated. And they were, in that order.

To this day, Church-supported anti-Semitism in the region revolves around a set of beliefs sponsored by the Church Fathers, among them the notion that Jews betrayed Jesus and their existence is proof of the authenticity of the Passion. These views are tightly held among a vast number of Hispanics. Jews were expelled from Spain in 1492, the same year Columbus' first voyage took place. The Expulsion Edict, issued in Granada in March, and written by Juan de Coloma on behalf of the Catholic Monarchs, Isabella and Ferdinand, "resolved to order all and said Jews and Jewesses out of our kingdoms and that they never return or come back to any of them." Pushing the Jews out from a land they had lived in since the Roman Empire brought an end to the cohabitation of the three major Western religions.

I'm distressed by the fact that the edict isn't better known, given its historical importance as well as its brevity. It is a rather intricate document, the first portion of which is devoted to justifying the decisive legal action taken by the government. That rationale is equally revealing. The monarchy believed that the sheer presence of Jews in the Iberian midst made "bad Christians" misbehave. That is, there were "good Christians" and "bad Christians." A successful nation would endorse the former while rejecting the latter. The edict uses the verb *judaizar,* featured in Hispanic lexicons for centuries, from Sebastián de Covarrubias's canonical *Tesoro de la Lengua Castellana o Española* to dictionaries of the early twentieth century: to judaize, meaning to spread the evil gospel.

Such a concept is ingrained in the Hispanic psyche. The word alone serves as a kaleidoscope to understand the changing modes of Iberian culture. The establishment of the Holy Office of the Inquisition as an institution endowed with the responsibility to fight apostasy, hypocrisy, and witchcraft, among other sins, is inseparable from the first modality of anti-Semitism. There has been much debate among historians as to the true function of La Inquisición. Did it persecute Jews? Was it designed, instead, as a mechanism against an emerging class with powerful influence: the *conversos*? Has its role been over-emphasized? Whatever the answers to these questions might be, it is undeniable that its sheer authority projected a long shadow on every aspect of life. There was fear that a double identity, Jewish in the privacy of one's home, Catholic in public, would result in punishment.

That fear spread widely. To be a Jew and to be a *judaizante* were different things: the former resisted conversion and, hence, was a lost cause; but the latter was all the more dangerous, a body-snatcher whose surreptitious ways undermined the foundation of Iberian civilization. The terms *castizo* and *honrado,* in vogue at the time of the transatlantic colonial enterprise, are apropos. None is readily translatable into English. They make reference to the pure blood in one's family, to the difference between a *cristiano viejo* and a *cristiano nuevo:* Old and New Christian, respectively. At the time of the colonial enterprise, this ethnic hierarchy, based on ancestry, shaped the Americas to the core.

Spain, after 1492, was mostly left without Jews, but not without anti-Semitism. For centuries a fascinating development took place, its impact still traceable nowadays: anti-Semitism without Jews. Just as Shakespeare wrote *The Merchant of Venice* without having been exposed to Jews in British society, so did some of the authors of the so-called Spanish Golden Age, like Francisco de Quevedo y Villegas, imagine Jews in their oeuvres without direct contact with them. The same goes for their successors, like Benito Pérez Galdós. In Spanish literature of the sixteenth century and onward, Jews are big-nosed money lenders. And while the country, democratic, representative, and enlightened since the 1980s, is currently a full partner in the European Union, on occasion one still stumbles on anti-Semitic remarks, especially among soccer fans.

In Latin America, anti-Semitism is grounded in the ethnic phobias that arrived from the Iberian Peninsula with the conquistadors, explorers, and missionaries. The first modality I listed, Church-sponsored, is pervasive. *Conversos* seeking to escape the Spanish Inquisition believed the colonies across the ocean were a safe haven. In spite of the prohibition by the Holy Office to allow apostates to emigrate, a wave of New Christian families traveled overseas, and along with them crypto-Jews. Cases like that of Luis de Carvajal the Younger, accused of proselytizing the Mosaic religion, were sacrificed in autos-da-fé in major urban centers like Lima and Mexico. To meditate on anti-Semitism in the Hispanic world, in particular in the Americas, without invoking the victims of the Inquisition in the New World, is to de-contextualize the phenomenon. Even though *conversos* are never mentioned in textbooks, their plight is the pillar on which subsequent hatred is built. The Catholic Church used them as anti-models. By burning them at the stake, in ceremonial gatherings attended by the masses, the message was clear: they were sinners because they refused to acquiesce and persisted in being different. Yet the presence of *conversos* was so widespread in Latin America that, according to specialists in onomastics, literally hundreds, if not thousands, of the region's patronymics, from Espinoza to Pérez, have Jewish origins.

One could argue that the impact of the Counter-Reformation, sponsored by the Catholic Church, which eliminated any possibility of free, open debate, left Latin America hobbled. Jews, harbingers of progressive thought elsewhere in Europe, were eliminated in Spain and banned from emigrating to the colonies, where dissent wasn't tolerated. When the independence movements began to emerge, a fever that spread like dominoes from 1810 onward, the revolutionary figures were often accused of being Jewish *conversos,* masons, and free-thinkers. For instance, attacks were unleashed against the parish priest Miguel Hidalgo y Costilla, the Mexican patriot and chief leader in the fight for independence from Spain, as a way to discredit his cause.

Ashkenazi immigrants arrived in the Americas roughly between 1880 and 1930, sponsored by philanthropists like Baron Maurice de Hirsch. Argentina was a primary destination. Their arrival, as well as that of thousands of immigrants from other origins, triggered an outbreak of xenophobia in the local population. This is the period in which *The Protocols of the Elders of Zion* multiplied, from Russia to Europe and beyond. In the Americas, there was an ingrained debate about their presence. On one hand, ideologues and politicians subscribed to the theories articulated decades earlier by thinkers like Domingo Faustino Sarmiento, who in his book *Facundo: Civilization and Barbarism* suggested that the only way for these emerging republics to become "civilized" was to eliminate the *gauchos,* since they represented primitivism, and to invite Europeans to settle the land in the hopes that they might build metropolitan habitats like those in the Old Continent. On the other hand, there were reactionary forces for whom the immigrants, and Jews especially, symbolized the destruction of the pristine nature of the place.

Among the chapters in the history of Hispanic anti-Semitism of the ideological modality is the Semana trágica, the Tragic Week. Some commentators have described it as the first and so far only *pogrom* (a Russian word meaning "a violent anti-Semitic outburst") in the Americas. But the fact that it was first and foremost labor unrest might put it under a different light. It happened in Buenos Aires in 1919. As Argentina was undergoing a process of industrialization and workers were seeking to organize, labor unrest took place with an obvious dose of anti-Jewish sentiment. Businesses were destroyed. How many people were killed is still a subject of debate. Some sources put it close to seven hundred dead and thousands injured. A number of them were Jews. Since then, anti-Semitic attacks based on ideology are sporadic. Their tone depends on circumstance. Different political figures have used anti-Semitism to their advantage, steering the population in a convenient direction.

When I was growing up in Mexico, anti-Semitic information would often make its way to newspapers. I remember reading comic-strips and watching TV shows where stereotypes were featured. Jews were accused of controlling major businesses. In 1982, when President José López Portillo nationalized the banking industry, he threatened to publish a list of those Mexicans who had taken money out of the country, a threat that remained just that. It was said that the list had a preponderance of Jewish last names. Similar incidents have taken place from Peru to Costa Rica. It isn't at all surprising when one considers that *The Protocols of the Elders of Zion,* published in inexpensive editions, is sold in magazine stands.

Since 1948, however, and more precisely since the Six Day War in 1967, the third modality of anti-Semitism, ideology-based, has materialized. Although it goes by the name of anti-Zionism, the misnomer cannot hide the same kind of xenophobia. This modality springs from left-leaning circles. In campuses across Latin America, maybe more intensively than in their U.S. counterparts, Israel is portrayed as a merciless aggressor whose only purpose is to annihilate the Palestinian population. The rhetoric reaches higher intellectual circles. Some years ago I was engaged with the Nobel Prize–winning Portuguese novelist José Saramago in a polemical discussion about it. After his visit to Ramalah, Saramago equated the Palestinian situation to the Nazi genocide. Needless to say, his opinions aren't exceptional. *Jews* and *Zionists* have become interchangeable terms, and in urban graffiti they appear to be synonyms for merciless capitalist usurpers and partners of American imperialism.

The apex of this modality of Hispanic anti-Semitism took place in Buenos Aires when, in July 1994, a terrorist attack left eighty-five people dead and hundreds injured. A car bomb was crashed against the building of the Asociación Mutual Israelita Argentina, the Jewish community center known by the acronym A.M.I.A. The entire building collapsed. President Carlos Menem, of Syrian descent, ordered an investigation, which dragged on for years and in the end offered no conclusive data, although Iranian top-ranking officials and Iranian-backed terrorist groups remain to this day the prime suspects. Some months earlier, also in the Argentine capital, the Israeli Embassy was the target of another terrorist attack.

These incidents signaled the vulnerability of Jewish communities in Latin America. A drastic change in attitude followed. Up until then, they didn't see the need for security, notwithstanding anti-Semitic aggressions of the first and second modality. Almost fifteen years later, prominent Jewish sites are under severe vigilance, especially during religious holidays.

These terrorist activities in Argentina and the anti-Jewish aggressions in other parts of Latin America I've discussed acquire a special quality when analyzed against centuries of Inquisitorial activity and in the context of ideologically driven anti-Semitism. They won't vanish into thin air; instead, they are manifestations of a unique type of hatred with deep cultural roots. A stereotypical image of the Jew is used to agitate the masses, to steer the electorate in a particular direction, and as an extension of the Middle Eastern conflict.

The impact of these manifestations in the United States is crucial. While, as the data released by the Anti-Defamation League suggest, Latinos born north of the Rio Grande increasingly reject anti-Semitic ideas, fringe organizations like the Nation of Aztlán, mostly through the Internet, incite hatred by spreading chauvinism. Connected to the independence-seeking view loudly articulated by Chicanos during the Civil Rights Era—that their original land is Aztlán and that Chicanos today live under U.S. occupation—this organization, as is clear from its publication, *La Voz de Aztlán,* denies the Holocaust and portrays Jews as abusive maquiladora owners, media manipulators, anthrax-spreading terrorists, and shrewd spies. It also supports the idea that Zionists were behind the attacks of September 11, 2001. Their editorials, reprinted in the Arab world, are intertwined with comments on poverty, voting rights, immigration, and bilingual education. The immigration marches last year allowed for the dissemination of these nativist opinions. Their emergence hasn't taken place in a vacuum. They ought to be linked to anti-Semitism in Latin America, although these idiosyncratic manifestations are clearly more ethnocentric in nature, belonging to the type of rhetoric associated with Louis Farrakhan and other extremist black leaders.

The only way to respond to Hispanic anti-Semitism is to understand it at its core.

My Mexican Shivah

IN MY VIEW, complaints about a film misrepresenting the source on which it is based miss the point. Once a writer sells the material and agrees to no longer be involved, the product is beyond his domain. He might as well sit back and enjoy the show, just like any other spectator.

A few years ago, Alejandro Springall came to visit me at Amherst. He dreamed of making a film about Mexican Jews and wanted me to write the story. I was intrigued by the invitation: I'm always in need of exploring with new forms; plus, I'm an unredeemed film buff. In fact, when I was an adolescent I seriously considered—as "seriously" as one does at that age—pursuing filmmaking as a career. Springall and I spent hours together at a Holiday Inn, including pulling an all-nighter, mainly sharing our experiences of growing up in Mexico City, a megalopolis today of about eighteen million people where Jews constitute less of 0.1 percent of the population. Yet the tightly knit, complex, entrepreneurial Jewish community has solid roots, as is evident in thriving neighborhoods such as Condesa, Polanco, and Tecamachalco, and in institutions like the Kehila, the Yiddish and Hebrew day schools, the legendary sports center, mikvehs and cemeteries, and its various youth organizations. Its ancestry isn't exclusively Eastern European, though; there is a significant portion of members identifying themselves as Sephardic, with ancestry in Syria, Turkey, and Lebanon. Some still speak Ladino.

I didn't know Springall before this, though I had admired his 1999 movie *Santitos*. He isn't Jewish, but he told me about dating Jewish girls and feeling at home in their milieu. Should a movie come out of it, I remember telling myself during our tête-à-tête, it would have the perspective of an affectionate outsider, which is more than fitting, given that Mexican Jews in my view retain a sense of uniqueness that makes them stand apart. We signed an agreement, and months later I sent Springall the first draft of *Morirse está en hebreo,* a ninety-page-long novella that was eventually collected in my book *The Disappearance.*

Springall's film, also called in Spanish *Morirse está en hebreo* and titled in English *My Mexican Shivah,* premiers at Lincoln Center's Walter Reade Theater on January 9 as the opening entry of the New York Jewish Film Festival. Co-produced by John Sayles and with an original score by The Klezmatics, it has a cast of theater and soap opera actors that includes my father, Abraham Stavans. The film was shot in a Polanco apartment like the one in the story. (I visited the set and even have a cameo appearance.) It belongs to the growing shelf of south-of-the-border movies about Jewish topics, from *The Holy Office,* about the sixteenth-century auto-da-fé of Luis de Carvajal the younger, to *The Last Embrace,* about Argentine-Jewish angst.

Aside from a brief opening and a funeral at the Ashkenazic *panteón,* the plot was Aristotelian in its structure. It's about the death of Moishe Tartakovsky, a patriarch in the Ashkenazic community. Unfolding in the background are the presidential elections of 2000 taking place, in which the ruling party, Partido Revolucionario Institucional, finally lost after holding on to power for seventy-plus years. The candidate who replaced PRI ruler President Ernesto Zedillo wasn't from a left-wing party, like Andrés Manuel López Obrador, who, speaking for the Partido Revolucionario Democrático in the elections of 2006, claims that, despite his defeat, he is Mexico's rightful president. The winner in 2000 was Vicente Fox, a former Coca-Cola executive from the conservative Partido de Acción Nacional. The nation's democracy was still untested then. Maybe the word is *immature.*

Immature is how at times I've felt we Mexican Jews perceive ourselves. Anti-Semitism is always latent in Mexico. It has been supported by the Catholic Church and by certain extremist ideological factions since colonial times. But the Jewish community ignores it, preferring to look inward. It's just as well, since my intention in *Morirse está en hebreo* wasn't to dwell on the political sphere per se. Without ignoring the larger national scene, I wanted to write an intimate portrait, a chamber piece, concentrating on the domestic side of a single family; the Tartakovskys would serve as a microcosm of a Diaspora that happens to be my own.

What has made each chapter of the Jewish Diaspora, from the destruction of the First Temple in Jerusalem to the present, different? The fact is that, like chameleons, we Jews "adapt and adopt," as a teacher of mine enjoyed saying; we assimilate to the environment by incorporating elements of that environment into our *Weltanschauung.* A leather businessman, Moishe Tartakovsky has a personality built around the dilemma of being a member of a small minority in a country monolithically Catholic. Why does he constantly feel like a traitor? Is Mexico his real home?

Since the 1970s, writers in Latin America have been pressured to conform to the magic realism made famous by Gabriel Garcia Márquez and others. While I've been interested in the style, I've resisted being enlisted into its ranks. It might be seen as ironic, then, that between the time I sent Springall the draft and its final publication, an uncle of mine,

Abraham Slomianski, also a family patriarch, died exactly the same death I had imagined for Tartakovsky. Talk about literature as a way of life, or else about life as a way to literature.

In any case, before his death, Moishe's family—his two children, Bernardo (a.k.a. Berele) and Esther; his grandchildren, Nicolás, Ari and Galia; his close friends and associates; his school sweetheart; the shiksa who was his lover; the maid, et al.—approached him as the glue keeping everyone together, for better or worse. They saw him either as idol or as villain, received either his gifts or his scorn. But they hardly spent any time together as a family unless he was around. So with his death, they face a challenge: What keeps them together now? And did they all see Moishe through the same lens? Was he a chameleon even among Jews? I wrote the novella in English with portions in Yiddish and Hebrew. The tone is humorous, although it isn't outright comedy.

Sadly, the political dimension was left out. The film isn't a reflection on the perils of young democracies and the role that minorities play in them. There are mariachis, paramedics, and other supporting figures, but they are marginal. Springall also endorses the symbolic, a decision I applaud. Two bearded Hasids—played by a pair of excellent amateur actors—take the function of a Greek chorus, offering insight into the story through comments delivered in the Yiddish I grew up with (but with subtitles, of course). But his adaptation is less than subtle, emphasizing the role I barely insinuated for my characters.

But I have no regrets. It is at once exciting and strange to see my fictions transposed onto the big screen. Springall turns the material into comedy by stressing the exoticism that results from Jews and Mexicans seated together in *shiva*. To me there isn't much exoticism there, only a mundane relationship based on centuries of misunderstanding. Art is about letting loose, about breaking boundaries, about usurping what isn't ours. In the novella *Morirse está en hebreo,* I sought to exorcise some of the demons of my past, to place them in historical context. I visualized myself in Tartakovsky's *shivah.* What I mourned was the ambivalence of Mexican Jews during the PRI years. Springall reinterprets the material in an exaggerated manner, one suitable in cinematic terms.

This time around, I'm the outsider.

Is José Saramago an Anti-Semite?

⟨✥⟩

IS JOSÉ SARAMAGO AN ANTI-SEMITE? The answer, unfortunately, might be allegorical. In March 2002, during a visit to Ramallah along with seven other delegates of the international Parliament of Writers, Saramago compared the situation of Palestinians in the Occupied Territories to the extermination of Jews in Auschwitz. His visit, and the remarks he made, brought along an uproar. Israelis are avid readers, and the Nobel laureate responsible for such masterpieces as *The Year of the Death of Ricardo Reis* and *The Gospel According to Jesus Christ* is an unqualified favorite. Or better, in the lucid Hebrew translations he *was* a favorite, but newly published and used paperbacks of his oeuvre were immediately returned to stores in Tel-Aviv, Haifa, and other metropolitan areas, as a sign of protest. The disapproval reached beyond the Middle East: a storm of opinion pieces in newspapers and magazines was felt in Spain and the Americas, and an outbreak of email responses traversed from France to South Africa and from Poland to Mexico.

My involvement in the affair wasn't that of a distant observer. I've been a passionate admirer of Saramago since the late 1980s, when I first reviewed him for the *Nation*. News of his assertions in Ramallah reached me in April. I was told that the novelist had articulated his thoughts more comprehensively—and, no doubt, more repulsively also—in a piece he published in *El País* in Madrid. Toward the end of the month I met him and his wife, Pilar, and I had a public discussion with him, at the John F. Kennedy in Boston. Saramago had been scheduled to tour the United States the previous year, but 9/11 put the schedule on hold. The international situation was quite tense when he appeared with Harold Bloom at the New York Public Library. The repeated terrorist attacks on Israeli civilians and Ariel Sharon's belligerence had pushed the Middle East to the edge. In his customarily apolitical manner, Bloom, I was told, had turned his comments on Saramago in Manhattan into an exercise in self-negation. He delivered an in-depth examination of his oeuvre and then . . . *silencio.* It was up to me to take the bull by the horns. But our dialogue was a disappointment.

I spent several days reading book-long interviews and essays published in Portuguese, as well as browsing through his *Journey to Portugal* and rereading his early- and mid-career novels. I also discussed his overt ideology with colleagues across the map, such as Saramago's friend in Porto Alegre, Moacyr Scliar. Then I asked Saramago himself, point blank, if he is anti-Semite. His answer was a rotund *no*. As he told a reporter of *Ha'aretz*, he told me that the role of the intellectual is "to make emotional comparisons that would shock people into understanding." He also said he wondered if "the Jews who died in Nazi concentration camps, were persecuted throughout history, or forgotten in ghettoes . . . , if that vast multitude of the wretched would not feel ashamed to see the vile acts their descendants are committing" in the Occupied Territories. And he added: "I wonder if having suffered so much would not be the main reason to spare others suffering."

Saramago and I talked for about an hour. It had been our desire to communicate in Spanish, a "neutral" tongue since he is unversed in English and my Portuguese is limited. But the organizers wanted us to have a simultaneous translator on stage, which became a distraction. In any case, I asked him about the precise nature of his remarks in Ramallah. He talked of meeting Yaser Arafat in his headquarters and also of traveling around Israel. He sought to persuade me and the audience before us that the Israeli press had taken his views out of context. But had it really? Was Saramago not sticking to his guns? In the end, the dialogue left me frustrated. I wished I had more time, and less intrusion tête-à-tête, to explore the issues in full.

To a large extent the American media seemed to have ignored the controversy. There were notices in the *Boston Globe* and in some other newspapers, but their impact was minuscule. In comparison, the decision by the English Department at Harvard University not too long ago to "disinvite" the Belfast poet Tom Paulin ("a poetic polemist" is how the *Guardian* in London describes him) as a result of the statement, in a poem by Paulin in the *Times Literary Supplement,* that Jewish settlers in the Occupied Territories should be assassinated, had strongly agitated reporters and editors from Los Angeles to New York. The disparity between these two reactions is symptomatic. Why, I wonder, was so little said about Saramago's remarks in the United States? Is it because the Iberian Peninsula remains a center without gravitas in our milieu? My assumption is that far fewer people have read Tom Paulin's poetry than, say, *Blindness,* which is Saramago's towering achievement and became a bestseller in the United States. But Paulin, born in Leeds, teaches at Oxford and Columbia and is part of our linguistic habitat. He is an Englishman—his father is English, his mother from Northern Ireland— whose dilemmas concern the American intelligentsia. Portugal, instead, is too remote, its concerns too provincial. Plus, anti-Semitism has been an essential feature of its history, hasn't it? The answer is yes, but hasn't anti-Semitism also been at the heart of England's quest for self-definition?

The appearance in English of his novel *A Caverna,* originally published in Lisbon in 2000, and lucidly translated by Margaret Jull Costa, is an opportunity to ponder Saramago's politics yet again. This is a brilliant novel of allusions and archetypes that opens with a quote from Plato's *Republic,* Book VII: "What a strange scene you describe and what strange prisoners. They are just like us." As is often the case in the later oeuvre of the Portuguese author, the coordinates of time and space are left unspecified, although, judging by the references to technology (TV, electricity, amusement parks) it quickly becomes clear to the reader that we're somewhere in *the present.* And how does that present become palpable? By the existence of a huge complex called The Center, made up of fashionable stores, entertainments, offices, apartments, i.e., a site of arcades and malls and "sensation zones" of the kind that invade Western societies today. The protagonist of *The Cave,* translated from the Portuguese by Margaret Jull Costa, is one Cipriano Algor, a sixty-four-year-old small-village potter whose life has been devoted to the making of pots and jars. He lives humbly with his daughter Marta and his son-in-law Marçal Gacho, who works as a security guard in The Center.

Cipriano regularly takes Marçal in his truck from their village to work in The Center. The trip is also made to deliver Cipriano's merchandise, which is sold at The Center. But early in the plot the protagonist is told by the authorities that his items are no longer sellable and that The Center shall no longer buy them. Customers nowadays "prefer plastic," he is told by the authorities. In other words, the change in consumer tastes has made Cipriano Algor redundant. In the hands of a lesser writer, one more pamphleteering in his nature, this premise would easily evolve into a predictable critique of capitalism. What makes Saramago extraordinary, at the literary level at least, is his extraordinary humanity—the depth and dignity with which he infuses his creatures. From the start his characters are designed as metaphors, but this doesn't make them cartoonish: they are made to represent higher values, but their individualized self is perfectly delineated. Cipriano reacts to the disastrous news with depression, but soon Marta, and to a lesser extent also Marçal, persuade him that senility isn't a synonym for death. There is hope for him if he is able to find it on his own terms. Uselessness is a state of mind.

The search takes Cipriano into an unexpected journey, one in which his values are tested radically. First, he stumbles upon a dog, which he calls Found and turns into his closest companion. With the encouragement and support of Marta, he also decides that if The Center doesn't want pots and jars, then he should think of another item to sell. He and his daughter come up with an idea: small figurines dressed in multiple ways. He offers them to the authorities, and to his surprise and ours, he receives a new commission. Suddenly, his life has meaning again. Or has it? Soon Martha finds out she's pregnant. Another twist of events occurs when Marçal is promoted. These benchmarks result in the decision by the three to leave their small village and move to The Center. Around the same time, in a visit to the cemetery, to the tomb of his late wife, Cipriano meets a widow, Isaura Estudiosa, and they begin an unlikely affair. It complicates the decision to move, but Fate in *The Cave,* and in Saramago's work in general, is spelled with a capital "F": it is implacable. The move eventually takes place. The tortured ins and outs of existence are shrewdly explored by Saramago in a style that is as lurid and dense as it is unremitting. Protracted paragraphs run for entire pages, sometimes for whole chapters. The incessant dialogue between characters isn't identified through quotation marks but is integrated into the flux of the narrative. An example:

> Cipriano Algor got up from the table. Have you suddenly lost your appetite, asked his daughter, seeing that there was still food left on the plate, I find it hard to swallow, my throat feels tight, It's nerves, Yes, it must be. The dog had got up too, ready to follow his master. Ah, said Cipriano Algor, I forgot to mention that Found spent the night under the stone bench keeping a watch on the fire, So one can learn from dogs too, Yes, what one learns above all is not to discuss what has to be done, simple instinct has its advantages, Are you saying that it's instinct that is telling you to finish the job, that in human being, or at least in some, there is a behavioral factor similar to instinct, asked Marta. All I know is that reason would have only one piece of advice for me, What's that, Not to be so stupid . . .

The result of this ornate approach is an overwhelming feeling of fatalism. Cipriano, Marta and Marçal seem to be sheer marionettes in a tale that unfolds without hesitation. Aren't we all? They aren't free to chose. Saramago, their creator, leaves them at the mercy of superior forces whose *raison d'être* they shall always ignore.

Up to this point, which is about halfway through, I had the sense I was in John Steinbeck's *The Pearl,* a tale of envy and dispossession in a small Mexican village, which Emilio "El Indio" Fernández turned into a successful film. Saramago is versed in the same kind of suffocation:

provincial people, largely uneducated, halfheartedly invited to become part of modernity. No sooner do they become infatuated by the neon lights ahead of them that they fall victims to their own ambition. But the most perplexing part of *The Cave* comes at the moment the three characters move to The Center. A set of surprises is in store. Cipriano, jobless as he is, roams the place without much to do, only to discover that such unimpeded movement isn't allowed. The dwellers of the place are asked to be happy, to enjoy the amenities, but not to test the limits of the site. There are doors that ought to remain closed, entire sections beyond the reach of average people, secrets that should be left unrevealed. His movement compromises Marçal. A relative with such curiosity, it is obvious, is a danger not only to himself but also to those closest to him. He ought to be stopped. But before Cipriano is stopped, an unimaginable development unfold in The Center: a magisterial discovery take place in its underground—a cave is located, and in it six people dead, three men and three women. Who are they, and why are they there? The authorities respond with *silencio* . . . until Cipriano, of his own will, descends to the tunnel, finds the cave. He also finds Marçal. The two are stunned by what their eyes see. Cipriano then decides to turn around:

> There was nothing more to do there, Cipriano Algor had understood. Like the circular route of a calvary, which will always find a calvary ahead, the climb back up was slow and painful. Marçal had come down to meet him, he held out his hand to help him, and when they emerged from the darkness into the light, they had their arms around each other, although they could not have said for how long they had been like that.

The protagonist understands that, lo and behold, "*those people are us.*" In due time he abandons The Center, returning to Isaura Estudiosa and his dog Found, which he left with her when he departed from the village. By now, though, the village isn't an option for him and his family either, and thus the five characters—Cipriano, Marta, Marçal, Isaura, and Found—are pushed to exile, their destiny an open question. The cave discovered at the core of The Center turns out to be Plato's famous parable of illusions, where people are pushed to live in darkness, observing a parade of shadows projected on the wall that are the result of the visual effect created by a bonfire.

The volume is mesmerizing and also emphatically mythical. That, of course, is Saramago's objective: to turn his plot into an *allegory,* which, as the Oxford dons put it in their iron-handed dictionary, is "the description of a subject under the guise of some other subject of amply suggestive resemblance." Needless to say, allegories were ubiquitous in the Middle Ages, but the rise of the novel as a literary genre has liberated us from their burden. Contemporary audiences are allergic to substitutes. They are used to calling things by their own names. Saramago pulls it off in *The Cave* because he doesn't force too much "alien" symbolism into his protagonist: he's presented as *Mr. Everybody,* and thus readers identify with his plight; but he is also naïveté personified. His emblematic self is made to mean something far beyond his own skin: Cipriano Algor is a concrete person, yes, but he is also an abstraction. In Saramago's pen, this device works superbly, infusing the novel with an excess of meaning that makes it irresistible.

But the same device fails miserably when Saramago works outside the boundaries of fiction. The Middle East is no doubt a quagmire of signification, but an intellectual of his stature ought to know better than to inject malleable biblical allusions into a process that in and of itself is frighteningly volatile. Evidently, in his Ramallah remarks the Portuguese applied the *"those-people-are-us"* mechanism to a circumstance that is exacerbated by the tendency to embrace allegory. The battle between Sharon and Arafat isn't a re-creation of an atemporal duel between Abraham's children. Instead, it is a confrontation between people whose claims to the same parcel of land are equally valid. Likewise, the encounter between Nazism and the Jews wasn't another scene in the clash between Christ and anti-Christ. Was Saramago naive enough to make a comparison designed "to shock people into understanding"? Is *shock* truly the way to bring enlightenment in a region overburdened by shocks of all sizes? On the international scene we are what we are and little else, and not some mythical remnant of a past. Would it make sense to compare the Portuguese people of today with the cruel colonizers of the Brazil in the sixteenth century? Ought Saramago, so righteous in his tone and tune, be perceived as a descendant of the vicious conquerors, which would make him accountable for their nefarious performance toward the aboriginal population?

His piece in *El País,* published on April 21, 2002, was an offensive diatribe that metastasized "the well-known biblical legend of the combat between the little shepherd-boy David and the Philistine giant Goliath" into a war of adolescent Palestinian stone throwers and hostile Israeli tanks and helicopters. But this connection is a mirage: excessive violence by the Israeli Army is at once a shame and a disgrace; conversely, the blind faith of Palestinian youngsters hypnotized by Hamas, who become portable bombs designed to kill civilians, is equally tragic. But the Israeli-Palestinian discord isn't a novel in which a creator manipulates his characters, extracting a meaning in their actions for the reader to digest. No, Auschwitz isn't an allegory, and neither is Ramallah. These two sites are calamitous on their own terms and ought to be understood in their proper context.

I've talked to Saramago, and although the dialogue we had left me dissatisfied, I don't believe he is an anti-Semite. No, I don't think we're in front of a case like T. S. Eliot's. The temptation to offer grandiose pronouncements about the Middle East has turned one too many sages into clowns. Usefulness is also a state of mind. Saramago is an admirable master at the peak of his talent, as *The Cave* proves. He is also a fool for using his reputation to misrepresent, and ultimately to confuse even further, a global conflict that isn't in need of obfuscating symbolism but of brave and tangible solutions. (I was about to end with a line suggesting that Saramago the intellectual and not the novelist seems imprisoned in Plato's cave, but I realized that that too is an allegory.)

Don Quixote at Four Hundred

❧

The Knight of the Sorrowful Countenance is turning four hundred. By some accounts, the first part of *Don Quixote of La Mancha*, Cervantes' masterpiece, published by Juan de la Cuesta, was available in Valladolid by Christmas Eve 1604, although Madrid didn't get copies until January of the following year. Thus came to life the "ingenious gentleman," who, ill-equipped with an antiquated armor "stained with rust and covered with mildew," with an improvised half-helmet, and atop a nag that had hooves "with more cracks than his master's pate," went out into a decaying world, where there were plenty of "evils to undo, wrongs to right, injustices to correct, abuses to ameliorate, and offenses to rectify."

Cervantes catches a glimpse of Alonso Quixada or Quexada, as the down-and-out hidalgo is known in the novel, at around fifty, the prime of one's life by today's standards but a synonym for decrepitude at the height of the misnomered "Golden Age" in Spain, a period also known, deceptively, as "the Age of Enlightenment." That, at least, is how the character is described from the outset: the protagonist, we are told, was weathered, his flesh scrawny, and his face gaunt. Cervantes gives us no reference whatsoever to his childhood and adolescence. In fact, we are only given a modicum of data about his affairs, including the fact that little sleep and too much reading of chivalry novels like *Amadís of Gaul* had finally succeeded in drying up his poor brains. Almost a thousand pages later, Don Quixote—or else, Alonso Quixana–lies in his death bed, a bit older and maybe wiser too. He is about to die an exemplary death, shaped as a physiological, spiritual, and social departure. But consumed as he is by the grief of countless defeats and frustrated too in his impossible mission to see his beloved Dulcinea of Toboso disenchanted, what does he die from? Is it melancholia? Or should we attribute it, yes, to his refusal to recognize the limits of old age?

Or better, does he actually die? By chapter 73 of the second part, published in 1615, Cervantes made sure Don Quixote is dead and buried. Some time before he had managed to release the sequel, an impostor from Tordesillas by the name of Avellaneda, impatient that Cervantes kept procrastinating, brought out an unofficial second part, a trashy follow-up that not only angered Cervantes but pushed him, probably sensing that his own death was close (he died on April 23, 1616), to complete the job. "Don Quixote's end," we are told, "came

95

after he had received all the sacraments and had execrated books of chivalry with many effective words. The scribe happened to be present, and he said he had never read in any book of chivalry of a knight errant dying in his bed in so tranquil and Christian a manner as Don Quixote, who, surrounded by the sympathy and tears of those present, gave up the ghost, I mean to say, he died." To be sure, in that chapter Cervantes makes sure no one else is ever capable of appropriating his creation again. "For me alone was Don Quixote born," he writes, "and I for him; he knew how to act, and I to write; the two of us alone are one." He even composes a riddle (hereby translated by Edith Grossman, as are the previous quotations):

> Careful, careful, worthless idlers!
> Let no one lay a hand on me;
> for this enterprise, O king,
> is reserved only to me.

The character of Don Quixote might be dead, but his ghost is restless. As the forerunner of anti-heroes and superheroes from Fantômas to Spiderman, his flawed ambition might not subdue giants and unravel pretend enemies like the Knight of the Wood, but it surely conquers your heart, precisely because he is ridiculed time and again, inhabiting a universe of his own concoction. Don Quixote is the ultimate symbol of freedom, a self-made man readily championing his beliefs against all odds.

No wonder the legion of admirers—and, in unequal measure, of detractors—is infinite. Other than the Bible, has any work in Western Civilization generated more ink? Operas, musicals, theatrical and film adaptations, as well as fictional re-creations based on the rendezvous of Don Quixote, keep piling up: Laurence Sterne was inspired by his misadventures in *Tristram Shandy;* Flaubert pays homage to him in *Madame Bovary,* as do Dostoievski in *The Idiot* and elsewhere and Milan Kundera almost anywhere. Isaac Bashevis Singer's "Gimpel the Fool" might be read as a reimagining of the knight's simplicity. These are only a handful of overt tributes. The list of invisible references is . . . well, invisible. And then come the multilayered interpretations of Don Quixote's pursuit. Anybody who is somebody has put forth an opinion, from Miguel de Unamunos, José Ortega y Gasset, Salvador de Madariaga, and Américo Castro, to name a handful of Iberians first, to Dr. Johnson, Diderot, Kafka, Thomas Mann, Lionel Trilling, Borges, and Nabokov.

Yes, at four hundred years of age, his birthday presents have been multifarious. Indeed, he has become a template: the eighteenth century believed the knight to be a lunatic; the Victorians approached him as romantic dreamer, trapped, just like artists and prophets, in his own fantasy; and the modernists applauded his quest for an inner language of his own, whereas the post-modernists adore his dislocated identity. Psychiatrists have seen him as a case study in schizophrenia. Communists have turned him into not only an altruistic soul but a victim of market forces too. Historians of ideas have portrayed him as a salvo in a Spain doomed by its own intellectual obscurantism. Some have seen *Don Quixote,* considered to be the authentic first modern novel in that it is a *bildungsroman* that traces the arch of its protagonist's life from point A to point Z, and the inner transformation it gives room to, not as a work of art but as an integral element in the design in which we live, as important as, say, the color green. But others have suggested that Cervantes himself was unworthy of his creation. One size fits all.

No doubt these echoes would have come as a surprise to Cervantes himself, a soldier whose old battleground glories kept him alive—in 1571 he was crippled in his left hand in the Battle of Lepanto against the Turks—and a tax collector with a tarnished reputation. He was a second-rate talent, and his dreams to succeed in literature were at times pathetic. He envied Lope de Vega, the dramaturge of a thousand *comedias,* and was looked down on by younger snobs like Luis de Góngora and Francisco de Quevedo. In short, Cervantes was an outcast, and, in spite of all the hoopla, he remains one in Spain today. What is the secret of his success? The answer, of course, isn't readily available. If it was, the publishing industry would have seized upon it long ago. One might wonder: would *Don Quixote* pass the test and be published today in New York? I frankly doubt it. It would have been deemed what editors call "a trouble manuscript." Years ago Umberto Eco imagined rejection letters for some classics. Here is the one I've come up with for this one:

Dear Señor Michael of Sirvientes (do I have the spelling right?):

We've now had the chance to read the long manuscript—a behemoth, really—you kindly sent us. While we appreciate your earnest attempt at developing the distinct personalities of the old chap and his fat servant, we've found the storyline to be problematic. You stuff the plot with one too many adventures that do little to advance the plot. There are too many characters whose fate the reader gets attached to but who suddenly disappear never to be heard again. Maybe another publisher will be willing to trim the book to approximately two hundred pages; we simply don't have the time.

Plus, what is one to make of the fact that Cide Hamette

Benegeli is said to be the true creator of the book? Is this true? At times this seems like an ingenious device. But we've had a word with our legal department on this respect. They would be anxious to bring out a novel whose authorship is uncertain. The file would be wide open to a copyright lawsuit. This problem is exacerbated by Mr. Benegeli's religion. Given the political situation in which we live today, as an Arab he would even have grounds for blasphemy, given the derogatory comments made of *moriscos* in your work. The comments on Catholicism and the Church are smoother, but we might also get caught for publishing them.

And the style!!! Advance apologies for asking, but did you take a writing course in college? You write carelessly. Your sentences twist and turn. You don't always seem to know where you're going and what you have in mind. Your vocabulary bank seems quite limited, given the size of your endeavor, and your use of adjectives is questionable.

In short, *Don Quixote* is not really for us. We do wish you success in placing it elsewhere. Let me conclude by saying that should you have something substantially shorter, preferably with some elements of magical realism, please don't hesitate to send it to us. We've also been looking for novels about ghetto life in New York and Los Angeles. If you do decide to try your luck at one, please keep drugs and violent crimes to a minimum. We usually get criticized by reviewers in this respect, although these books do get adopted in college courses.

Happily, Cervantes proves how foolish it is to pursue publishing through formulas. The manuscript of the first part was sent (possibly under the title of *El ingenioso hidalgo de la Mancha*) to the Counsel of Castilla for permission to print it. It then went to the Inquisitorial censors for approval. In neither of these stops did it suffer defeat. Around August 1604, Cervantes tried in vain to enlist a celebrity to compose a poem eulogizing his protagonist, as it was the custom of the time to include such praise at the outset of a novel. But he came up empty-handed: his narrative was too low-brow for them. He decided to compose the burlesque poems himself, much in the way Walt Whitman, failing to receive any critic attention for *Leaves of Grass* when it was freshly published, decided to write an anonymous review himself.

The first part of the novel was quite successful early on. The first printing was of eighteen hundred copies. It was brought back to press repeatedly, and different editions were released. By the time the second part appeared, a decade later, *Don Quixote,* was, *en totto,* a runaway bestseller. It has remained one ever since. In my personal library I have some eighty different versions and variations, including the ones made for children, the illustrated ones by Gustav Doré and Salvador Dalí, as well as translations into Yiddish, Korean, Urdu, and versions of the partial Spanglish one I myself have published. I guess my collection is proof of my passion. In my estimation, Cervantes' masterpiece is the best, most profound secular book ever written. How many times have I read it? Impossible to say: perhaps three dozen times. There are chapters I've studied with detective zest, to the degree that I've memorized entire portions: the first and second chapters, of course, but also chapter 6, in which the priest and the barber scrutinize Cervantes' own library and dispense comments on his half-baked earlier oeuvre; the debate on the opposition between the pen and the sword in chapter 38; the episode of the Cave of Montesinos; the section on finding the original Arabic manuscript in Toledo; the interpolated novella about the captive, which reseambles Cervantes' own plight in northern Africa; the portion where a discussion on translation takes place in Barcelona; and the magisterial concluding chapter.

The best edition available in Spanish is the two-volume-plus CD-ROM authoritative one prepared by Francisco Rico. Aside from the text, it includes just about everything: maps, diagrams of armor used in Cervantes' time, drawings of domestic utensils, annotations, glossaries, a more-than-two-hundred-page bibliography and an even longer index, an appreciation of Spain in the seventeenth century, a survey of chivalry novels . . . In English alone, there are close to twenty different full-fledged translations, from Thomas Shelton's in 1612 and Peter Motteux's in 1700 to Tobias Smollett's in 1755 and John Ormsby's in 1885, from Samuel Putnam's in 1949 and J. M. Cohen's in 1961 to Burton Raffel's in 1995 and Grossman's in 2003. A few of these translations are astonishing examples of originality, but others are outright plagiarism cases. Translation is a form of appropriation. I like to believe that the fact that Shakespeare's tongue has reinvented Cervantes so frequently is proof of the lasting value of his morals in the Anglo-Saxon world: Don Quixote is a self-made fighter, an individualist eager to defend his principles until the end. It is also a story about reaching beyond one's own confinements, a lesson on how to turn poverty and the imagination into assets, and a romance that reaches beyond class and faith.

Unlike the Old and New Testaments, the Al-Qran, and the Bhagavad-Gita, Cervantes' novel doesn't have the attribute of the sacred. Or does it? Over time, it has been seen as the boilerplate through which to understand the ethics and esthetics of the Enlightenment. And in the age of relativism, it might well be that it has, after all, become the Bible of the liberal world. To be an underdog supported by others including the state, to be a fool content with his delusions—is that what modernity is about? And is what Cervantes does a way to push those delusions into a platform of action? There is a plethora of authors whose names have been turned into adjectives: Dantean, Proustean, Hemingwayan . . . But how many literary characters have undergone a similar fate? "Quixotic," "Quixotism," and "Quixotry," according to the *Oxford English Dictionary,* are variations of a "Quixote," "an enthusiastic visionary person like Don Quixote, inspired by lofty and chivalrous, but false or unreliable ideals."

The enthusiastic visionary is about to start his fifth century, still as vibrant and mischievous, as resourceful and controversial as ever. How is that for longevity? Even in the age of Viagra, it is a hell of a journey.

Javier Marías' Hubris

V. S. Pritchett, whose essays are an invaluable companion, a sort of Dante's Virgil in the navigation of modern literature, once described *Don Quixote* as "the novel that killed a country by knocking the heart out of it and extinguishing its belief in itself forever." This is no doubt an incisive statement, and perhaps truthful too. If so, it should be expanded to say that the novel also artfully extirpated Spain from Europe's intellectual conscience. For beyond Cervantes, where are its influential figures to be found in the international sphere? This is not to say that the country has given up on literature. On the contrary, tens of thousands of books (non-fiction, poetry, and as much fiction as mushrooms spring in a forest after a rainstorm) are published annually at home. The number of awards has multiplied dramatically in the last couple of decades: every major publisher has its prize, and parades its winners with unrestrained flair. But does anybody abroad really pay attention?

If this diagnosis—that the Spanish novel is in a centuries-old hiatus—sounds improbable and even a bit offensive, I suggest an exercise in improvised criticism. Stop for a moment at your local bookstore to find, say, a dozen Iberian novels, classics and commercials, on the shelf. I bet the task defeats you. You might stumble upon a title by Camilo José Cela, whose Nobel Prize, like that of his fellow Spaniard, Jacinto Benavente, only accentuated his obscurity; and you will surely come across the "brainy" thrillers of Arturo Pérez Reverte, probably the most popular Español of all time . . . But beyond these, what? It would be easy to blame the publishing industry for this failure, but most editors, especially at university presses, are liberals; censorship is not a principle they endorse. The fact is, even in an atmosphere such as ours, fastidiously allergic to foreign cultures, far more literature from France and Germany, even from Italy—not to mention the "quick eastbound trip" of scores of Britons—and fiction in particular, is released in the United States. Spain simply isn't trendy; its intellectual life is of no consequence.

The problem, in part, is internal. It is symptomatic that whenever an Iberian's letters are discussed at home, critics recur to similes: "Benito Pérez Galdós was *our* Dickens," it is said, "and Juan Benet *our* Faulkner." In all fairness, these comparisons are often to their advantage: a handful of essayists, and chiefly poets, fare better: Unamuno and

Ortega y Gasset, still not fully translated into English, are the owners of pungent, incisive voices not stilted by time that are delightful to read; and Federico García Lorca, along with poets of the Civil War (Machado, Cernuda, et al.), is a true giant. But a quick survey of the landscape in fiction does evidence a kind of wasteland: Miguel Delibes, Carmen Martín Gaite, Rafael Sánchez Ferlosio, Alvaro Pombo, and younger figures like Almudena Grande, Juna Luis Cebrián, César Antonio Molina . . . Are these recognizable names? So even if his remark isn't taken at face value, Pritchett, I think, is on to something of significance: the country's literary flame might not have been extinguished altogether with *Don Quixote,* but it surely burns at a low intensity. Spain is in a permanent state of eclipse.

Beyond national borders one of the very few heralded talents of the last decade is Javier Marías. His work has been timidly appearing in bookstores, praised in literary supplements and review pages. But it remains, not surprisingly, largely ignored by readers. But he has much to offer, even if it isn't consistently breathtaking, and a push should be made to bring him to the attention of a wider audience. From his 1971 debut novel *Los dominios del lobo* on to collections of essays like *Literatura y fantasma,* his books have sold in excess of 3.2 million copies, mainly in Europe and Hispanic America. Sales and quality don't always match, but they do in his case. He has been translated into some twenty languages. It is time Americans also woke up to a skillful *littérateur.*

Marías (*née* 1951) is a grounded *madrileño,* the son of a prominent cultural critic. Figuratively, he is one of Borges' grandchildren, although Proust should also be taken as a prominent inspiration: his themes are circular and metaliterary; and his style is meditative to the point of cantankerousness. Infatuated by British fiction since an early age, he has been, aside from a practitioner of fiction, a translator of high caliber who has made Hardy, Conrad, and Yates sit comfortably in Cervantes' tongue. His rendition of Laurence Sterne's *Tristram Shandy* is especially noteworthy: it brings the original back to life without ever mimicking it. This talent, it ought to be said, is no meager achievement in a culture with a miserable history of translation, one made of uninhibited displays of ineptitude and misinformation. HarperCollins and Harcourt first tried to publish him with little success in the United States in the 1990s. New Directions, the small, estimable New York publisher founded by James Laughlin, has now taken over the effort. It is relaunching a few of Marías' titles and a novel previously available only in England as *hors d'oeuvre,* along with a main dish made of a fresh collection of stories, *When I Was Mortal,* and also *Dark Back of Time,* a bizarre experiment in fiction—described by the author as a "false novel." The effort is laudable: although I'm sure it won't change the global status of Iberian fiction, it should at least make the exercise of browsing through a shelf for invigorating fiction from Spain a bit less frustrating. And it should place the ball in the reader's court: from now on anybody who doesn't read Marías is doomed

I used the word *bizarre* in the last paragraph. It fits him to the dot, for he enjoys exploring the eerie, mysterious, and supernatural—what Cortázar once described as "lo neofantástico"—in a way that is reminiscent of Stevenson, Wells, and W. W. Jacobs (author of the legendary tale "The Monkey's Paw"). But, to return to the similes, the figure he ought to be equated with, with hesitation, is Henry James: he has the same syncopated prose and introspective inquisitiveness, plus he uses equally long, torturous sentences. But, unlike James, he isn't quite a novelist, even though, for lack of a better term, he is invariably portrayed as one. Under close scrutiny, it is clear that Marías' narratives are made of disconnected segments, fragments that are abrupt and constantly interrupted by side effects that seldom add up to a whole; his train of thought functions as a spiral: one scene leads to another, and then another . . . *ad infinitum.* Still, the result is rewarding because he is a literary pugilist who understands literature as a game of mirrors.

This is not to say, of course, that everything he touches turns into gold. I've just reread him in the lucid translations by Margaret Jull Costa and Esther Allen: the pedantry and sense of superiority over his readership that I came across the first time around, when I discovered Marías in the original half a decade ago, strike me as more protruding. He loves to fashion himself as donnish, a little like Oscar Wilde. This pomposity comes across even in the author's photos. He invites you to his universe, but once you're in it, he shrieks: Look at how divine, how gifted I am! The effect might be chilling, and the persevering reader needs to put it aside, to be oblivious, in order to enjoy the material in full. There is little that is humble in him.

His sermonic quality is explicit in *All Souls,* based on his two-and-a-half-year experience at Oxford, that institution that has turned "donnishness" into a profession. It is part of the trend of so-called campus fiction that includes David Lodge, Jane Smiley, and Philip Roth. The volume's narrator is a Spanish lecturer who observes the ridiculous pomposity of academics, devoted to obscure themes, painfully aware of their overall insignificance, people for whom, as Marías puts it, "simply being is far more important than doing or acting." The adventures he comes up with are sheer fantasy, although his characters, among them faculty and bookstore owners, have actually recognized themselves in the various portrayals. The narrative suffers from homogeneity: Marías' erudite monologues all sound the same. But perhaps that doesn't matter, for the author doesn't seem to be looking for full-fledged characterizations; instead, his is a tangential disquisition about Spain from without, a study of an Iberian intellectual abroad in the spirit of James's *Daisy Miller,* a American's rendezvous in the Old Continent. Marías zooms in on the dislocation of one lonesome, perplexed Spanish observer in the land that Doctor Johnson once emulated with the chant: "Ye patriot crowds, who burn for England's fame." He never ponders issues of national identity. And yet, this is a book about a self-imposed "high-brow" traveler, a stranger in a strange place.

My personal favorite among Marías' books is *Tomorrow in the Battle Think of Me,* originally released in 1994 and the recipient of Venezuela's prestigious Rómulo Gallegos Prize. It is a complex, centripetal whodunit about the reverberations of a sudden death. The protagonist is a scriptwriter in Madrid who has an affair with a married woman while her husband is in London. As her child goes to bed and she begins to undress, she is taken ill and collapses grimly. The narrator's consciousness is vividly mapped out. The leitmotif is the quest for morality in a dissolute universe. Marías ponders large philosophical themes, such as the role of memory and morality in human affairs, by intertwining the individual in a larger picture. A quote:

> . . . no one knows anything for sure, not even what they do or decided or see or suffer, each moment sooner or later dissolves, its degree of unreality constantly on the increase, everything travelling towards its own dissolution with the passing of the days and even the seconds that appear to sustain things but, in fact, suppress them: a nurse's dream will vanish along with the student's vain wakefulness, the tentatively inviting footsteps of the whore, who is possibly a sick young man in disguise, will be scorned or go unnoticed, the lover's kisses will be renounced. . . . And, as if it was just another insignificant, superfluous tie or link, the murder or homicide is simply lumped in with all the crimes—there are so many others—that have been forgotten and of which no record remains and with those currently being planned or of which there will be a record, even though that too will eventually disappear.

This is the book Marías was destined to write by the Emersonian High Spirit and is unquestionably the introduction to him. Its exposition is hypnotizing, and its plot plays tricks on us: it falsifies its routes by pushing to its denouement. Also of notice is *A Heart So White,* portions of which take place in Havana and New York, about a thirty-four-year-old husband haunted by the demons of suicides by women (his father's first wife, his mother's sister, his aunt Teresa). It has brought Marías the applause of many, including Francis Ford Coppola and Salman Rushdie, and is considered his best. It might well be: it is an anti-detective story about genealogy and sin. (The title pays homage to *Macbeth*: "My hands are of your colour; but I shame / To wear a heart so white.")

In contrast, Marías' collection of stories, *When I Was Mortal*, is of a minor key. It appeared in 1996 and is made of material published in anthologies, as well as in periodicals like *El País* and *El Correo Español*. The short tale constrains Marías as a form and pushes him to summarize in a way that does him a disservice. His is an elastic vision that fits better the longer narrative. Also, these are all pieces drafted on commission, which isn't necessarily bad. In fact, Marías states in his foreword that this didn't "compromise them." He then goes on to craft an *ars poetica* that again recalls Henry James:

> You can write an article or a story on commission (though not, in my case, a whole book); sometimes even the subject matter may be given and I see nothing wrong in that as long as you manage to make the final product yours and you enjoy writing it. Indeed, I can only write something if I'm enjoying myself and I can only enjoy myself if I find the project interesting. . . . It is perhaps worth reminding those sentimental purists who believe that, in order to sit down in front of the typewriter, you have to experience grandiose feelings such as a creative "need" or "impulse," which are always "spontaneous" or terribly intense, that the majority of the sublime works of art produced over the centuries—especially in painting and music—were the result of commissions or of even more prosaic and servile stimuli.

The best tales in the volume are peopled by victims of mistaken identities, unexpected friendships, and professional liars. In one titled "In Uncertain Time" Marías explores the fanaticism surrounding soccer in Spain in particular, and Europe in general. In another one, "Everything Bad Comes Back"—clearly autobiographical in tone—a melancholic translator of Burton's *Anatomy of Melancholia* ponders his place in the world. And yet another one, "On the Honeymoon," reproduces the same subplot of *A Heart So White,* and also several of its paragraphs, thus acknowledging Pierre Menard's lesson: a same page used twice is a different page.

By far the brainiest, most emblematic and abstruse book by Marías, and the most demanding one, is *Dark Back of Time,* about . . . well, everything and nothing. This is what Italo Calvino described as a *hypernovel*, although I'm inclined to describe it as a meditative essay. But to pigeonhole it seems preposterous, for its strength lies precisely in its amphibious, anarchistic structure. This, after all, is a nonlinear *opera aperta* that functions as a circuitous rendezvous through the realms of knowledge and the imagination. It mixes autobiography with fiction, truth with lies, so as to show the extent to which an author—Javier Marías himself—is enriched and also cursed by his oeuvre. Marías' overall journey, with stops in *Tristram Shandy* and *All Souls* and also explorations of figures such as John Gawsworth and Wilfrid Ewart, accompanied by a long list of cameo appearances, parades in front of our eyes.

G. K. Chesterton, in a mini-biography of Stevenson, offered some thoughts on the role of the critic. He argued that reviewers lately—he wrote it in 1928—had been in the business of "depreciating" Stevenson, of "minimizing and finding fault" with his work. He suggested that the matter that mainly interested him, and the one critics should always be on the lookout for, "is not merely [a writer's] prose, but the large landscape or background against which he was posing; which [the writer] himself only partly realised, but which goes to make him a rather important historical picture." That, I think, is the way Marías ought to be perceived: the merit of his books is unquestionable, but the niche he has made for himself in Spain must be understood. He isn't really a writer's writer, as I've seen him described, but a writer's reader: his oeuvre invites us to engage in a rereading of the Spanish tradition beyond the nation's borders, in an unconstrained, cosmopolitan fashion. Marías' worth is to be found in his disinterest in *lo español*. Indeed, he might be among the last to try rescuing his country by refurbishing its belief in itself. Of course, that attribute precisely might be the one that makes him such an enthralling Spaniard today.

The Jews of Sosúa

୴ଊଊ

AT THE MUSEUM OF JEWISH HERITAGE, a not-to-be-missed exhibit, on display until July 25, focuses on the Jewish refugees during World War II who settled on the northeastern shore of the Dominican Republic. This little-known episode is part of the yet-to-be written history of the Holocaust in Latin America.

The participation of the Spanish-speaking world (Spain included) in World War II, in particular in regards to Jewish refugees, is complex. In countries like Argentina, Uruguay, Bolivia, Paraguay, and Chile, Germans and Jews who were together in concentration camps, as guards and prisoners, at times settled in the same neighborhood. The cases of Adolf Eichmann and Josef Mengele, spotted at different points by survivors, are the most famous. But there were hundreds of others whose lives intersected in twisted ways. (José Emilio Pacheco, a Mexican poet and essayist, wrote a novel about it, still unavailable in English: *A Distant Death.*)

In this constellation, the case of Sosúa, a coastal town in the Dominican Republic, is unique. Notwithstanding their record for having a relaxed immigrant policy, a majority of Latin American countries refused to open their doors in the mid-1930s to Jewish refugees. That posture didn't change in the next decade, with some exceptions. As early as 1935, the Dominican Republic, led by dictator Rafael Leónidas Trujillo Molina, suggested that his country would welcome as many as one hundred thousand refugees from Europe. That approach was ratified in July of 1938, after the Evian Conference, called by President Roosevelt to discuss the problem of Jewish refugees.

That Trujillo, known for his repressive regime, would invite Jews to the island, promising them religious freedom, might seem ironic. Like other Latin American caudillos before him, he wanted to accelerate capitalism. In any case, that isn't the only irony of the story. The American Jewish Joint Distribution Committee was instrumental in the arrangement, supporting the effort by creating a subsidiary, the Dominican Republic Settlement Association. This entity, known as DORSA, secured funds and provided educational, financial, and diplomatic support. In October 1939, Roosevelt personally endorsed the idea. American help dried up as the U.S. Department of State dragged its feet. In the end, only a few hundred refugees arrived in Sosúa. The lackluster assistance was yet another embarrassment for the United States. In contrast, the reception the refugees received from the average Dominican was solid. The Sosúa episode was indeed a success in large part as a result of this grassroots embrace.

Sosúa was a rural habitat. For shtetl Jews, the landscape would have been somewhat similar to what they were used to in the Pale of Settlement: arid, tropical, more humid, but equally provincial. Instead, the majority of newcomers to the Caribbean island were urban and middle class, hence their dismay at the living conditions. What kind of response did they have? The black and white photographs at the Museum of Jewish Heritage, along with other memorabilia collected by the curators, evidence the disappointment experienced by the refugees. The place was remote, rudimentary, challenging in every way. "No maps were in existence," a settler, Félix Bauer, wrote in his memoirs. Another one, Barbara Steinmetz, described Sosúa as "just a piece of land with a few buildings on it . . . and very sparsely populated." And a third refugee, David Kahane, stated: "There were two barracks and a few shacks. No electric lights, and the mosquitoes were humming."

Shock gave way to some degree of comfort, which metastasized into gratitude. From the start Sosúa locals were friendly. They interacted with the newcomers, doing business with them, striking friendships. The relationship was fruitful. Over time, it resulted in strong collaboration and even marriage. Yet in spite of Trujillo's goodwill, the total number of refugees to Sosúa never reached beyond five hundred, with another two hundred passing through it. The last group of settlers arrived in mid-1947, having spent the war in Shanghai. The small number speaks to the missed opportunity this episode in Holocaust history allowed. How many thousands could have been saved in the Dominican Republic had the U.S. government been more decisive?

Marion A. Kaplan, a professor of modern Jewish history at New York University and the author of *Dominican Haven: The Jewish Refugee Settlement in Sosúa, 1940–1945,* a book published to accompany the exhibit, puts the cipher in context. "In comparison," Kaplan argues, "about 100,000 Jews reached Latin America and the Caribbean between 1933 and 1942, and about 160,000 came to the U.S. between 1933 and 1942." Kaplan adds: "But numbers do not convey the full story. The United States, for example, only once fulfilled its yearly quota of German-Austrian immigrants between 1933 and 1944, and that was in 1939, after the shock and empathy that emerged in response to the open violence against Jews in Germany on November 9, 1938, known as the November Pogrom, or Crystal Night."

For years I've dreamed of visiting Sosúa. While the photographs on display at the exhibit aren't a substitute, they make my dream tangible. Jews and Dominicans, their religious and ethnic selves evident, appear near cattle on a dairy farm. There are calves, horses, and roosters nearby. A settler drives a tractor. Four male swimmers lying on the beach smile at the camera. Children work the land. A long shot of the dorms shows a couple of inhabitants at the door. A thirteen-year-old celebrates his Bar Mitzvah. People congregate around a faucet of potable water that is being inaugurated.

I find these pictures strikingly familiar. They are touching in their immediacy. In spirit, they might appear similar to those of Yiddish-speaking immigrants to Moisés Ville and other settlements in the Argentine Pampas, where Jews coexisted with *gauchos*. (They were immortalized by Alberto Gerchunoff in his somber volume of vignettes *The Jewish Gauchos*. Conversely, in Brazil, the quite different Jewish life in the pampas is the subject of a humorous disquisition in Moacyr Scliar's *The Centaur in the Garden*.) Yet the tenor is dramatically different: again, the Sosúa refugees came from an upper social scale. Their escape from the Old Continent took place at a time of extreme desperation.

Today only a handful of the original settlers in Sosúa remain. The majority left a long time ago, mostly for the United States, where they intermingled with the American Jewish community the way other Jews from Latin America did: in a renegotiation of their collective identity. Trujillo was assassinated in May of 1961. The Dominican Republic remains one of the poorest nations in the Western Hemisphere. Sosúa is currently a tourist attraction, among other reasons because of its sex trade. The synagogue still stands, and there is a museum that remembers the Jewish presence more than half a century ago. The companion book indicates the gratitude of those who lived in Sosúa, summarized by a settler, Paul Cohnen, who is quoted thus: "We owe the Dominican Republic so much. After I became more comfortable I donated land for people who had worked for me for 27 years. I'm proud to do it. I've donated land and money for the school." Others described their Caribbean interval as "a second life."

Delano

John Gregory Dunne

⚬∞⚬

FORTY YEARS AFTER ITS ORIGINAL PUBLICATION, *Delano: The Story of the California Grape Strike* retains not only its freshness but its urgency too. John Gregory Dunne's book centers on a five-year strike organized by César Chavez and the National Farm Workers Association (NFWA) of 1965 that, in retrospect, stands as one of the most acrimonious in American labor history. It catapulted Chavez onto the national stage, opposed a marginalized, largely undocumented minority with grape vineyard growers in the Great Central Valley of California, especially the town of Delano, and revitalized the base of a number of prominent political figures, including Robert Kennedy. At a time when the struggle for civil rights was defining a young generation of Americans, the strike—in Spanish, *la huelga*—placed Mexican-Americans on the nation's radar. It legitimized the grassroots inspiration of the Chicano Movement and might be seen as an early sign of the United States recognizing itself as diverse and heterogeneous in demographic terms.

Thus, given the historical benchmark that the Delano strike became in history books and the amount of journalists on the scene, it is surprising that few eyewitness accounts of the upheaval are available. As the unrest moved toward its third year, Dunne believes, the strike was "mired in quicksand." Yet the amount of media interest was immense. The grape boycott orchestrated by the Farm Workers worked on a number of levels precisely because radio, TV, and newspapers kept the pulse of the clash alive while generating half-hearted sympathy toward them among consumers nationwide. I say *halfhearted* because the average American didn't quite embrace the NFWA's demands. They did refuse to buy grapes in major stores, and marches were organized in large urban centers. But the strike unfolded as a distant event reported on prime-time news, one in hundreds that torpedo the general public on a regular basis. To this day the agitation hardly raises an eyebrow. It hasn't made it to the elementary-school curriculum.

Maybe it shouldn't surprise anyone that little of lasting value about the event has survived. There are several accounts addressing the demonstrations of Chicanos in the Southwest at the end of the 1960s and in the early 1970s, and there is a collective biography of La Causa by

Jacques Levy, a mosaic-like re-creation of the Mexican-American leaders and their odyssey. And Peter Matthiessen's *Sal Si Puedes*, released in 1969, is equally extraordinary, although it focuses more on Chavez as a man. Delano is only a passing chapter in them. In comparison, Dunne's volume stands as the single most authoritative chronicle of *la huelga* in the Valley—indeed, when a slightly different version of it was first published in the *Saturday Evening Post*, it was called "The Strike"—as well as an eminently readable record of the factors behind the labor confrontation, the negotiations that went on to resolve the dispute around grapes and what was then known as "agribusness," and the magnetic but radicalizing personality of Chavez, which evolved as the process moved along. It's as if John Steinbeck's *The Grapes of Wrath* had been reimagined in the 1960s and rendered into fractured Spanish. The *New York Times* said: "John Gregory Dunne's book is an exceptionally incisive report on the anatomy of the strike; a colorful, perceptive examination of its impact on the community; and an analysis of actions of both employers and labor so realistic as to make it important reading for current students of economics and public policy." And the *San Francisco Chronicle* described it as "a sensitive rendering of the atmosphere that permeates the great battle of Delano."

The book is an anomaly for other reasons. Its author wasn't known then, nor would he eventually make a reputation, as a left-leaning reporter of working-class protests. Responsible for a dozen screenplays that include *True Confessions* and *Up Close & Personal*, co-authored with his wife Joan Didion, and books like *Dutch Shea, Jr.* and *Playland*, Dunne is famous for his Hollywood inside stories and his essays on culture in the *New York Review of Books*. Dead in 2003 at the age of seventy-one (his death and that of his daughter, Quintana Roo, are the topic of Didion's prize-winning memoir *The Year of Magical Thinking*), he was of Irish descent, a native of Hartford, Connecticut, and a Princeton graduate who, soon after college, got a job at *Time* magazine, where he mostly wrote on a number of disparate issues, especially under the foreign news section. Soon after leaving *Time*, he convinced the editors of the *Saturday Evening Post*, then an in-depth weekly to which Didion also contributed, to assign him to the Mexican strike in the Valley. His life-long interest, as discussed by George Plimpton in a *Paris Review* interview of 1996, was Dunne's "extraordinary grotesqueries—nutty nuns, midgets, whores of the most breathtaking abilities and appetites," which Dunne explained as a perverse fascination of a lapsed Catholic, adding that "the nuns and the monks were far more valuable to me than my four years at Princeton." In any case, he was amazingly patient in his pursuit of every detail about the NFWA, its demands, its impending impact on the country's future. It was the first and, as it happens, the only time Dunne would focus his considerable talent as a literary observer of the labor-force revolution shaking America in the Vietnam years. The result is a strikingly balanced picture of the animosity that prevailed in Delano and an invaluable document allowing us to appreciate the volatility in the air at the time. (In the same interview, Dunne argues that "writing is a sort of manual labor of the mind.")

A lucid, intelligent, clear-headed stylist, Dunne in *Delano* has the unmistakable viewpoint of an outsider. His first paragraph places us on Highway 99, the road that takes him from Los Angeles to Delano. His exploration of the places he visits is multilayered. Sooner or later he zooms in on the agricultural past of the Valley, its changing population since the Gold Rush, the importance of the grape industry, the techno-logical tools used in it, and the presence of Mexican migrants. He settles on Chavez as his protagonist, surrounded by a galaxy of supporting characters. Neutrality is the keyword: Dunne's objective is to deliver a nuanced narrative summary of events without endorsing any one ideo-logical stand. The impartiality works well, even if at times one gets the impression that the conflict he's exploring doesn't concern him fully, that it's only remotely linked to his own vision of the nation's future. Is this because Dunne was a Northeasterner with a different sense of the country's social texture? His freelance effort would serve as his intro-duction to California, although in the end the magnetism of the state would come to him from the other quarters, namely the rich and famous in Hollywood, and not the beaten and downtrodden in the San Joaquin Valley.

There is a quasi-scientific tint to Dunne's evaluation. He reflects, with astounding fidelity, on the labor debacle, allowing his curiosity to go as far as possible, at one point even applauding the grape boycott, but remaining reluctant to be swept away by the charisma and energy of the underdog. The approach does create complications and might be said to be inadvertently lopsided. I'm in awe, for instance, at the how the Mexican *huelguistas* are portrayed in *Delano:* as a group in need of rep-resentation, offended, voiceless; yet their viewpoints aren't personal-ized. Prominent growers, teamsters, politicians, even religious leaders, are identified by name. The NFWA, instead, is an acronym. Dunne doesn't side with them; he just isn't ready to compromise his own emo-tions and loyalties. Still, at the core of his book is César Chavez, whose mission, I get the impression, made Dunne skeptical, even uncomfort-able. (Chavez is said to belong to that "inarticulate subculture of farm workers upon whom the Valley depends but whose existence does not impinge heavily on the Valley consciousness.") In *Delano,* Dunne tells a story that perfectly illustrates his reluctance to judge. When he returned to the Central Valley years after having finished his story, he tells us, a highway patrolman stopped him for driving too fast. "You were going 85 mph in a 70 mph zone," the agent tells him. After requesting Dunne's driver's license, the patrolman asks about Dunne's occupation. He answers the questions. "Do you know about the grape strike here? That's a good story," the patrolman says. Dunne replies that he'd been writing about it for a magazine. "Is that a liberal magazine or a conservative magazine?" he wonders. Response: "They let you think pretty much what you want." The patrolman continues:

> "You ever met this Cesar Chavez?"
> "Yes."
> He was closing his summons book. "He a communist?"
> "No."
> The youth was silent for a moment. Then he unbuttoned his shirt flap and took out his pen. He reopened his summons book. "You were going 85 mph in a 70 mph zone," he said.

Yet as *Delano* progresses, Dunne warms up toward Chavez, who maybe even somewhat wins the reporter's heart. While he understands the hopes deposited in him, his spirituality based on Christian values, his ambition and shrewdness yet polarizing strategies as a leader, his messianic drive, he sees him less as a solution than as a mystery. "The curious thing about Cesar Chavez," Dunne states, "is that he is as little understood by those who would canonize him as by those who would condemn him." He perceives him through an edgy lens as a rural folk hero. "To the saint-makers, Chavez seemed the perfect candidate. His crusade was devoid of the ambiguities of urban conflict. With the farm workers there were no nagging worries about the mugging down the block, the rape across the street, the car boosted in front of the house. It was a cause populated by simple Mexican peasants with noble agrarian ideas, not by surly unemployables with low IQs and Molotov cocktails. . . . The saintly virtues he had aplenty; it is doubtful that the media would have been attracted to him were it not for those virtues, and without the attention of the media the strike would not have survived. But Chavez had the virtues of the labor leader, less applauded publicly perhaps, but no less admirable in the rough going—a will of iron, a certain deviousness, an ability to hang tough in the clinches."

What is most striking to me about the picture that emerges of Chavez in the last sections of *Delano* is that it's in the past tense. Dunne sees the *huelga* in Delano as a fait accompli. He predicts that in urban centers where what he calls "ethnic and cultural pride ungerminated for generations" will explode one day: "Drive down Whittier Boulevard in East Los Angeles, a slum in the Southern California manner, street after street of tiny bungalows and parched lawns and old cars, a grid of monotony. The signs are unnoticed at first, catching the eye only after the second or third sighting, whitewashed on fences and abandoned storefronts, the paint splattered and uneven, signs painted on the run in the dark of the night, '*Es mejor morir de pie que vivir de rodillas*'—'Better to die standing than live on your knees.' The words are those of Emiliano Zapata, but the spirit that wrote them was fired by Cesar Chavez."

Dunne analyzes the picture before him and connects the dots. He talks about issues of ethnicity and about the low self-esteem he sees in the Mexican-American population. And he understands the allure of extremism. "What the barrio is learning from the blacks is the political sex appeal of violence," he affirms. "The vocabulary of the dispossessed is threat and riot, the Esperanto of a crisis-reacting society, italicizing the poverty and discrimination and social deprivation in a way that no funded study or government commission ever could." Dunne doesn't emphasize how charged the word *Chicano* is but is certainly aware that the concept of assimilation—as previous waves of newcomers understood it—has changed dramatically. Possibly because racism and discrimination are rampant, or because Mexico is just *del otro lado,* on the other side, the pressure to conform to the mainstream cultural patterns in the United States is no longer there. But Dunne's prognosis is local. He mentions the term La Causa but doesn't expand it beyond the Southwest. There is little connection in *Delano* between the NFWA and the Puerto Rican Young Lords. This limitation, needless to say, isn't Dunne's exclusively. The entire Civil Rights Era continues to be viewed today in black and white. Few were able to prophesize that Chavez's ordeal was the announcement of "brownness" as a mode of thinking.

Dunne's account was published in book form by Farrar, Straus and Giroux in 1967, with black-and-white photographs by Ted Streshinsky that are considerably more biased toward the NFWA than the reportage. Four years later, a revised, updated edition appeared, in which Dunne brought full circle his chronicle by explaining how the strike was resolved and the way Chavez moved from grapes to lettuces. By the mid-1970s that edition was out of print, and the Delano strike was out of sight. Since the mid-1980s, a young generation of Latinos, a vast number of them of Mexican descent (in the year 2005 approximately sixteen out of every twenty Latinos had roots in Mexico), has come to the fore, seeking clues to understand its recent and remote past in the United States. On the surface they look to be less connected with radicalism than with the embrace of middle-class commodities. The barrio might even now be a time bomb but pop culture—raeggatón, Hollywood, sports—allows for the disenfranchised to feel attached to the nation's soul. And war: the number of *mexicanos* in the armed forces is considerable. Even if *la huelga* isn't a daily topic of conversation for them, their need to identify heroes and benchmarks is legitimate. The conditions of itinerant farm workers in the Southwest have changed somewhat in the interim, not always for the better. Mechanization has become a factor embraced by the growers to increase production. The workers' living provisions are, for the most part, less miserable. The wages have increased, though they've never kept up with inflation. The long hours of penurious physical effort remain in place, and the use of pesticides is another decisive element affecting worker's health. Worse, the negative appreciation of Mexicans in the United States as subhuman is more pervasive than ever, as attested by the labyrinthine and never-ending national debate on immigration. *Parasites* is the noun used by a prominent CNN commentator.

As Dunne concludes his reportage and jumps back on Highway 99, he reflects on the effect of Chavez on the people. In the end, he realizes the strike didn't sink in quicksand. He wonders at the impact of the newly found Chicano labor management. "Denied to blacks," he states, "assimilation for years robbed the Chicano community of a nucleus of leadership. Today the forfeiture of this newly acquired cultural aware-ness seems to the young Chicano a prohibitive price to pay." But while the 1970s would be a decade of political consolidation, the 1980s and 1990s would emaciate the ideological fat accumulated by Chaves and his peers. As Dunne departs Delano, he does see that bumper stickers that read "Boycott California Grapes" and "Buy California Grapes" are now fading.

A Master's Voice

Edmund Wilson

⚬∞⚬

LITERARY CRITICISM IS IN DEEP TROUBLE in the United States today. Aside from a couple of lucid voices (Louis Menand, for instance), what passes for reflection on books and literary themes is generally of embarrassing quality. Perhaps the assumption is that, in the Internet age, blogs have taken over as open forums of debate, making redundant the space allocated in periodicals for literary analysis. At least that's the corollary one gets from the recent space shrinkage of book-review sections. The fact is that media corporations have little patience for serious insights. They are interested in instant gratification. Trashy books about diets, sports, the reckless life of celebrities, and trying one's luck in business are the crop of New York every season. They don't require much thought. The more literary ones sell far less, hardly ever justifying the investment. In other words, literature is about making a buck. If it doesn't bring money, it's too complicated. Why waste time and energy discussing it? Also, the news media is now less about spreading information than about brainwashing people. The less you think, the more stable the status quo will be. No wonder the country as a whole feels like Disneyland.

At this point, some readers will say: there goes Stavans again with his admonitions. But I'm not the only one bored. Look at Charlie Rose: does he look as if he's excited about the state of American culture? Worse even, I spend my days among academics in the humanities, a vast majority of whom make a profession of being pretentious. Writing for them is about obfuscation: rather than enlightening a discussion, they make it more obscure. The state of literary criticism among them is even more dismal: it is self-obsessed, self-contained, and self-referential, hiding behind terminologies only a small group of initiated readers are able to grasp. But not much happens when they do. This is because this type of reflection is utterly useless. It's a shame students have to waste themselves in graduate schools in order to produce totally illegible writing. Its impact on the world per se is nil—or worse.

I'm afraid the publication by the Library of America, on its twenty-fifth anniversary, of the first two volumes of Edmund Wilson's oeuvre won't change the tenor of the game. Nothing will at this point. We confuse democracy with a cacophonous shrieking of ideological arguments. Civility has been forgotten, and so have patience and introspection. Still, the Wilson volumes might serve, for the small audience who might dare to open them, as a reminder of an age not too distant from ours when literature mattered. The latest titles of Faulkner, Eliot, Hemingway, Pound, Stein, and Dos Passos were reason enough to rush to the bookstore. They had an urgency to them, a vitality, a pathos. That's because the idea of culture was important to Americans: What makes us distinct from Europe? How does America mature as a nation?

Wilson, the dean of twentieth-century American critics, used his pulpit in the *New Republic,* the *New Yorker, Vanity Fair,* and other magazines, as well as in books, as a thermometer of that culture. His style was terse, provocative, engaging. His erudition was emphatic but hardly condescending. It was his idea, toward the end of his life (he died in his old house in Talcottville, New York, in 1972, at the age of seventy-seven, and is buried in Wellfleet, Massachusetts), to orchestrate in the United States a publishing venture like France's La Pléyade that would make available the classics of American literature in enduring editions edited in lighthearted fashion by men of letters but without a needless critical apparatus that ends up drowning the reader. It took his work too long to enter that illustrious library—but there it is now, astonishing in its lucidity and comprehensiveness, admirable as a chronicle of some of the crucial decades in the twentieth century, from the 1920s to the 1960s.

Edited by Lewis M. Dabney, who is responsible for a biography of Wilson as well as for organizing some of his diaries, these two volumes by the Library of America open with pieces on Willa Cather, Sherwood Anderson, Malraux, Lytton Strachey, e. e. cummings and Stephen Crane, and move to Wilson's meditations on modernism in his legendary *Axel's Castle,* which is a lesson in clarity (it includes essays on Yates, Valéry, Joyce, Proust, Eliot, and Stein, and a bonus piece on Rimbaud). Wilson is never afraid to speak his mind. His objective is to offer an esthetic appraisal of his subject matter. The first-person voice appears on every page. But it isn't enough to be opinionated. His explorations combine the individual and the historical. A Princeton graduate, he was attracted to Marxism as a map allowing him to comprehend the social, economic, and cultural forces that define any group of people.

The second volume stresses Wilson's interest in the intersection of the transitory and the permanent. He writes about detective fiction and bestsellerdom. He follows the career of his favorite authors: Do they burn up? Are they able to reach beyond their early success? He reacts with brio to the publication of *For Whom the Bell Tolls* (he praises Hemingway's courage to "dramatize" the events of America's recent past and his resistance to engaging in "partisan journalism"), *Dangling Man* (Saul Bellow's book is "an excellent document on the experience of the non-combatant in time of war"), and *The Power and the Glory* (Graham Greene "reduces [his Mexican priest] to crawling on his belly for spiritual self-preservation while he fights with dogs for bones and keeps his morale up with brandy; and the reader is not even sure that the author has managed to redeem him").

Yes, Wilson is a socially conscious patrician literary critic in the tradition of Matthew Arnold. He hardly pays attention to black and other ethnic writers. American literature is written by white, Ivy League–educated brats. And the majority of his legacy—certainly the material included in these inaugural volumes—is fragmentary in nature: an assemblage of snapshots. He rightfully sought what he liked but also ignored much that ultimately became essential. In due time Wilson wrote in more sustained fashion semi-monographic books about Marx (*To the Finland Station* might well be his finest work), the Dead Sea Scrolls, the American Indians, the income tax, and the Civil War, scheduled for forthcoming installments of the Library of America series. In other words, it would be easy to dismiss him as deaf to what the nation would become only a few decades later: a messy sum of heterogeneous parts made, shaped by a dramatic immigration drive from the so-called Third World that transformed, at its core, the ethical structure of the country. But while Wilson was no prophet, he was a consummate dilettante with an enviable critical eye. He didn't vituperate, like Christopher Hitchens; nor did he look down at popular art as an unworthy manifestation by insignificant earthlings, as George Steiner used to do.

To read him is to know the true worth of criticism. The critic is a compass that helps one to navigate the cultural map. The critic greases the engine, providing context without forcing a particular interpretation of a text at the expense of others. In short, the critic shows that literature is about thought, about morality, about transcendence. Too bad such vision is now gone. Nowadays we babble.

Homage to Ryszard Kapuściński

RYSZARD KAPUŚCIŃSKI made globe-trotting reportage alluring. In an age of ephemeral information, his engaging, thought-provoking dispatches from various war zones (Angola, Iran, Congo, Algeria, Cuba, Zanzibar, El Salvador, and Uganda, among others) gave readers a sense of history in the making. Born in Pinsk, Belarus, in 1932, he died in Warsaw earlier this year, at the age for seventy-four, having witnessed twenty-seven coups and revolutions and being sentenced to death four times. And even though Warsaw was home, he was a foreigner even there. For to be a foreigner for him was to be alive, to reject complacency.

His half a dozen books, among which my favorite is *The Soccer War,* are invaluable documents. In a nervous world such as ours, where authenticity is an endangered quality, Kapuściński was interested in the large strokes of history. Still, he always sought the local, the habitual, and the mundane wherever he went. And he didn't fail to stress in them the autobiographical. A story comes to life only when the author allows his ego to be exposed. There is no such thing as objectivity, even for journalists. What is important is not what happens but what people make of it.

His last book, *Travels with Herodotus,* was a delicious coda to his oeuvre. Melodiously translated by Klara Glowczewska, its topic was the reporter itself: how he became a traveler, the forces that shaped him, the aspirations he nurtured. Call it *The Education of Ryszard Kapuciski.* The structure, however, is far more complex. Made of approximately thirty small chapters, the vertebrae keeping them together is a rhetorical conversation the author maintains with Herodotus, the Greek historian, whom he first encountered as a student, when he read *The Histories* in the early 1950s, after the Soviet-sponsored government had delayed its Polish translation. No wonder: Herodotus was a relativist, a restless traveler eager to understand differences in culture.

Soon after Kapuściński discovered him, he too became a peripatetic wanderer. His career as a journalist took him from New Delhi to Khartoum, from Addis Ababa to Dakar, and after the collapse of Communism, from Georgia to Armenia. At every turn, he opened his copy of *The Histories* to find solace and companionship. He realized he was retracing Herodotus' path, at least intellectually. The historian's voyages to Egypt, Libya, and Italy, and his quest to seize the meaning of history at the time of the Peloponnesian War, served as mirror to his own quest.

The book offers parallel narratives: Kapuściński wanders as he wonders in what sense the past is different from the present. The overall effect of this juxtaposition is enthralling. Descriptions of the milieus he sent his dispatches from are accompanied by meditations on the act—and art—of being a first-hand observer. What, he asks, is the difference between the historian and the journalist? His response comes in the form of a series of rhetorical questions. "What set him into motion? Made him act? Compelled him to undertake the hardships of travel, to subject himself to the hazards of one expedition after another?" Kapuściński reply is straightforward: Herodotus came up with an ambitious task: "to record the history of the world. No one before him had ever attempted this. He is the first to have hit upon the idea." Then he adds: "Many centuries before us, he discovers an important yet treacherous and complicating trait of human memory: people remember what they want to remember, not what actually happened. Everyone colors events after his fashion, brews up his own mélange of reminiscences."

Kapuściński set an equally arduous task for himself: to be a witness of major events and to make readers remember them as a mare magnum of conflicting viewpoints. A citizen of a nation, Poland, repeatedly beaten by more powerful forces, he tested Europe's boundaries by exploring the effects of colonialism. But he wasn't exclusively interested in the relationship between the haves and the have-nots. He believed human behavior to be far more complex. Like V. S. Naipaul, his magnet was the unruly nations, the feisty, amorphous Third World, although his coordinates were less Manichean. He wasn't interested in patrons and servants, the civilized and the barbarian. Instead, Kapuściński was attracted to attempts, foolish as they might be, to make sense of chaos. With the exception of the former Soviet Union, the places he visited were, almost exclusively, "without the mediation and, to some degree, without the knowledge and consent of Europe." And what did these places have in common: turmoil.

Turmoil and the need for redemption. Indeed, what makes his legacy appealing is Kapuściński's forceful pounding of Europe's condescension toward others. As a result of its arrogance and condescension, the continent, in his eyes, had become parochial. In response, he struggled, as much as possible, not to "fall into the trap of provincialism." Toward the end of *Travels with Herodotus* he quotes an essay by T. S. Eliot on Virgil: "In our time," he states, "when men seem more than ever to confuse wisdom with knowledge, and knowledge with information, and to try to solve the problems of life in terms of engineering, there is coming into existence a new kind of provincialism which perhaps deserves a new name. It is a provincialism not of space, but of time, one for which history is merely a chronicle of human devices which have served their turn and have been scrapped, one for which the world is the property solely of the living, a property in which the dead hold no share."

To confuse knowledge with information . . . I'm in awe at Kapuściński's legacy. He was the real thing—and the rarest: a humbling thinker.

Language and Colonization

❧

SOME YEARS AGO, I wrote an essay called "Translation and Identity,"* in which I tackled the role that the Spanish language played during the conquest of the Americas. I pondered the fact that the arrival of the Iberian conquistadors forced a reconfiguration of almost every aspect of life in the New World: political, religious, sexual, military . . . ; but I expressed dismay that another important aspect, language, was seldom contemplated in textbooks. What kind of verbal negotiation took place as conquistadors, explorers, missionaries, and other Iberians interacted with the native population? What was the reaction of the local population to the arrival of a foreign tongue whose cadence was unlike anything they had heard before in the Aztec and Inca empires? I also discussed the strategies used by interpreters such as Melchorejo and Julianillo, and by mistresses like Doña Marina, who functioned as cultural bridges between both civilizations.

My essay concentrated on the campaign by Hernan Cortés in the capture of Tenochtitlán, narrated by, among others, Bernal Díaz del Castillo in his book *The Conquest of New Spain*. My intention now is to take my disquisition a step further, investigating the role that language played during the almost three centuries that constitute the colonial period in the region: from 1521, when the last of the Aztec rulers, Cuauhtémoc, is tortured and dies at Cortés' hands, to the first attempt at independence by Father Miguel Hidalgo y Costilla, in Mexico in 1810. In fact, my scope is comparatively smaller: I want to focus almost exclusively on the sixteenth century, when a heated debate on the purpose and future of the Spanish language in the Americas took place.

In other words, I'm interested in the slow penetration that *el español* made among the pre-Columbian population. How did an entire continent submit to the colonizing language? What types of institutions were established to foster the spread of Spanish? How did linguistic resistance manifest itself? And was there code-switching among the *mestizos, ladinos,* and *cholos*?

I don't intend my reflections to be solely devoted to the history of Spanish in the New World. I'm interested in an entire philosophy of life. To what extent did language become a conduit in the propagation of

The Essential Ilan Stavans (Routledge, 2000), 231–40.

European values? How was it employed in the establishment of a mentality that, in the end, owes as much to the Iberian Peninsula as it does to the aboriginal civilization? What philosophical investigations needed to take place for *el español* to become what Borges once called *el orden de las cosas,* the order of things? My hunt springs from a particular curiosity. For a decade, I've concentrated on the history and development of Spanglish, a hybrid form of communication, mainly in the United States, that results from the clash of two tongues, those of English and Spanish cultures, and, ontologically, of two civilizations, Anglo and Hispanic. There are three strategies Spanglish speakers engage in to make themselves understood: (1) code-switching and code-mixing, (2) simultaneous translation, and (3) the coining of a vast number of new terms that are neither in English nor in Spanish (*wáchale, friquiar, marqueta . . .*). Spanglish is spoken by millions of people, some of whom are monolingual while others are bilingual (Spanglish and Spanish, Spanglish and English) and even trilingual (Spanglish, English, and Spanish), and I've come to the realization that the phenomenon is the result of complex circumstances. Among them is the astonishing demographic growth of the Hispanic minority in the United States (close to forty-seven million in 2007), its mobility as a result of temporary jobs, the influence of Spanish-language media in the country, and the effect of federally funded bilingual education programs whose resources were equally applied to language instruction in English and Spanish.*

My central thesis is that Spanglish in present-day America (a term referring not only to the country but to the continent as a whole) is a state of mind. Among Spanish speakers nowadays, 88 percent describe Spanish as their full-first language, and the remaining 12 percent have it as a second or third language. In Spain, the number of Catalan, Gallego, and Vasque speakers has grown since the death of General Francisco Franco and the arrival of democracy. In the Americas, where more than 90 percent of the total number of Spanish speakers live, almost two dozen aboriginal tongues (Guaraní, Aymara, Quechua, Nahuatl, Tolteca, Zapoteca, Mixteca, etc.) play an influential role.

Talking about language purity in the Hispanic world is preposterous. The varieties of Spanish used in Argentina, Chile, Venezuela, Nicaragua, and Guatemala differ from the type used in Spain. There used to be a time, at the dawn of the colonial period, when that Iberian variety served as the unchallenged model against which the colonies set

*Antonio Alatorre's influential *Los 1001 años de la lengua española* (3rd ed., Fondo de Cultura Económica, 2002), written from the perspective of a Latin American linguist and translator (Alatorre was born in Mexico), features a section on Anglicisms in Spanish but doesn't contemplate more fully code-switching, code-mixing, and the emergence of Spanish as a linguistic alternative.

their standards. In spite of what the scholars of the Real Academia Española de la Lengua and purists in the Spanish-speaking world might believe, that is no longer the case. The Hispanic world has grown to be a decentralized entity in a number of areas, language being a crucial one. Renaud Richard's *Diccionario de Hispanoamericanismos** offers a rich assortment of *latinoamericanismos* whose importance is global: *burrito, huevada, ñato,* and *simpatía*. Indeed, the frequent complaints by intellectuals this side of the Atlantic against the paternalistic opinions from Spain about the abuse Spanish undergoes in Buenos Aires, Bogotá, and Mexico City are more strident than they used to be. Jorge Luis Borges, in his essay called "Las alarmas del doctor Américo Castro,"† ridicules the Spanish philologist for thinking that Iberians are more refined in their speech.

In any case, I want to shift my attention now from the present to the past. The early part of the colonial period in the Spanish colonies was also fertile ground for linguistic cross-pollinization. At the end of the fifteenth century, Castilian, the language brought by the Spanish conquistadors, entered a landscape brewing with native tongues. Was there an equivalent—keeping the distance between environments, of course—to bilingual education, schooling efforts to make Indian students proficient in the conquering language while advancing their knowledge of their mother tongue? Was there cross-fertilization between Spanish and the various aboriginal tongues? Did it amount to a full-fledged phenomenon with recognizable patterns that is similar to Spanglish?

Before I start, it is essential that I set the proper context. When Columbus embarked on his first voyage across the Atlantic Ocean, Spanish had recently become a unifying force in the Iberian Peninsula. The Catholic Monarchs, Ferdinand and Isabella, in a process known as La Reconquista, were successful in campaigning against outside forces to create a unified nation. The nascent country had existed in a Babel-like state. However, by 1492, as a language Spanish had metamorphosed from a regional dialect to the language of the empire. To a large extent, the force behind that transformation was the lexicographer, humanist, and grammarian Antonio de Nebrija (1444–1522), whose academic career evolved first at Universidad de Salamanca, then at Universidad de Alcalá de Henares. Nebrija was the author of influential philological studies as well as bilingual lexicons, such as *Introductiones latinae* (1486),

---

* Cátedra, 1997.
† Included in *El lenguaje de Buenos Aires* (Emecé, 1968). Borges' essay, first published in *Sur,* is a review of Castro's *La peculiaridad lingüística rioplatense y su sentido histórico* (Losada, 1941).

Diccionario latino-español (1492), *Vocabulario español-latino* (circa 1495), and *Tabla de la diversidad de los días* (1499). His *Gramática de la lengua castellana,* released in 1492, just as the Genoan admiral was organizing his first trip cross the Atlantic Ocean, and as the Catholic Monarchs, Isabella and Ferdinand, were ready to expel the Jews from the kingdom, established Spanish as a tool in the effort to homogenize the population.

Nebrija had qualms with the pedagogical approach that Spaniards had in his time toward their linguistic heritage. Latin was a tool for education. The educated elite employed it in intellectual debates. But in his view, Spain wasn't rigorous enough about the proper usage of Latin. Thus his life-long objective was to reestablish, through a clear-cut pedagogical method, the glories of the Roman language in the peninsula. He wanted priests, writers, teachers, and students to take it more seriously. Plus, Nebrija was eager to fix the rules of the vulgar tongue, *el castellano* (from the region of Castile). By forcing it to abandon its anarchic syntax, his dream was to make it more elitist, less a jargon of the ignoramuses. As a Renaissance humanist, he believed that language is the key to who we are. Thus, he worried that Spanish spelling was unsystematic, proving that the people who used the language had a penchant for anarchy. His solution was to append the written language to its oral counterpart. Nebrija's motto might be said to be his overall philosophical approach to culture: "escribir como pronunciamos y pronunciar como escribimos"—to write how we speak and to speak how we write. He endorsed the opinion that language must represent nature in simple, straightforward fashion.

In the prologue to his *Gramática* (1492), which he wrote for Queen Isabella, Nebrija analyzed the evolution of language from the Tower of Babel to the fifteenth century. Of course, the engine behind his vision of history wasn't science but myth. He pondered the development of pre-biblical tongues, then reflected on Hebrew and Greek, and finally reached the topic of Latin, which, in his eyes, was the highest manifestation of perfection. The prologue—in old Spanish—includes the following passage (the italics are mine):

> Cuando bien conmigo pienso, mui esclarecida Reina, τ pongo delante de los ojos el antigüedad de todas las cosas que para nuestra recordación τ memoria quedaron escriptas, una cosa hállo sáco por conclusión mui cierta: que siempre *la lengua fue compañera del imperio;* τ de tal manera lo siguió, que junta mente començaron, crecieron τ florecieron, τ después junta fue la caida de entrambos. I dexadas agora las cosas mui antiguas de que a penas tenemos una imagen τ sombra de la verdad, cuales son las de los assirios, indos,

sicionios τ egipcios, en los cuales se podría muy bien provar lo que digo, vengo a las más frescas, τ aquellas especial mente de que tenemos mayor certidumbre, τ primero a la de los judíos.

For Nebrija, hence, the Spanish language is a companion of empire.

What aboriginal tongues were in use in the Americas as the Spanish conquistadors, explorers, and missionaries arrived? An estimate of the overall population varies enormously from one historical source to another. Some historians believe the number to be between 13 and 18 million; others push for a far larger cipher of 180 million. The latter is certainly too inflated but is connected to the decimation of the Indians through warfare, malnutrition, and epidemics. Even if the actual number of people from Alaska to the Pampas is around 45 million, it is still bewildering (no adjective does more justice) that, according to Díaz del Castillo, Cortés was able to vanquish the Aztec Empire with only 200 soldiers. (Other chroniclers put it at 670, but the adjective still holds). Similarly, Francisco Pizarro, in his conquest of Peru, had a battalion of equal size: 200 soldiers against the army of Atahualpa of 80,000. How did such reduced forces end up bringing down two of the most magisterial empires ever? The answer is complicated and needs to be approach regionally. First, there was the misconception among the Aztecs that Quetzalcóatl (i.e., a bearded man in an iron suit) would soon return from his cosmic journey; and second, the Iberians were far more technologically developed in warfare, using gunpowder (inherited from China) in their colonial quest. The effect was equally fatal in Peru. In his encounter with Pizarro, Hernando de Soto, and the Spanish invaders, Atahualpa became complacent. A leading historian of the conquest of Peru once said, sarcastically, that while the Inca emperor was planning to have Pizarro for lunch, Pizarro had him for breakfast.

The Aztec and Inca empires at the time of the Iberian invasion were amorphous entities. They themselves function as mechanisms where the forces of integration and separation were shaped by their conquering pursuits. The "Aztec Empire" is a misnomer referring to a collation of three powerful Mesoamerican people: the Mexicans and their allies, the Texcocans, and the Tlacopans. The partnership is known as *la triple alianza,* the triple alliance. Its height took placed in the hundred years preceding the arrival of Cortés. Together these three entities are often described as Nahuas because of the language they used: Nahuatl, of the classical sort, to distinguish it from the Nahuatl spoken nowadays by bastions of the Mexican population. Centralized in Tenochtitlán, the partnership, while consolidated in religious, economic, and political terms (they had a tributary system of government), was loose in linguistic terms.

While Nahuatl was the *lingua franca* of Mesoamerica (with two varieties, one known as *pipiltin* that was used by the nobles, and *mcehualtin* that was used by the lower strata), subaltern tongues were in much demand among the Aztecs. It is estimated that in the early part of the sixteenth century there were approximately 2,000 languages in the Americas, 350 of which were in use in Central Mexico alone, the region covered by the Aztec Empire, in and around the Tehuantepec Isthmus onward to the Pacific coast of Guatemala. Like the Greeks, the Aztecs believed that whenever they conquered a neighboring power, the way to submit them to their culture was through translations of the Aztec code of law into their colonized tongue. That was a job done by *nauatlatos,* which in Nahuatl means interpreter.

Compared to the Aztec Empire, the Inca Empire was larger in size, covering more than 772,000 square miles on the Pacific coast of South America, passing through present-day Ecuador, Peru, Bolivia, Colombia, Chile, and Argentina. Its capital was the city of Cuzco. The method it used to dominate other cultures was through peaceful assimilation. The empire should best be seen as a federation. It was divided into four parts called *suyus.* The complex structure that resulted from invasions allowed for multiple forms of worship. The central command in Cusco encouraged the sun god Inti, but other loyalties coexisted in the Andean region. Quechua, which is spoken by roughly ten million people today (it's one of the official languages in Bolivia and Peru), was the dominant vehicle of communication, followed, in descending order, by Aymara, Puquina, and scores of other tongue.

The arrival of the Spanish forces dramatically changed things. Top in the order of needs identified by Iberian missionaries was a survey of the hierarchy of aboriginal languages. This needed to be done in order for the Indian population to be instructed in the catechism. But first, that hierarchy established the concept of *lenguas generales,* a term used for describing the most sophisticated and frequently used tongues in the colonies. They were Nahuatl and Quechua. A debate ensued among educators and the centralized imperial power in Spain as to what approach to take to implant "civilized values."

The survey performed by missionaries convinced many of them that teaching Spanish to the natives was an effort destined for defeat. Aside from the discrepancy in numbers—depending on the source, by the mid-sixteenth century the ratio varies from one Spaniard for twenty thousand Indians to one Spaniard for fifty thousand—there were also spiritual implications. The Royal Crown believed it was in the best interest of everyone to use Spanish as the language of business, education, and religious affairs. An *orden de enseñanza,* i.e., educational law, promulgated by Emperor Charles V on June 7, 1550, established the following:

> As one of the main things we desire for the good of this land is the salvation and instruction and conversion to our Holy Catholic Faith of its natives, and that also they should adopt our policy and good customs; and so, treating the means which could be upheld to this end, it is apparent that one of them and the most principal would be to give the order so these people may be taught our Castilian language, for with this knowledge, they would be more easily taught the matters of the Holy Gospel and gain all the rest which is suitable for this manner of life.

Yet scores of friars and other religious leaders chose to ignore this legislation. Recognizing the scope of their endeavor, they often fell prey to disillusionment. In a response sent to the emperor that same year, Fray Rodrigo de la Cruz wrote:

> Your Majesty has ordered that these Indians should learn the language of Castile. That can never be, unless it were something vaguely and badly learnt: we see a Portuguese, where the language of Castile and Portugal is almost the same, spend thirty years in Castile, and never learn it. Then are these people to learn it, when their language is so foreign to ours, with exquisite manners of speaking? It seems to me that Your majesty should order that all the Indians learn the Mexican language, for in every village today there are many Indians who know it and learn it easily, and a very great number who confess in that language. It is an extremely elegant language, as elegant as any in the world. A grammar and dictionary of it have been written, and many parts of the Holy Scripture have been translated into it; and collections of sermons have been made; and some friars are very great linguists in it.

Other Catholic friars expounded a similar rejoinder. Fray Juan de Mansilla, General Commissioner of Guatemala, in an epistle to Charles V drafted in 1551, explained:

> We are too few to teach the language of Castile to Indians. They do not want to speak it. It would be better to make universal the Mexican language, which is widely current, and they like it, and in

it there are written doctrine and sermons and a grammar and a vocabulary.

The Indians resisted the colonizer's tongue in all sorts of ways. Isolated populations in the Yucatán Peninsula, for example, retained Mayan as their private language, which people learned in childhood at home and in school. In the urban centers where Indians congregated for work, only fundamental linguistic tools were adopted, enough to satisfy the masters. Whenever they needed to go beyond this, the Indians would pretend to have a short memory. Or they would claim not to have talent or energy to accomplish the task. Of course, their negative reaction is understandable. The pride in their aboriginal culture made them resist. "El Inca" Gracilazo de la Vega, quoting Blas Valera, tells this anecdote in his *Comentarios reales:*

> Whence it has come about that many provinces, where when the Spaniards entered Cajamarca the rest of the Indians knew this common language [*quechua*], have now forgotten it altogether, because with the end of the world and Empire of the Incas, there was no one to remember something so convenient and necessary for the preaching of the Holy Gospel, because of the widespread oblivion caused by the wars which arose among the Spaniards, and after that for other causes which the evil Satan has sown to prevent such an advantageous regime from being put into operation. . . . There are some to whom it appears sensible to oblige all the Indians to learn the Spanish language, so that the priests should not waste their efforts on learning the Indian one. This opinion can leave no one who hears it in any doubt that it arose from failure of endeavor rather than stupid thinking. . . .

Along the same lines, Fray Domingo Santo Tomás, one of the canonical lexicographers of the colonial period, wrote in his treatise on Quechua, *Arte de la lengua general del Perú* (1560):

> It is of note that the Indians of Peru, before we Christians had come to them, had certain and particular modes of swearing, distinct from ours. They had no assertive oaths, such as "by God" or "by heaven," but only execrations or curses . . . e.g., "if I am not telling the truth, may the sun kill me," they said: *mana checcanta ñiptiy, indi guañuchiuancmancha.* . . . Once when I asked a chieftain in a certain province if he was a Christian, he said: "I am not yet quite one, but I am making a beginning." I asked him what he knew of

being Christian, and he said: "I know how to swear to God, and play cards a bit, and I am beginning to steal."

Still, the proselytizing effort unfolded even amidst complaints, pushing along with it the spreading of the Spanish language in the region. Even before the conquest of Tenochtitlán, twenty copies of Nebrija's *Arte de la lengua castellana* were delivered in Hispaniola in 1513, sent from the governmental Casa de Contratación de Indias. But Nebrija wasn't an educator. What the providers of Spanish in the America needed was a large artillery of pedagogical material: dictionaries, grammars (known as *artes*), and textbooks in Spanish became a priority of the Royal Crown. Within the next hundred years, almost all the lexicons published in the Americas were from Spanish to other tongues and not the other way around. That is, the emphasis by the Iberian educators was placed on teaching, not on learning. Also significant is the effort by friars to identify speakers of aboriginal languages and use them to decodify the surviving codices and other material from the pre-Columbian past.

Historian Nicholas Ostler, in his book *Empires of the Word*,* profiles this need as appearing "the first time in the world." Ostler suggests that, unlike previous empires at the global stage, no civilization had ever taken upon itself as ambitious a task as to educate a large mass of people in the use of its imperial tongue. Previous empires like the Phoenicians, Hebrews, Greeks, Romans, Byzantians, Aztecs, and Incas had used their language as a mechanism of usurpation. To various degrees, they had forced their subalterns to adapt to their manners by making them become fluent in the colonizers' parlance. But the Spaniards went a step further: they orchestrated a transoceanic campaign to educate by means of the importation of printed books, which in turn were disseminated by the Catholic missionaries. These educators weren't always Iberian dwellers. Scores of them were creoles and *mestizos,* such as "El Inca" Gracilazo and Fernando de Alva Ixtilxóchitl, a descendant from the line of Texcoco kings.

The printing press, first established in Nueva España (Mexico today) in 1535, fostered the spread of manuals and translations designed for the aboriginal population to become acquainted with the colonizers' *Weltanschauung.* Immediately, there appeared volumes in Nahuatl, Quechua, and other native tongues. For instance, the first book published in what is today Mexico was *Breve y más compendiosa doctrina cristiana* (1539), which appeared in the *lengua mexicana,* a code name for Nahuatl. It was followed by Fray Alonso de Molina's *Doctrina cristiana breve tra-*

*HarperCollins, 2005.

ducida en lengua mexicana (1546) and Fray Andrés de Olmedo's *Arte de la lengua mexicana* (1547).

Not only schooling was used in the imposition of Spanish. The Royal Crown understood that the domestic realm was a fundamental habitat wherein to implement language loyalty. At this level, the topics of ethnicity and language become juxtaposed. For racial miscegenation was a desired goal. In 1503 the Royal Court recommended to the governor of Hispaniola that some Christians should marry some Indian women, so that "they may communicate with and teach one another." Clearly, the connection between marriage and schooling was appreciated in the Iberian Peninsula as essential to the spreading of Catholic values. And, indeed, the rise of *mestizaje* that resulted from the cross-breeding of Spaniards and Indians is a byproduct of the sixteenth century.

Arguably the most significant system implemented by the Spanish conquerors was the *encomienda*. A conquistador was granted a trusteeship over a group of aboriginal people. This was a form of economic property. The relationship between the *encomendero* and his Indians served as an obstacle in the process of integration between Europeans and natives. But it also fostered an atmosphere whereby Indians needed to know basic Spanish in order to respond to their requests. The phenomenon of *mestizaje* fostered enough ambivalence for the duality of cultures, Iberian and aboriginal, to give place to a third option: a local concoction nurtured by these two sources yet also self-sufficient. The formation of a native Spanish was also a byproduct of the same phenomenon. Words like *mezcal, hamaca, piñata, canoa, elote,* and *platicar* defined its idiosyncrasy. *El español mejicano* is a manifestation of the *mestizo* self. Likewise the *cholo* variety used by Peruvians.

Our knowledge of languages in contact allows us to deduct that, depending on the location, the Indians engaged in code-switching and code-mixing, forming misconstrued sentences whose syntax alarmed their educators. Regrettably, there's a scarcity of primary sources allowing us to appreciate the verbal negotiations that took place in the private and public realms. Still, the work of chroniclers like Fray Bernardino de Sahagún and Fray Toribio de Benavente "Motolonía" (in Nahuatl, "the poor one") is useful in determining the cross-pollinization. Sahagún's *History of the Things of New Spain* (1579), published bilingually in Nahuatl and Spanish, was designed as both an evangelical and an ethnographic resource to convey the Aztec past and to explain it to the native population. Motolinía believed that world salvation would ultimate happen in the Americas. His interest in language showcases the transition he hoped the aboriginal population would make to Spanish in order to be redeemed. Interestingly, unlike what happened in the British colonies, where the Old Testament was translated by John Eliot in 1659 (and published in 1663) from Latin into aboriginal languages, the project of rendering the biblical text in Nahuatl and Quechua wasn't part of the agenda of the Royal Crown. Such an endeavor was controversial in the Holy Office of the Inquisition, where the translation was judged to be a heretical act. Even having the Hebrew and Latin transferred to Spanish provoked strong reactions.*

I'm puzzled by the question: was there an equivalent of Spanglish, a hybrid tongue mixing Spanish and the *lenguas generales* or other native parlances? Where two clearly defined linguistic groups come into intense contact for an extended period of time, a third option results in the mouth of speakers. But the missionaries disregarded the evidence because for them the in-between vehicle of communication was an abomination, neither here nor there and, hence, unworthy of attention. Whenever a Nahuatl speaker faced the problem of not knowing a Spanish word, he would insert a Nahuatl noun and then use a modifier. A pirate was described as an *acalco tenamoyani*, "one who robs people on a boat." Similarly, the law became *tlamelahuacachihualiztli*, "doing things straight." The linguistic negotiation became even more intense. In their native Nahuatl, speakers incorporated Spanish words. A *caja* was a wooden chest, *puerta* became a swinging door, and a church was a *santa iglesia*. Quechua also engaged in similar exercises. Furthermore, "El Inca" Garcilazo described the way the Indian population lived in one language but communicated in another. He offers samples of Quechua terms incorporated into *el español* and vice versa.†

Did such back-and-forths result in a perfectly delineated third option? It's hard to say. More evidence is needed to assert such a claim. However, an adaptation of the Iberian mind to the landscape is already evident in translations done in the Americas, which often adapted material to a regional setting for the benefit of the reader. In 1579, a rendition into Nahuatl of a Latin version of Aesop's fables was published. In the Latin original, it says that "a lion once heard a frog croaking; he turned toward the noise thinking it was some great beast; when he saw the frog by the pond he went up and squashed it." In Nahutal, it reads: "A jaguar once heard a frog, screaming and croaking a great deal." The jaguar was frightened and thought that it was a large front-footed animal: "To quiet his heart, he looked around him in all directions. When

*See my essay "La imaginación restaurada," in *El español en el mundo* (Círculo de Lectores, 2004), 107–25.
†Jayne A. Sokolow, *The Great Encounter: Native Peoples and European Settlers in the Americas, 1492–1800* (M. E. Sharpe, 2003), 132.

he came to the water's edge, the jaguar was very angry and ashamed of being frightened by such a small creature."*

Should Spanish then be seen as a great equalizer during the colonial period in the Americas? Only to a certain extent. It enabled Catholicism to set roots. Yet its propagation wasn't achieved without endless obstacles. The defiance and lack of enthusiasm of the natives generated dismay for the Royal Crown, which responded by changing its views as it went along and depending on who was in power. That the aboriginal population was reluctant to become fluent in Spanish repeatedly frustrated legislators. In 1578, King Philip II ordered that religious educators appointed to teach Indians should have some knowledge of their tongue, at the very least one of the *lenguas generales*. And in 1560, he established chairs in indigenous languages in Mexico City and Lima, announcing that "knowledge of the general language of the Indians is essential for the explanation and teaching of Christian doctrine."

In his classic *Historia de la lengua española*,† Rafael Lapesa devoted the last section (70 pages, out of the book's total 690) of a chapter entitled "El español actual" to the Spanish used in the Americas. Lapesa's succinct appreciation doesn't allow a complete picture of the challenge faced by the regiment of Iberian lexicographers at the outset of the colonial period. Nor does is explain the debate between *el español* and the *lenguas generales*. This isn't unique. A wide-ranging historical analysis of the disputes of the time is essential for a consideration of linguistic identity in the Americas. Especially now that the explorations surrounding Spanglish in the United States have drawn light to the linguistic cross-fertilization of a large minority population, it is crucial to recognize the path that Spanish took on its search for continental domination. How is it that from a tongue of a minuscule army, it metamorphosed during the so-called Age of Independence into the common language of millions of people? It is estimated that in 1810, the year marking the first attempt at secession from Spain, there were 6.7 million inhabitants in the Americas. Approximately 45 percent of them (more than 3 million) were either Spaniards or *mestizos* for whom Spanish was their first language.

By the beginning of the seventeenth century, the social, political, and linguistic landscape in the Americas had been transformed. When Shakespeare staged his play *The Tempest* in 1611, set on a Caribbean island (i.e., Carib), it was widespread knowledge that the European languages were the instrument of control in the colonies. Shakespeare has

*Sokolow, 133–34.
†Gredos, 1942. Its 11th edition appeared in 1981, a decade before Lapesa's death.

Caliban complain to Prospero (Act I, scene 2): "You taught me language, and my profit on it is I know how to curse. The red plague rid you for learning me the language." Yet Spanish didn't quite take hold in a homogenized manner throughout the colonies, at least not to the degree the colonizers wished. The *lenguas generales* didn't altogether disappear. On the contrary, literature in Nahuatl, Quechua, Aymara, and other tongues flourished in the form of religious poetry and plays (known as *autos sacramentales*). The fact that they are still in use is proof of the duality of the endeavor. The fact that four hundred million people use Spanish today is proof of success. It's the third most popular language in the world after Mandarin and English.

The Unfathomable César Aira

❧

AFTER THE RABELAISIAN MOVEMENT known as El Boom in Latin American letters came along a period of exhaustion. And revolt, too. There was, for instance, a group of authors that included the Chilean Alberto Fuguet and the Bolivian Edmundo Paz Soldán who ascribed to the generation of McOndo. Their objective was to turn magic realism on its head. But their novels were flat and repetitive and, in most cases, DOA. Then there were the five Mexicans responsible for the "Crack Manifesto." Their esthetics was far more ambitious: to shape a novel in Spanish unburdened by language and geography. This resulted in interesting examples, among them Jorge Volpi's *In Search of Klingsor,* about the Nazis and the making of the atomic bomb. *Interesting,* of course, is a demeaned word: it used to mean "appealing" but nowadays is a synonym for "all right," maybe even "tolerable."

Interesting is the last adjective I would use to describe Roberto Bolaño, by far the most inspiring talent from south of the border to come since the 1970s. A Chilean who lived for years in Mexico and ultimately settled near Barcelona before he died in 2003, at the age of fifty, Bolaño created an oeuvre that is slowly making its way into English, in renditions by Chris Andrews, released under the aegis of New Directions. His hypnotizing style and restless approach to plot are at once refreshing and humbling.

More imaginative, although also less consistent, is the astonishingly prolific Argentine César Aira, whom Bolaño once described as the type of "eccentric" whose prose, "once you start reading [it], you don't want to stop." Bolaño's portrait isn't quite accurate: born in 1949, Aira has published almost sixty books, from criticism on Edward Lear and Alejandra Pizarnik to editions of the poetry of Osvaldo Lamborghini to a vast number of novels. In the novels I've read, like the untranslated *El congreso de literatura,* about a writers' conference where one of the participants decides to clone Carlos Fuentes, the premise is better than its execution. Aira's dreams are emblematic and never conventional. When he's in top form—and it's seldom the case—he can be utterly astonishing, as in *An Episode in the Life of a Landscape Painter,* published in Spanish in 2000, also translated by Andrews.

This novella-cum–artistic meditation is about Johann Moritz Rugendas, a nineteenth-century German artist and colleague of explorer Alexander von Humboldt. Rugendas visited Chile, Argentina, and Mexico in the hope of recording the flora and fauna through an art conceived as "physiognomic totality." During a trip to the Pampas, he is electrified by a convergence of nature and spirituality. The impact of his experience handicaps him physically and psychologically. And his quest to see the Indians of the region ultimately crowns his descent to hell. More than fiction, it is an imaginative chronicle based on Rugendas' correspondence and other historical sources from the era. To which Aira adds the novelistic touch: *el beso de la fantasía.*

That his protagonist is a European attempting to scientifically codify what he sees—Rugendas is a child of positivism—allows for an unforgettable opportunity to see Latin America through the eyes of a foreigner. Better even, the foreigner, Rugendas, is re-imagined à la Russian doll by a native, Aira, thus inviting the reader to be simultaneously outsider and insider. Another one of his books, the Kafkaesque *The Hare,* appeared in English in 1997, without fanfare, among other reasons because of its dissipated quality. In *An Episode in the Life of a Landscape Painter,* his concentration is absolute, and it pays off handsomely. The book is excellent.

Another one of Aira's most famous works is *How I Became a Nun,* a fictionalized autobiography about a protagonist, a six-year-old savant called César Aira, who dies at a young age. Or does he? The reader is offered all sorts of perplexing clues about Aira. He is sometimes described as a boy and sometimes as a girl. But the narrative isn't about transgender mutation. In fact, it doesn't have a single sexual scene. And, by the way, it isn't about becoming a nun either, although the first line is perfectly clear:

> My story, the story of "how I became a nun," began very early in my life; I had just turned six. The beginning is marked by a vivid memory, which I can reconstruct down to the last detail. Before, there is nothing, and after, everything is an extension of the same vivid memory, continuous and unbroken, including the intervals of sleep, up to the point where I took the veil.

To attempt a synopsis of the plot is to fall prey to its bizarre connections and probably to undermine Aira's efforts, for his point, if he is said to have one, is to defy logic, to prove that autobiographical writing is a sham, a travesty, a game of mirrors. Is it always us who are the protagonists of our own lives? Do we ever know what that life is about?

The action of *How I Became a Nun* takes place in Rosario, Argentina. César Aira, Pop, and Mom have just moved into a lower-class neighborhood from a small town called Coronel Pringes (where the real Aira was born in 1949). The beginning shows Aira being forced by Pop to try ice cream for the first time. It turns out the ice cream has cyanide poison. Angry at the ice cream seller, Pop kills him, for which he gets an eight-year prison sentence. Soon a portion of the Rosario population is dying of poison. But Aira doesn't care. Why should he? Life is too precious for him. And so, the reader gets a taste of his experiences: her encounter with dolls, his acquaintance with a neighborhood friend called Arturo Carrera, a disquisition about dyslexia. In the end, the ice cream vendor's wife comes back with a vengeance.

And what is the vengeance about? I won't reveal it.

The novella has a taste of the early, unspoiled Paul Auster, of Felipe Alfau's masterpiece *Locos: A Comedy of Gestures,* and of Bruno Schulz's *The Street of Crocodiles.* Aira's true ancestor is the Uruguayan Felisberto Hernández, a forgotten master—his best stories are about an inundated house, the fetishism of dolls, and a terrific one called "Around the Time of Clemente Collin"—whose career as a pianist in silent-screen movie theaters appears to have shaped Hernández's imagination . . . and Aira's.

Nevertheless, the publisher is trying to make other connections. It is promoting *How I Became a Nun* as a modern-day *Through the Looking Glass,* but this is yet another false clue. Yes, Lewis Carroll wrote about children, but he also wrote *for* children. Aira, even though his character is prepubescent, doesn't give a damn about childhood. Worse, she doesn't give a damn about growing up.

So, does he care about anything? Only one thing: the unfathomable.

This is experimental literature at its best, an exposé unlike anything around today. We get to know César Aira better than his parents ever did, better even than his friends, perhaps better even than he knows himself. Of course, we never really know anything for sure. Nor should we.

Renegade Bolaño

❦

NOT SINCE GABRIEL GARCÍA MARQUEZ, whose masterpiece, *One Hundred Years of Solitude*, turns forty this year, has someone from Latin America redrawn the map of world literature so emphatically as Roberto Bolaño does with *The Savage Detectives*. He is such a rewarding author, I wish I could go in prison just to have endless time to read him.

As the title suggests, the material in *The Savage Detectives* has the shape of a detective story, yet one that stretches the genre to its limits. The narration is polyphonic: The first part is told by Juan García Madero, a transient member of the "visceral realists." The second is a maze of testimonials by a plethora of people, real and fictional, about the Mexican literary world from 1976 to 1996. (I bet an army of bored graduate students in Spanish departments will waste years attempting to disentangle the maze.) And the third part returns to 1976 and García Madero, who delivers a denouement as eccentric as it is graphic. The reader reaches the end recognizing that everything is a joke and that words are insufficient to chronicle metaphysical searches such as the one engaged in by this pair of no-do-gooders who recall Don Quixote and Sancho.

Cervantes' masterpiece serves Bolaño as pretext and subtext. The entire book is episodic, alternating between discussions of literature, misadventures, and stories within stories. Middle-class angst is ubiquitous. Sex is performed—and depicted—prodigally. The scenes of García Madero's initiations into a world of frenzied hedonism are the best of the kind I've read. There's a hilarious episode in which the "visceral realists" attempt to kidnap Octavio Paz, who is accurately portrayed as stiff and formal. In another irreverent section, Carlos Monsiváis, a solipsistic cultural commentator who lives with his mother, is visited by Belano and Lima in a branch of the famous chain restaurants known as Sanborns, only to be shown as being equally aloof, disconnected from the true undercurrents of Mexican literature. The cumulative effect of these satirical episodes is astonishing. Everyone in these episodes is looking to understand Belano and Lima, but fails to do so. It's a Rashomon-like quest: truth, it becomes clear, is evasive, unattainable. That, indeed, is the tone of the entire novel. As Belano and Lima try to find Cesárea Tinajero, the reader tries to understand them as characters. Yet Bolaño doesn't want us to succeed. He fills his characters with contradictions, just as he makes them feel unhappy that in the end they actually find Tinajero in the Sonora Desert. What matters isn't the solution to the puzzle but the effort of assembling the parts of the puzzle into a whole.

One part of that puzzle comes early in the novel's second part, when a mythical female, Auxilio Lacouture (Bolaño's names are at once trite and magical), makes an appearance. She's a Uruguayan woman who moved to Mexico in the 1960s, became involved in the student uprising of 1968, when she locked herself in a bathroom as the government soldiers were about to reclaim a building taken over by some protesters, and presents herself, irreverently, as the "Mother of Mexican Poetry." The part on Lacouture lasts less than a dozen pages, but after *The Savage Detectives* first came out in Spanish, Bolaño expanded the material into a novella, *Amulet*, which was first published in 1999 and has now been gorgeously rendered into English by Chris Andrews. The tone is witty, and wit is also behind Lacouture's voice. "But one thing stopped me from going crazy," she argues at one point. "I never lost my sense of humor. I could laugh at my skirts, my stovepipe trousers, my stripy tights, my white socks, my page-boy hair going whiter every day, my eyes scanning the nights of Mexico City, my pink ears attuned to all the university gossip." Allegorical in tone yet lacking in plot, it is, in my estimation, among the lowest points in Bolaño's distinguished career. Still, it fits the puzzle he has constructed, imagining Cesárea Tinajero, a poetess, alone in a bathroom, devoting her energy to making Mexican poetry fresher, less stilted than it was at the time.

By far the most hallucinatory element in *The Savage Detectives* is its bizarre, exquisite Spanish. Having spent years studying linguistic varieties across the Americas, I've never come across a chameleon talent like Bolaño's. He writes in a Mexican Spanish with an Iberian twist but with an impostor's accent. How ironic that the best Mexican novel of the last fifty years ended up being written by a Chilean.

The Chilean-born Bolaño moved with his parents to Mexico in 1968, returned to Chile in 1973, only to be caught up in the Pinochet coup d'etat, and settled eventually in Catalonia, Spain. Much of the time before his untimely death in 2003, at the age of fifty, he was obsessed with being an outcast. He was vicious in his attacks on figures such as Isabel Allende and Octavio Paz, accusing them of being conformists, non-daring in their oeuvre, more interested in personal fame than in art. In poems, stories (some of them included in *Last Evenings on Earth*), novellas (like *Distant Star* and *By Night in Chile*), two mammoth narratives (the one under review and *2666*), and a collection of essays (called, in Spanish, *Entre paréntesis*), he built such a flamboyant, stylistically distinctive counter-establishment voice that it is no exaggeration to call him a genius.

The Savage Detectives alone should grant him immortality. It's an outstanding meditation on art, truth, and the search for roots and the self, a kind of road novel set in Mexico in the 1970s that springs from the same roots as Alfonso Cuarón's film *Y tu mamá también*. Its protagonists are Arturo Belano and Ulises Lima, fringe poets professing an esthetics they describe as "visceral realism." Their hunt for a tangential ancestor by the name of Cesárea Tinajero takes them to the Sonora Desert, portrayed by Bolaño as a land of amnesia.

Yet he left another extraordinary book—arguably the most daring, ambitious literary project a Spanish-language fiction writer ever embarked on: *2666*. Although it isn't altogether satisfying, not in the way *The Savage Detectives* is, its messiness is, in and of itself, a sign of sheer genius. Bolaño wrote this mega-narrative (in Spanish it has 1,125 pages) in the last years of his life, with a death sentence over him: he knew he had liver disease and would soon die of it. So he gathered every bit of his energy to complete the manuscript. As he was completing its final touches, he collapsed. What we have isn't quite a finished manuscript. Ignacio Echevarría, a Spanish critic and Bolaño's friend, who heads Bolaño's estate, made some minor changes and sent it to the printer.

This was not exactly how Bolaño wanted it, though. The book is divided into five parts, almost all of them the length of a novella. Wanting to leave his family some financial resources, he requested that each part be released separately. But Echevarría and Bolaño's Barcelona publisher, Jorge Herralde, opted for one volume, believing it would give readers a sharper sense of the author's intention. The U.S. publisher, instead, is almost having it both ways: the novel is appearing in a single tome as well in a box made of three paperbacks, one of which includes three novellas.

Overall, the central narrative motif in *2666* is moral inversion: good *is* evil, and vice versa. Bolaño's penchant for sarcasm makes that motif treacherous. His sentences circumvent the heart of the story, proudly announcing that storytelling should always be a zigzagging line.

Ciudad Juárez, the U.S.-Mexico border town where hundreds of *señoritas* have been assassinated with impunity by one or more serial killers in the last couple of decades, is where a large part of the plot takes place. Some other portions take place in Italy, England, France, Spain, Mexico, Chile, and the United States. In *2666,* Bolaño calls Ciudad Juárez by another name: Santa Teresa. He portrays it as the world's dumpster. Nothing in this maze is real.

In one novella, a group of international literary critics looks for

Benno von Archimboldi, a Pynchon-type German author and eternal Nobel Prize nominee who disappears from the public eye and might have ended up in Santa Teresa. In another, a black reporter for a Harlem magazine arrives in Santa Teresa to cover a boxing match only to realize there's a larger story to be told in the place. In a third part, a philosopher, Amalfitano, and his daughter make their way to Santa Teresa. The diverse plots, the last having Archimboldi at its core, intersect à la Alejandro González Iñarritu, by way of serendipitous connections between characters.

Several sections feel incomplete, as if Bolaño was merely accumulating material. And the last novella, about Archimboldi himself, is somewhat of a disappointment: the mystery behind most of *2666* is fleshed out in an easy way, depriving the core of the plot of a religious value. Up until that point, the novel (is that what it is?) feels like a tribute, if not a rewriting, of Borges' pseudo-review "The Approach for Al-Mu'tasim," just as *The Savage Detectives* was a stepchild of Cortázar's *Hopscotch*.

According to Echevarría, Bolaño intended the narrator of *2666* to be none other than Arturo Belano, one of the protagonists of *The Savage Detectives* and Bolaño's alter ego in most of his mature work. Although this isn't entirely clear, there are some clues signaling that this was something the author envisioned for *2666* as he was completing the endeavor.

By his own account, Bolaño started writing at the age of eighteen. He was an unredeemed smoker, ate poorly, and slept irregular hours. Literature for him was a mania, if not also a form of martyrdom. His last decade of life, from 1993 to 2003, was remarkably prolific. Starting in 1993, he published almost a book a year, sometimes more. His fiction started out by dealing with topics such as the death of Peru's poet César Vallejo in Paris and the excesses of fascism in Chile. He rewrote a story by Borges and imagined an encyclopedia of Nazi authors in Latin America. He refused stipends from the literary establishment, submitting his manuscripts to contests in order to get the little money he needed to go on.

In his late teens, he made an irrevocable decision: never to enter a classroom again. Since then, everything he learned was through reading. Indeed, I'm convinced that Bolaño worked his deepest revolution as a reader: He chose his own predecessors, forcing us to rethink the canon while taking every opportunity to ridicule that canon as a manufactured commodity useful only to appreciate bestsellers. He didn't want to write bestsellers; on the contrary; he enjoyed carving out a career against the wishes of the literary status quo.

Witnessing Bolaño's canonization in academia has been fascinating. Barely a decade ago, he was a *don nadie,* a supreme nobody, and currently he's a consummate dandy: the *New Yorker* puts its imprimatur on him, he's a household name at the MLA convention, and he's taught as providing a refreshing perspective, a kind of Jack Kerouac for the new millennium. Bolaño is rapidly becoming a factory of scholarly platitudes. More than a year ago, I had a student who wrote his senior thesis on him. He started early in his junior year with a handful of resources at his disposal. By the time he finished, the plethora of tenure-granting examinations was dumbfounding: Bolaño and illness, Bolaño and the whodunit, Bolzano and the Beatniks, Bolaño and eschatology . . . Since then, interviews, photographs, emails—everything by him is perceived as a discovery, even though they were never lost.

The rapture must have been the same when Borges, long a commodity among of a small cadre of followers in Argentina, shared with Samuel Beckett the International Publishers Prize in 1961. Suddenly, from one day to the next his oeuvre, available in his native Spanish, in French in the renditions of his friend Néstor Ibarra, and in minuscule quantities in English, became, through translation, an overnight sensation around the world. Prior to the "unmasking," his passionate readers used to talk of being in a private club where they had Borges exclusively to themselves. After the success, there appeared to be a cheapening of the author's quality, the feeling of treason that comes when sharing with the masses what belongs to a limited few.

Bolaño would have laughed at the abundance of accolades he has garnished since the late 1990s. Did he ever imagine himself being anointed *the* novelist of the early twenty-first century? His arrival in Spanish departments is particularly intriguing. His mordant tongue frequently attacked the holy cows of Latin American letters, and for good reason: Octavio Paz, Isabel Allende, Diamela Eltit . . . He described them as complacent, solipsistic, tedious. In response, Bolaño built his own parallel esthetic tradition, a rebel's gallery of outlaws and pariahs with Borges—in particular, the Borges of tales like "Three Versions of Judas" and "The Gospel According to Mark"—as its gravitational force.

And yet, he's now moving steadily to the center of the curriculum in Spanish departments. Not a moment too soon, I might add, although there are obvious drawbacks. The abuse the "Boom" masters have undergone in Spanish-language classrooms has gone on for too long. How many times should Carlos Fuentes' *Aura,* Gabriel García Márquez's *Chronicle of a Death Foretold,* and Elena Poniatowska's *Dear Diego* be taught during a lifetime: twenty, forty, sixty? Bolaño's novellas are delightful in that they make the wrong ideological links: their ultra-conservative cast is perceived admirably. In *Nazi Literature in the Americas,* for instance, a catalog of perversion (again, emulating Borges' *Universal History of Infamy*) is expounded as a web of interconnection. And in *By Night in Chile,* an Opus Dei priest and literary critic reveals his connection in Chile to the Pinochet regime. Are politics in the Southern Cone this repulsive?

Not only does Bolaño's ideology (the Left is weak, the Right is bizarre) produce a welcome whiplash to students in Spanish departments. His ascending prestige, and therein his other enchanting quality, also break into a thousand little pieces the traditional boundaries of Latin American letters. It's impossible to describe him across geographic (i.e., national) lines. On the page this Chilean's Spanish is the most dazzling Mexican Spanish I've ever read by an Iberian author. In other words, translation is at the core of Bolaño's endeavor: not the standard rendering of a sentence in one language into another, but the reimagining of a country's linguistic self through another, and another . . .

Bolaño didn't hold academic life in any esteem. Knowledge, he seems to have suggested, comes to us in chaotic ways, when we least expect it: not in the classroom, not through formal instruction. Whenever he portrays academics in his oeuvre, they are dissatisfied types, looking for signs of intelligence everywhere but in their own profession. The model student for Bolaño is irreverent, intolerant, and self-taught.

In any case, therein the lesson to be learned from Bolaño: all revolutionaries end up dead or co-opted by the system.

Happy Birthday, Señor Neruda!

⌘

"LADIES AND GENTLEMAN, I never found in books any formula for writing poetry; and I, in turn, do not intend to leave in print a word of advice, a method, or a style that will allow young poets to receive from me some drop of supposed wisdom." Thus spoke Pablo Neruda on December 13, 1971, upon receiving the Nobel Prize for Literature. He had become by then *the* poet of Latin America par excellence. The Stockholm committee acknowledged Neruda "for a poetry that with the action of an elemental force brings alive a continent's destiny and dreams." That continent was known—maybe still is—for being trapped in a hundred-year labyrinth of solitude. But Neruda added: "There is no unassailable solitude. All roads lead to the same point: to the communication of who we are. And we must travel across lonely and rugged terrain, though isolation and silence, to reach the magic zone where we can dance an awkward dance."

Neruda turns one hundred this year, and his journey has never been more tangible. He is the emblem of the engaged poet, an artist whose heart is literally consumed by passion. That passion is defined by politics. Gabriel García Márquez called him "the best poet of the 20th century—in any language." The blurb might be over-inflated. There is already little doubt, though, that Neruda is among the most lasting voices of that most tumultuous (in his own words, "the saddest") century. He is surely one of the most popular poets of all time, his books, from his romantic *Twenty Love Poems and a Song of Despair* to his masterpiece *The Heights of Macchu Picchu* and his memorable and endlessly mutating poems about Isla Negra, selling millions of copies in dozens of languages.

Ever before his death in 1973, at the age of sixty-nine, Neruda was an icon of the young: at once eternally idealistic and impossibly hyperkinetic. Among his own idols was Walt Whitman, whom he called an "essential brother." Whitman personified for Neruda the crossroads where poetry and politics meet—or don't—and the commitment to use the pen as a calibrator of one's age. After a self-centered start, he published *Canto General,* the endeavor that made him dutifully famous, written over a decade (1938–49) that encapsulated the atrocities and peace treaties of World War II. *Canto General* offered a cinema-scope portrait of the Americas, the United States included, that still is unprecedented.

Everything is included: its mineral structure, its flora and fauna, the tribal struggles of its pre-Columbian past, the sweeping swords of the conquistadors and liberators, up to a picture of average workers in factories at midcentury, anonymous in their jobs, on strike to improve their miserable labor conditions. Though Borges and Neruda are polar opposites, there is something almost Borgesian in Neruda's task: yes, as the Nobel announcement had it, he attempted to reduce the universe— or, at least, *a* universe—into a single book. Poetry today appears to have lost that ambition, supplanting it with an endless need to emphasize the autobiographical. Creative writing workshops do little but manufacture inane poems by consent. In spite of his refusal to leave us a manual of style, Neruda's oeuvre displays a clear pedagogy: it puts poetry and history side by side.

This isn't to say that Neruda is foolproof. The evidence points to the contrary. His best poems feel as if created by not as temperate a person as one is likely to imagine—"I Explain a Few Things," for instance. But he also left us an overdose of bad poetry. How could he not when his five-volume *Obras Completas,* published in Spanish in 1999, totals more than some six thousand pages? While editing *The Poetry of Pablo Neruda,* I often thought of Truman Capote's comment on Jack Kerouac: he didn't write, Capote said, he simply typed. Neruda's late oeuvre is passable at best and disheveled at worst. Indeed, Alastair Reid, one of Neruda's most accomplished English translators, told me I was doing a disservice by releasing, in between covers, some six hundred poems by the Chilean laureate, organized so as to show the overall arc of his career. But an unsmoothed Neruda is better than a censored Neruda, even when that censorship has nothing to do with politics and all to do with esthetics. To fully appreciate the sublime, it helps to meddle with the unworthy.

The most attractive yet delicate aspect of Neruda's posterity has to do with his ideological odyssey. He was simultaneously a witness and chronicler of most of the decisive events of the twentieth century. From the remoteness of his childhood he heard the bangs of the Great War unravel, was a published poet in Spain in the 1930s (he befriended Federico García Lorca), traveled through the Soviet Union, saw the rise and demise of Hitler, made it to Cuba after 1959, opposed the U.S. invasion of Cambodia and Vietnam, and was in Chile when General Augusto Pinochet orchestrated a coup—on the other 9/11—against the elected Socialist president Salvador Allende. In fact, Neruda often posed as a politician: he was a senator in Chile and also a presidential hopeful; plus, at various moments and different geographies he was a diplomat.

All of which didn't manage to dissipate his naïveté. In a poem he imagined Franco in hell: "May you be alone and accursed, / alone and awake among all the dead, / and let blood fall upon you like rain, / and let a dying river of severed eyes / slide and flow over you staring at you endlessly." But he was also a staunch supporter of Stalin, which prompted him to write cheap red propaganda. He also imprudently embraced Fidel Castro: "Fidel, Fidel, the people are grateful / for words in action and deeds that sing, / that is why I bring from far / a cup of my country's wine." And in the early 1970s he wrote a book called, embarrassingly, *Incitación al Nixonicidio*—in English, "Invitation to the Nixonicide."

Still, Neruda is a torch-bearer. On campus in the 1970s he was a favorite. The Beatniks made him a role model. But then the neo-liberals of the 1980s turned him into an archaism. In 1995 came Michael Radford's film *Il Postino,* based on a novella by Neruda's compatriot Antonio Skármeta. Since then, he is enjoying a renewed appeal, intensified this year by the festivities surrounding his centennial. Students embrace him because he sought fairness and didn't shy away from resistance. The Communism Neruda so fervently embraced has lost its gravitas, but another larger-than life conflict has taken hold. How would he react to the current atmosphere where civil liberties are under threat in our country, which prides itself as fundamentally democratic? And what would his take be on the misconstrued War on Terror? In his Nobel speech he said he had no manual to offer to the next generation. His poetry is anything but programmatic: it is fluid, rambunctious, centrifugal.

His unstoppable commitment to freedom during the Spanish Civil War has enormous currency nowadays. After the terrorist bombings in Madrid last March, the electorate voted José María Aznar out of office in a clear rebuttal to his foreign policy in Iraq. His indictment of careless corporate globalism in poems like "United Fruit Co." if anything became more urgent. And his anger against limitations of press expression, from Venezuela to Saudi Arabia and North Korea, feel as if finished just this morning. But I'm especially thinking of Neruda's deep if conflicted love toward the United States. Throughout his life, he made sure to distinguish between the people of the United States and its government. He acknowledged the honesty and noblesse in the American masses but reacted irritably when that honesty and noblesse were betrayed by politicos. Elsewhere in the poem, Neruda stated: "What we love is your peace, not your mask." He stressed the element of peace again, putting it in a larger context:

> You come, like a washerwoman, from
> a simple cradle, near your rivers, pale.

Built up from the unknown,
what is sweet in you is your hivelike peace.
We love the man with his hands red
from the Oregon clay, your Negro boy
who brought you the music born
in his country of tusks: we love
your city, your substance,
your light, your machines, the energy . . .

Then, of course, there's the domestic Neruda, whose "elemental odes" are, well, elemental, i.e., they celebrate with Buddhist concentration the mundane, insignificant objects surrounding us: a stamp album, an artichoke, a hare-boy, a watermelon, a bee, a village movie theater . . . What do they say about us? And what do we, their enablers, say about them? I presume it's my trade, but the ones I never stop rereading are the odes to the book ("A book ripens and falls / like all fruits, / it has light / and shadow"), the ode to the dictionary (". . . you are not a / tomb, sepulcher, grave, / tumulus, mausoleum, / but guard and keeper, / hidden fire") and the two ones to criticism ("With a single life / I will not learn enough. / With the light of other lives, / many lives will live in my song"). These are items always at my side, but somehow Neruda makes me see anew.

Over time I've learned to understand an aspect in Neruda I had failed to spot and my students recurrently point to: his humor. This aspect on occasion appears connected to religion, which, needless to say, was not his dish *du jour,* a factor that highlights one of Neruda's limitations in reaching readers today. He ignored God and dismissed faith as irrelevant. After reading dozens of his poems compressed in a single semester, a student of mine said, a bit pompously: a life experienced only through the heart is nothing but tragedy; one approached solely through the mind is comedy; and one seen through Neruda's eyes is sheer drama—poignant and droll. What mesmerized the student was that the Chilean bard had resisted, to the extent that it is possible, the traps of cynicism. He took human behavior seriously but also knew how to laugh.

Although, as death approached him, perhaps he did become sarcastic. In "The Great Urinator," a poem left unpublished (it is part of the posthumous *Selected Failings*) he portrays God peeing bronze-colored, dense liquid rain from above. The urine falls on factories, cemeteries, gardens, as well as churches. It flows inexhaustibly underneath doors and in avenues, backing up drains, disintegrating marble floors, carpets, and staircases. It is a scene taken out of a Hollywood disaster movie: how do people react? Neruda's answer is hilarious: everyone is frightened but, oops, there are no umbrellas. And "from on high the great urinator," the poem states (in John Felstiner's rendition), "was silent. . . ." What does all this mean? True to form, Neruda doesn't sort out the imbroglio. Again, he has no wisdom to dispense. Or has he? The last stanza reads:

> I am a pale and artless poet
> not here to work out riddles
> or recommend special umbrellas.
> Hasta la vista! I greet you and go off
> to a country where they won't ask me questions.

Happy birthday, Señor Poeta!

Felisberto Is an Imbecile

❦

"FELISBERTO HERNÁNDEZ is a writer like no other," Italo Calvino announced once, "like no European or Latin American. He is an 'irregular,' who eludes all classifications and labelings—yet he is unmistakable on any page to which one might randomly open one of his books." This is a sharp eulogy by the author of *If on a Winter Night, a Traveler . . .*, as trustworthy as they come, for I've tried it myself: I've browsed aimlessly in the impish Spanish prose in Felisberto's three-volume *Obras completas,* released posthumously in 1983, some twenty years after his death, and the effect is daunting: the voice is unlike anything one comes across anywhere in literature—a voice broadcast directly from the Unconscious, poignant, "irregular" in the best sense of the term. Rubén Darío, Nicaragua's famous *modernista* poet, whose death in 1916 made it chronologically impossible for him to relish Felisberto, used the term *el raro*—the eerie—to describe the disposition of people like Edgar Allan Poe, the Count of Lautréamont, and Paul Verlaine. Felisberto would have made the cut too: "If all my life and my being were judged by a few incidents," he believed, "it would be rightly determined that I was a complete imbecile." To be a success as an imbecile, one needs to work hard at it, and Felisberto more than made the effort.

I've used his appellation because that seems to be the way everyone referred to him, not only in life but also since his death in 1964, at the age of sixty-two. In fact, there is, so to speak, a Felisberto Cult, not only in his native Uruguay, but all across Latin America, and in certain regions of Europe—a club for the initiated in the occult exercises of his imagination. This cult has been prolific as of late: I've counted no fewer than six biographies of him in the last couple of decades (actually, some are no more than mere hagiographies), as well as three times that amount of banal academic studies. This isn't quite an industry, but it surely is a sign of increasing enthusiasm. It is an enthusiasm that began beyond Felisberto's own borders when Borges published one of his stories in the elite journal *Sur.* Since then, others have paid tribute to the author of the legendary novella *The Daisy Dolls:* Rosario Ferré has a volume entitled *El acomodador,* a sort of explicative meditation that is succinct and thought-provoking; and what would Julio Cortázar . . . ah, who would Cortázar—another *raro* in Darío's canon—have become had it not been for Felisberto? Truth is, the Argentine read it too late in life to be properly influenced by the Uruguayan, so it is impossible to say that stories like "House Taken Over" and "Blow Up" have a Felisbertian drive. But as Cortázar himself acknowledged, the other "other" of the River Plate exerted so powerful a spell over him, that, in retrospect, even *Hopscotch,* his masterpiece, reads like a variation—a massive one, for sure—of enchanted tales like "No One Had Lit a Lamp" and bewildering essays such as "How Not to Explain My Stories." Felisberto was first and foremost a pianist, not of the type who end up in Carnagie Hall but of the kind who accompany silent movies. He gave a concert in a club in the Argentine city of Chivilcoy in 1939. So it happens that Cortázar worked there as a college teacher at the time. "Do you realize how close we were?" the author of *Hopscotch* wrote in a letter-qua-prologue. "I believe we would have *recognized* each other in that club where everything would have projected us toward each other, and I would have invited you to my little room to offer you a *caña* and show you some books and maybe, who knows, some of the stories I was writing then and never published . . ." A few lines later, Cortázar shrieks: "Felisberto, I will always love you."

And so will I. Esther Allen, whom I've learned to trust as a translator of Javier Marías and José Martí, ought to be thanked for this fine collection of two novellas and four stories. Almost a decade ago, Luis Harss, famous for the groundbreaking volume of literary reportage *Into the Mainstream,* issued a similar volume under the name *Piano Stories.* It included one of Felisberto's most celebrated pieces, "The Flooded House," a Kafkesque parable with political undertones about a home inundated with water. And it contained *The Daisy Dolls,* a critique of fetishism and capitalist society, in which a bizarre couple exists surrounded by life-size dolls that awaken feelings of adultery and incest. Allen has been careful not to replicate the material in the previous collection. It is always difficult to attempt a summary of a plot delivered by Felisberto, simply because his stories are as close to plotlessness as is possible without succumbing to utter chaos. A handful of leitmotifs run through them, among them autistic behavior, the piano, and outbursts of faked emotion. I have read one too many atrocious *nouveau romans* that, I realize, might be described thus: uneventful, impressionistic. I fear for the comparison, which might deliver the mistaken impression that Felisberto doesn't write and instead simply types. In the masterful "The Crocodile," for example, a good-for-nothing man becomes a traveling salesman. He finds it impossible to sell his merchandise: women's stockings. In despair, he dreams of flying into nothingness until he chances upon a superb solution. I quote:

I felt unusually impatient; I longed to leave that shop, that city, that life. I thought about my country and about many other things. And suddenly, just as I was beginning to calm down, I had an idea. What would happen if I started crying right in front of all those people? It struck me as a very violent thing to do, but I'd been waiting to do something out of the ordinary, to put the world to the test, for a long time. I also needed to prove to myself that I was capable of great violence. And before I could change my mind I sat down in a little chair backed up against the counter and with all those people around me I put my hands to my face and began emitting sobbing noises. Almost simultaneously, a woman let out a loud cry and said, "A man is weeping."

To do something out of the ordinary, to put the world to the test—the protagonist is soon turned into a model salesman inside the company, admired by his peers. People call him "the crocodile" because of his talent for spilling empty tears. And he, in satisfaction, perceives himself as "a bourgeois of anguish." The desire to perform violent acts is turned by Felisberto into a buffoonery: he makes fun of bravery among the wealthy and educated, in truth ridiculing their environment as flaccid and inoffensive.

In "Mistaken Hands," orchestrated as an irrelevant exchange of correspondence between two society ladies, he pokes fun at the tradition of the epistolary novel made famous by, among others, Samuel Richardson and Choderlos de Laclos. Irene and Margarita, the protagonists, have a trite objective: to write letters. They ought not be about anything in particular, as long as they are sent and received. "The external result of this desire," Margarita states, "is that I take immense joy . . . a feeling of calm, slow delight that wants to go forth and encounter unexpected things and, at the same time, awaits them." Curiosity is at the heart of their dialogue, but it is a curiosity that is a target in itself: dissolute, self-absorbed. Again, a critique of the Uruguayan bourgeois is at the core: life for the correspondents has too much time to waste, too few goals in sight. At one point, Irene lists the events she would like to happen. Her bucolic description is a triumph of platitudes:

I would be sitting on the grass in the woods.
   I would be thinking of other things that had nothing to do with the woods.
   But suddenly I would be distracted and would scan the great trees from top to bottom.

After that, the trees' great trunks would interrupt my view of the people going by some distance away.

One of those people would stir up some dust as he walked, and I would realize that he was walking down a dusty path. . . .

Felisberto left us with a total of ten books, including only two novels. He paid for the publication of the first four. His style was compressive: nothing of his is longer than one hundred pages. Esther Allen, in her prologue to *Lands of Memory,* suggests that he required absolute silence in order to write. This is ironic, since he was far happier as a musician than as a literati: at nine he began to play the piano, at twelve he was a regular in cinemas, and at twenty he was touring small towns.

The musical choice wasn't entirely his own: in school he was a poor student, and he was easily distractible. He gave this description of a recital at a convent school: "When I sat down at the piano and realized I was distracted, I began summoning myself with all my force, as if I was struggling to wake up from a dream. Once I'd been playing a while and was fully within myself, I looked at all the girls' faces, and their attention wasn't scattered any longer; now they were paying concrete attention to me, now they were observing the mystery that was mine." Felisberto also considered himself an inventor and was the owner of a failed bookstore. (His father had been a plumber and the owner of a construction company.) He married a number of times and divorced just as many. His wives supported him and also *lo soportaron*—i.e., bared his countless improprieties. Felisberto lived in Paris for a couple of years with a grant from the government. He had come under the wing of Jules Supervielle and Roger Caillois. Supervielle understood Felisberto well after reading *Around the Time of Clemente Colling,* which is the lengthiest in Allen's selection. This novella is a disquisition . . . on what? It is narrated in the first person by the same naive, innocent, imbecile voice that often appears elsewhere in Felisberto's work. It is shaped as a reminiscence of musical lessons, recitals, and the apprenticeship and initiation of a young musician into the artistic world. Clemente Collins, its center of gravity, is a blind teacher of piano and harmony, known as Mesiu Colén.

The evocation and explanation of Collins' mysterious manners give room to a tempo that throws the reader into a state of somnambulism. Although nothing much happens, we feel exhausted at the end. "You achieve originality without seeking it in the least, by a natural inclination toward depth," Supervielle wrote to Felisberto. As for Caillois, who was instrumental in introducing Borges in France, he hoped to do the same with Felisberto: make a name for him in Europe. He orchestrated an anthology of the Uruguayan to be translated by his wife, Yvette, but the project never materialized. At the time it is known that Felisberto was immersed in Marcel Proust, and that he read Freud too. It might be said that his landscapes were those of psychoanalysis, but I find this suggestion ridiculous: Felisberto was, like all hunger artists, in touch with profound chambers of the mind. If his creatures perform acts decipherable to Freudians, it is because his was also the realm of dreams, and in dreams, as Ezra Pound had it, begin responsibilities. By the way, like all hunger artists too, Felisberto died impoverished and unknown.

Allen offers us a catalogue of his obsessions. Partially, these are: a black cat, balconies, raised platforms, upper tiers, blindness, trains and streetcars, and a glimpse of his own face in two mirrors that met at a right angle, showing him half his head attached to the ear of the other half. The list is useful since blindness and sound serve as dialectical counterpoints in *Lands of Memory:* characters seek light but live in obscurity; they are driven by the inner sound they hear, like free spirits dancing around a bonfire. I've often wondered what the right definition for *imbecile* is.

Does it mean "weak" and "feeble"? Felisberto is the type of imbecile that broadens our horizon. Earlier on I used the term *kafkesque* to describe him; it might be misleading. Kafka depicted a somber universe with no room for redemption. There is little humor in him, at least from my viewpoint. Felisberto is akin to the eerie and the uncanny, but his is a joyful, not a terrifying, disposition. He appears to laugh at his own condition, or at least to indulge in its jazzy rhythms without much anxiety. His images are dreamlike: irrational, disconnected, funky. "At a given time," he once wrote, "I think a plant is about to be born in a corner of me. . . . I must take care that it does not occupy too much space or try to be beautiful or intense, helping it to become only what it was meant to be."

Edmund Wilson, in his piece "A Dissenting Opinion on Kafka," collected in *Classics and Commercial,* stated that Kafka appears to be "a human shadow thrown on the mist in such a way that it seems monstrous and remote when it may really be quite close at hand, and with a rainbow halo around it." Wilson advised against turning Kafka into a theologian and a saint who is able to justify emotions of incompetence and self-contempt. He questions if we must really accept the plight of his creatures as parables of our predicament. In Felisberto's oeuvre one also gets a pursuit of an evasive, almost unattainable utopia.

Trapped in absurd circumstances, his characters desperately look for ways of escape. If they find them, these are nothing but subterfuges. This is because his universe, it strikes me, is built as a hall of mirrors: everything is a hallucination. I doubt Wilson would have liked the

Uruguayan: he probably would have found him senseless and mannered. That is because the author of *Axel's Castle* had a dry sense of humor and a clear distaste for allegory. Felisberto also wasn't allergic to allegory. His stories are meaningful precisely because they are meaningless.

In his attack on Kafka, Wilson quotes one of the Czech's aphorisms. "One must not cheat anybody, not even the world, of its triumphs." Then, aphoristically, Wilson queries: "What are we writers here for if it is not cheat the world of its triumphs?" This lucid, memorable line might be used as the motto of the Felisberto Cult, for what is his literature about exactly if not cheating us out of ourselves? This *raro* does so at once splendidly and loquaciously, with flair, respect for the nonsense of life, and a titter or two.

Macondo Turns Forty

❧

GABRIEL GARCÍA MÁRQUEZ's *One Hundred Years of Solitude* celebrates its fortieth birthday this year. This is also the author's eightieth, and he received the Nobel Prize for Literature twenty-five years ago. Maybe it's a coincidence of numbers, but Gabo, as García Márquez is known among friends, has never been so popular. Celebrations are scheduled in countries like Spain, Cuba, Colombia, and Mexico. And an inexpensive anniversary edition of the novel, published under the aegis of the various branches of the Real Academia Española de la Lengua, overseen by the author, and with a first printing in the millions, is on sale throughout the Spanish-speaking world.

Gabo's fame is nothing new. It came almost overnight in 1967, with the hoopla surrounding the book's publication in Buenos Aires by Editorial Sudamericana. It was translated into three-dozen languages. For a while, almost everyone on the globe seemed to be reading the book. But with a population of more than 450 million, the Spanish-speaking world is larger and more complex today. No other artist in it comes even close in reputation.

Before *One Hundred Years of Solitude,* Gabo was respected as a journalist and the author of a handful of books, including *No One Writes to the Colonel,* about a poor, forgotten army man and his wife in a tropical town, who, as he anxiously awaits his military pension, considers selling a rooster whose value in cock fights might be the family's only ticket to redemption. Already there and in Gabo's stories there were references to Macondo. And after 1967, at midcareer, it didn't seem possible that Gabo could supersede himself. He went on to write an admirable shelf of novels, from *Love in the Time of Cholera* to *Memoirs of My Melancholy Whores.* They might be more measured, maybe even more mature, but when it comes to depth all of them pale in comparison.

One doesn't need to be a Spanish speaker to appreciate its beauty and complexity. Gregory Rabassa's 1970 rendition, published by an adventurous Harper & Row editor, Cass Canfield Jr., has been described—perhaps with a touch of irony—as being better than the original. Yet, as in the case of Flaubert's *Madame Bovary* and Tolstoy's *War and Peace,* it's better to appreciate it without the veil of translation.

The legend behind its composition isn't unlike that of Samuel Taylor Coleridge's poem "Kubla Khan." Gabo and his wife, Mercedes, living in Mexico in the mid-1960s, were on their way to a vacation in Acapulco in their Volkswagen when he was struck by the muse of inspiration. They turned around, and in subsequent months Gabo hid from everyone. Borrowing money, Mercedes became his guardian angel, bringing him food, keeping away strangers. A handful of chapters began circulating among friends, among them Julio Cortázar and Carlos Fuentes, who publicly referred to what they read as a tour de force.

Ours is the age of mediated kitsch. A single episode of a Mexican *telenovela* is watched by far more people on a single evening than all the readers of Gabo's novel, maybe of his entire oeuvre. But like the firefly, the soap opera perishes almost the second it stirs up its audience's passion. *One Hundred Years of Solitude,* instead, is imperishable. Yet, when read closely—as I've been doing this semester, with an battalion of approximately fifty extraordinary students, comparing it to the biblical narrative, the poem of Gilgamesh, the Icelandic Sagas—it's clear that first and foremost we're in front of a melodrama, albeit a magisterial one, with syrupy scenes of unrequited love, sibling animosity, and domestic back-stabbing. Gabo's original title was *La Casa,* but it could have been called something like *Blood & Passion.* But isn't that what all good novels are about, a roller coaster of emotions presented under a pretentious façade?

But the signature mix of exoticism, magic, and the grotesque that Gabo employs doesn't come from the world of soap operas. Known as "magical realism"—a category loosely connected to what the Cuban writer Alejo Carpentier, in the prologue to his novel *The Kingdom of This World,* drafted after a trip to Haiti, portrayed as "lo real maravilloso"— the category has achieved such ubiquity and elasticity as to become meaningless. For a while it denoted an attempt to erase the border between fact and fiction, between the natural and the supernatural. But its current use is chaotic: it is as useful in cataloguing Gabo's second-rate successors, such as Isabel Allende, as it is in understanding Franz Kafka's middle-class exposé *The Metamorphosis* and Lewis Carroll's perversely innocent *Alice in Wonderland.* Salman Rushdie's baroque hodgepodge of dreams and nationalism in *Midnight Children,* Najib Mahfouz's labyrinthine novels about Cairo, and Toni Morrison's phantasmagoric meditation on slavery in *Beloved* have all been linked to magical realism, with various degrees of success.

Gabo, however, is its acknowledged fountainhead, and for good reason. At the beginning of *One Hundred Years of Solitude,* Macondo is a small, nondescript town on the Caribbean coast of Colombia, made of twenty houses built on the edge of a river with clear waters running over large stones resembling prehistoric eggs. (The town was modeled after

Gabo's birth place, Aracataca, which, forty years after the novel's debut, is still a dusty place without running water.) In twenty symmetrical chapters, each made of approximately twenty dense pages, a third-person narrator—is it Melquíades the gypsy?—chronicles, with frightening precision, its rise and fall, exploring its geographical, temporal, ideological, and cultural dimensions. In spite of the title, the narrative time spans more than a century.

The Buendía genealogy is made of dozens of archetypical figures surrounded by a cast of thousands. Technology arrives in Macondo early on. It will have disastrous consequences. It ranges from ice and the daguerreotype to war artillery. The need to belong shapes each of the Buendías and their entourage, from Coronel Aureliano Buendía, modeled after the real-life military hero Rafael Uribe Uribe, who fought in Colombia's War of a Thousand Days, to Remedios the Beautiful, whose beauty is so overwhelming she ends up ascending to heaven. There's an epidemic of insomnia, a rainstorm of small yellow flowers, a woman who eats earth, a clairvoyant, and a character obsessed with photographing God. The novel's matrix is Ursula Iguarán, a patient, down-to-earth woman, the closest one gets in Macondo to Mother Nature, who keeps the family afloat over almost a century. Afloat but not together: Ursula's progeny doesn't know how to love healthily.

Indeed, the novel's central motif is incest: the Buendías don't seem capable of targeting their sexual desire anywhere else but endogenously. This Hieronymus Bosch–like Garden of Earthly Delights is narrated in a flamboyant style but with equanimity, as if nothing was out of the ordinary. There are references to buccaneers and adventurers like Francis Drake and Walter Raleigh, as well as to accounts of Spanish explorers and missionaries to the Americas in the sixteenth and seventeenth centuries. But *One Hundred Years of Solitude* is also full of tricks. Gabo himself shows up in the latter part, and he makes coded references to his friends and colleagues, such as Carpentier, Julio Cortázar, and Carlos Fuentes. It might all be a joke, the reader finds himself thinking as the novel reaches its climatic conclusion.

Or is it? Fortunately, *One Hundred Years of Solitude* hasn't been turned into a film, a process that usually ends up diminishing the value of the literary source. In one of his op-eds, Gabo wrote of an offer he received from Francis Ford Coppola to sell the rights for a cinematic adaptation. He declined, among other reasons, because he wanted Macondo not to be imprisoned in our imagination in the form of a set cast. (Some of his other novellas and stories, from *Eréndira* to *Chronicle of a Death Foretold*, have made it to the big screen, with atrocious results.)

Should a novel be read as a map of the author's life? In 2002, Gabo published the first installment of his autobiography: *Living to Tell It All.* (By then, Rabassa had been replaced by Edith Grossman as his official translator, in part the result of a publisher's dispute.) It contains keys to deciphering the origin of images and motifs. But should one be looking for explanations in a novel that begs to be read autonomously, as a door to a parallel reality? Wouldn't it be better to let it exist freely and uninterrupted? My suggestion is to leave biography outside. Take the case of Gabo's politics, which to scores of readers, especially Cuban exiles, are a troubling factor. Since youth he was a leftist. In the 1960s he followed the intellectual wave and embraced the Cuban Revolution. But with the Heberto Padilla case, many switched sides, denouncing Fidel Castro's regime not only as intolerant but as hypocritical. Gabo didn't take that path. He remains a loyal friend of Havana, never condemning Fidel's abuses. He has even become an occasional broker in the diplomatic relations between the U.S. and Cuba.

Should the commemoration of Gabo's achievements this year be turned into a referendum on his ideology? The same question was raised—yet again—in 2004, when Pablo Neruda's centennial gave place to accusations of his having written not poetry but propaganda. It doesn't take too many smarts to realize that in Latin America the crossroads of literature and politics is particularly messy. Borges received a medal from Augusto Pinochet. Mario Vargas Llosa was a presidential candidate in Peru in 1990, under a Thatcherite platform. It's impossible to disentangle these forces. But why do it? My opinion is that precisely that messiness is what makes *One Hundred Years of Solitude* so compelling, since the novel itself addresses the obstacles Latin America has encountered on its road to democracy.

My own relationship with the book has changed over time. I first read it in my teens and was transformed by it. It was the late 1970s. By then Gabo's impact was already being described as noxious. He had reinvented Latin America through his pen, infusing the region with magnetism. After World War II, the novel had underdone a period of insurmountable depression: after Kafka, Proust, Joyce, and Beckett, it seemed to have reached a dead end. Gabo and his peers came back with a vengeance. The novel, they announced, is alive and well, though not in the Old World but in the New.

Such was his talent that second-rate writers imitated him in uncritical fashion. My generation was still at awe, but it didn't want to be eclipsed by him. We too embraced William Faulkner, Gabo's model, but we were from urban centers and, thus, didn't empathize with his worldview. We wanted to write not from and about the tropics but about anything and everything, as Jorge Volpi has done with Nazism and the making of the atomic bomb in *In Search of Klingsor,* and Rodrigo Fresán has with Peter Pan in *Kingston Gardens;* or like Edmundo Paz-Solán's diatribe on anti-globalization in *Turing's Delirium,* and Ignacio Padilla's chess match on a train leading to the Austro-Hungarian Empire's Eastern Front in *Shadow Without a Name.* The tension with Gabo and the so-called Latin American literary "boom" was also a leitmotif in the life of Roberto Bolaño, a Chilean exile responsible for *The Savage Detectives,* for whom *One Hundred Years of Solitude* was too parochial. For Bolaño the novel as a literary genre needed to be feisty, oppositional, and unsanctimonious.

In my forties, I've returned to Gabo's masterpiece and have done so with brio. Along with Cervantes' *Don Quixote,* it decodes the DNA of Hispanic civilization as a whole. It's a "total" novel designed by a demiurge capable of creating a universe as comprehensive as ours. I've now decided to embark on a biography of Gabo. Who is he? How did he come to write such a masterpiece? What made him the right surveyor of his people? How did he manage to turn *One Hundred Years of Solitude* into the best *telenovela* ever? The novel, in my estimation, has done something astonishing: it has survived, accumulating disparate, at times conflicting rereadings. Isn't that what a classic is, a mirror in which readers see what they are looking for?

At the Same Time

Susan Sontag

Susan Sontag, who died at the end of 2004, has begun her second career. A portion of her diaries has recently been published in the *New York Times Magazine*. Annie Leibowitz, Sontag's partner in the last years of her life, released a book-length autobiographical portfolio, a series of photographs about Sontag's battle with cancer. In one of them she's sick as a dog, while in another she's naked, her emaciated body proof that suffering serves a public role. Sontag's correspondence is being edited. And now a volume of her last essays and speeches is available.

Not that these efforts are unworthy. Up until the 1990s, Sontag's efforts in criticism, for which she is best known, are all about posturing. Her ruminations on the French *nouveau roman,* the movies of Ingmar Bergman, camp as an esthetic modality, and the uses and abuses of photography, and her views on illness as a social metaphor, made her the talk of the town. And that's what she wanted: to be known as an intellectual spitfire. Her fiction, especially *The Volcano Lover* and *In America,* brought her accolades too, and she thought of herself as a novelist. But Sontag was mostly a self-reflecting thinker. She had the smarts as well as the guts. As a woman in a world dominated by men, she enjoyed being the center of attention.

Before thinking, a thinker observes. Those observations need to be shaped in the form of plain, articulate sentences. In her early career she wasn't in pursuit of clarity. In fact, she was prone to obfuscation. But as she matured, the need to impress gave way to a genuine desire to communicate lofty ideas in a tidy, non-convoluted style, an attribute well represented in *At the Same Time.* The volume includes Sontag's comments in the *New Yorker* on the events of September 11, 2001, which placed her at the center of an international uproar. Read in retrospect, they couldn't be more unambiguous. She stated that those carrying out the terrorist attacks against the Twin Towers were not cowards, as countless politicians and media pundits were suggesting: "If the word 'cowardly' is to be used, it might be more aptly applied to those who kill beyond the range of retaliation, high in the sky, than those willing to die themselves in order to kill others." Sontag also talked about the politics of democracy being replaced by psychotherapy.

Equally brave was an article in the *New York Times Magazine,* originally called "The Photographs *Are* Us," in which she deplored the abuses in Abu-Ghraib, describing them as a national shame. Her audacity was all the more admirable when one considers that others like Noam Chomsky and Michael Moore deliver a similar message but with far less elegance. For elegance was what Sontag was about: the point for her wasn't only to denounce, but to do so with flair.

It's evident from *At the Same Time* that she used her last opportunities in front of the microphone to spread a gospel she had only recently become enamored with: the gospel of freedom. Sontag used the opportunity of being honored with international awards (the Jerusalem Prize, the St. Jerome Lecture on Literary Translation, the Oscar Romero Award, the Friedenspreis Speech) to meditate on the power on language and the fledgling sense that words still have weight in a world ruled by electronic transactions. She was always obsessed with Europe, and as she matured, she modeled herself as an intellectual in the old tradition, one capable of pondering the most mundane aspects of life but also of condemning the abuses of power by those in control of others.

Of course, she was always a rebel. Yet there's a difference between the Sontag who opposed the Vietnam War and the Sontag who stood up against the invasion of Iraq. The first was a fashionable anti-establishmentarian from the United States. The second was a conscientious dissenter who happened to be an American. That detachment from her native country, that sense of increasingly becoming an outsider, is crystal clear in her last work. Reading these pieces one never gets the impression of encountering a thinker in the tradition of Emerson, Twain, Mencken, and Edmund Wilson. Nor does she have anything in common with ethnic essayists like James Baldwin and Richard Rodríguez. Her connections aren't even British: not Virginia Woolf and not Orwell either. Sontag writes and sounds like a Renaissance woman misplaced in the twenty-first century.

Her posterity isn't up for grabs. Quite the contrary, she's undergoing a far more complex transformation. A leading thinker of our age is being metamorphosed, as a second career, into the matron saint of chic resistance.

Black Studies vs. Latino Studies

❦

EARLIER THIS YEAR, the *New York Times* ran a front-page story by reporter Felicia R. Lee about an academic conference in Harlem in which hundreds of participants, among them Henry Louis Gates Jr. and Kim D. Buttler, were scheduled to discuss the state of Black Studies in the United States today. A couple of weeks earlier the U.S. Census Bureau had released information that confirmed Hispanics to be the largest minority in the nation with a total of thirty-seven million, a status reached faster than originally anticipated. Judging by the media coverage, the news was exciting to Latinos, whose time had come as a defining political and cultural force, yet it apparently sent chills in some quarters, among them African Americans. Lee ended up focusing on the impact of Latinos on the scholarly debate at the conference, which is unfortunate. The headline of her article, published on February 1, 2003, read: "New Topic in Black Studies Debate: Latinos."

I wasn't present at the Harlem event. My knowledge of its content is based on online briefs and personal conversations. By most accounts, the conference barely addressed the bridge between Black and Latino Studies. It was Lee and her editors who pushed the topic. The result is a cornucopia of quotes that is often misleading. A couple of typical examples: "African-Americans and the African-American leadership community are about to enter an identity crisis, the extent of which we've not begun to imagine," proclaimed Gates from Harvard. And: "There is something . . . profound in the DNA of the country that is tied to the enslavement of Africans, the trauma of slavery and the legacy of disenfranchisement," said Noliwe Rooks from Princeton. She added: "[That doesn't] change because there are more Latinos in the country."

The accumulation of comments such as this leaves the reader disoriented, open to dangerous conclusions: is lower-class status in American society a privilege of blacks, one Latinos are about to usurp? It is, indeed, an offensive question, but the underlying, "silenced" implication of the *New York Times* piece is that, when it comes to research money in academia, the lower the social status of a minority group, the wider the chances of funding research on it, and the more plausible it is to see topics that pertain to that group reflected in the curriculum. So have Latinos replaced Blacks as the new poor, and might that coveted position catapult them into wider recognition on campus?

Of course, there is nothing "new" in poverty. From the Dominican Republic to Bolivia and Argentina, poverty remains, for centuries, intensely ingrained. The northbound continental odyssey of people toward *el sueño americano* is, to a large extent, a consequence of that condition. Although there is, happily, a growing Hispanic middle class in the United States, Latinos are at the bottom of the ladder: abuse of undocumented labor remains a curse, language proficiency a handicap, teenage pregnancy is the highest in any group, and drop-out rates from middle-school students onward are dismal. But my intention in this essay isn't to digress on larger social issues but to look inside the classroom. I want to use the misguided newspaper article as an excuse to discuss the divergent paths of Latino Studies and Black Studies. For although a handful of suggestions made at the Harlem conference might be provocative, as conveyed by the *New York Times,* I'm not sure they point us in the right direction. What are the historical roots and the intellectual scope of Latino and Black Studies? Is there a bond that unites them? Or are their differences more striking than their similarities? More important, even, is the Hispanic demographic explosion a clear sign, as stated by the reporter, that the age of Black America is over in academia?

Imagine, for instance, a similar caption: "Roll over, Jewish Studies . . . Here Come Latinos." Or a similar headline making Latino Studies the "pushy" friend of Asian Studies. But why not? Since 1492, when the Americas were pushed precipitously to modernity, an array of outsiders has made them their own stage: explorers, missionaries, chroniclers, and immigrants from everywhere on the globe, from Spain and Portugal to, among other origins, Africa, Italy, France, China, Eastern Europe, the Arab world, and the United States. The area is an authentic melting pot, and Latinos north of the Rio Grande represent that hodge-podge: white and black and brown; Catholic, Muslims, Protestants, Jews, and Buddhists; and from different national backgrounds, such as Cuba and Puerto Rico, Colombia and Brazil, Mexico and El Salvador. Given this multiplicity, why then aren't there more ties established between Latino Studies and other area studies? Why is the sole connection always made with Black Studies?

The answer isn't complicated: Black Studies and Latino Studies have a similar birth date in the Civil Rights Era, although not everyone is aware of it. The study of Spanish as a language, and of Spain and the Americas as political and historical subjects, goes back to the late nineteenth century, but it was after the Spanish-American War of 1898 and the Mexican Revolution that started in 1910 that these concerns found a more solid, albeit marginal, seat on campus. But Latino Studies per se—i.e., the discipline devoted to Hispanics in the U.S.—wasn't on the radar until the 1960s, when Chicano and Puerto Rican student activists, in the Southwest and New York respectively, pressured for representation. Unlike, say, Jewish Studies, which has developed in large part thanks to off-campus philanthropy, Latino Studies, just like Black Studies, started from the bottom up. In fact, when compared to other area studies, outside funding sources remain minuscule, a reflection, no doubt, of the economic status of Latinos in society at large.

The term *Latino* is relatively young: it came about in the late 1980s and 1990s, to oppose the use of *Hispanic* in government documents since the Nixon administration. There was no Latino Studies in the 1960s simply because a pan-Hispanic rubric encompassing all national groups from the Americas was still inconceivable. Through marches, sit-ins, building takeovers, and protests, Chicanos, by then already the largest subgroup within the Latino minority, forced administrators to implement programs about the Mexican America in which they lived in metropolitan centers and rural areas. From UCLA to the University of New Mexico, programs echoed the patterns of life at home and on the street. Similarly, Puerto Ricans in New York struggled to open up the classroom to the experience of Nuyoricans like Bernardo Vega and Jesús Colón at institutions like Hunter College. Then, as the Hispanic minority in the United States grew exponentially in the 1980s, the need to go beyond the national prism to a more continental one began to be emphasized: not only the experience of Chicanos but also that of Guatemalans, Salvadorans, and Nicaraguans needed to be addressed in the Southwest and, slowly but surely, in the Midwest and Northeast too. And Cuban Studies and Dominican Studies also made their way from the University of Miami to City College of New York.

Today the compartmentalization is still quite noticeable. Latino Studies is a staple in institutions on the East Coast, especially in the North, whereas in California, Arizona, New Mexico, Texas, and Colorado the weight remains on Mexican American Studies. Is this fragmentation unique? Not in the least: other area studies came from similar challenges. Jewish Studies, for instance, places an emphasis on American Judaism, the Holocaust, and the Arab-Israeli conflict. The presence of Jewish themes from other regions of the globe, and especially the Sephardic tradition that ponders the Jewish Diaspora from the Iberian Peninsula and its dissemination in the Ottoman Empire, Italy, the Netherlands, and the Americas, is still, unfortunately, eclipsed as a subject of attention. Likewise, in Black Studies the stress on race, slavery, and the American Civil War is clear, and the tension with African

Studies per se and with themes that relate to the Caribbean and Brazil, and to immigrants from Haiti, Jamaica, and the Bahamas, often takes a toll not only in the classroom but in the camaraderie between faculty members.

This compartmentalization aside, the rapid growth of Latino Studies in the 1990s is welcome news. Professors, students, and administrators recognize it as the "hot" kid in the neighborhood. Clearly, it follows the interdisciplinary model: as in the case of Blacks, the argument is made, intelligently no doubt, that to understand Latinos one needs a multiplicity of tools used by anthropologists, historians, sociologists, political scientists, literary critics, and cultural studies specialists. None of these disciplines alone would be able to perform the job: the whole is a sum of the parts, each of which needs a focus. This pluralism is exciting, but it also generates bewilderment. And envy, too. Iberianists and Latino-Americanists, for instance, sometimes express themselves in reference to Latino Studies colleagues with a mixture of at once effusion and confusion. Will Latino Studies end up devouring the efforts by specialists of Latin America? In other words, is the interest in the complex civilization south of the Rio Grande dying out?

Clearly, everybody is a bit puzzled, including administrators. At institutions where Latino Studies exists in areas with a growing Hispanic population, where the student body is pushing for the implementation of a program that reflects their needs, the question arises: Where should the discipline be seated in the curriculum? Should it be placed in Ethnic Studies and/or in American Studies? Should it instead be part of Latin American Studies departments? Or should it be autonomous, with a center that in numerous ways mimics the autonomy of Black Studies? I am, as an adviser, invited regularly to talk to presidents, deans, and faculty, and the answer to the question always depends upon the needs, and internal structure, of each institution. At Amherst College, where I've taught for a decade, it emerged some years ago. It is also on the plate of President Lawrence H. Summers at Harvard University. Last year, when part of the African American Studies faculty left after a strained relationship with the president, other members of the faculty proposed a center of Latino Studies. The rationale was three-fold: demographics, demographics, demographics. But the argument was partly made through comparison, and it sounded like the litany of a younger sibling complaining of lack of attention, at least judging from the media reports: why allocate money (endowed professorships, research funds, handsome and spacious facilities, etc.) to African American Studies and not to Latinos, an unquestionable force in the U.S. already?

The initial reaction of President Summers was similar to the one I heard at Amherst and other Northeastern colleges and universities: if the institution bends this time, it will have to do it again; Asians are likely to come next, and after that the Arabs, and then . . . The ultimate consequence will be an impossible Balkanization. Blacks are a special case because of slavery. But are they really? The argument, it strikes me, makes sense but is unsustainable: why can't each of the siblings get a fair, equal share of support and attention? The problem isn't opening up to Latinos, and then to other groups, but to have done so to Blacks. How does one correct such a "mistake," as one dean in an institution in Pennsylvania described to me the emphasis on Black Studies? (Her view, by the way, wasn't stained by racism, as far as I am able to attest, but by a drive toward equality: the abundance of love toward one child sends chills to the other. Plus, she was black herself.) Truth is, it is a difficult question, and each administration responds to it differently. In any case, the challenge of where to place Latino Studies on campus, where autonomy is out of place, is equally unavoidable: when placed in Ethnic and/or American Studies, the weight is placed on Hispanics in the U.S. as a minority; when placed in the Spanish department and/or in Latin American Studies, the suggestion is made that Latinos are an extremity of the Spanish-speaking Americas in El Norte, and thus the focus isn't national but transcontinental and global.

Either way, the problem is larger than university life. A few weeks ago, for example, I got a copy of the two-volume set *Reporting Civil Rights,* an astonishing compendium of newspaper pieces and essays published by the Library of America, which, culturally, is our La Pléyade, in charge of disseminating, and keeping in print in excellent editions, American literature. From pieces by James Baldwin, Murray Kempton, and the "Letter from Birmingham Jail" by Reverend Martin Luther King Jr., the mosaic of voices was far-reaching. Anybody who is somebody was included . . . except, obviously, Chicanos, Puerto Ricans, and other Latinos. Not a single speech by César Chavez or Dolores Huerta, not one report on the grape boycotts and the struggle of the United Farm Workers Union. Weren't those also highlights of the Civil Rights Era? Aren't those actions and words also quintessential to our collective memory? The volumes are slated to be used in the classroom for educational purposes, and they should be—but who is to speak for Latino history then if even in canonical endeavors such as this we are but ghosts, speaking loudly through silence?

Honestly, Black Studies have paid marginal attention to Latinos. It might be a question of language, at least of verbal ambivalence: Spanish, after all, remains one of the crucial keys to understanding the Hispanic condition in the United States. Bilingual education, for better or worse, brings people together and apart, and for decades Latinos have been defined by it. I've seen syllabi on African American culture: little, if anything, relates the vast majority to the Americas. (Caribbean Studies are different, no doubt.) In the last few years, efforts have been made to discuss race in Brazil, but, unfortunately, these remain inconsequential.) Yes, Langston Hughes visited Cuba; Dizzy Gillespie and Latin jazz go hand in hand, thanks to Machito, Paquito D'Rivera, and others; in his autobiography *Down These Mean Streets,* Piri Thomas explores the labyrinthine roads of Blacks and Puerto Ricans; and Latino baseball players like Nomar Garcíaparra entered the game in the footsteps of Roberto Clemente and, before him, Jackie Robinson . . . Yet beyond those instances, what? There is a deeply rooted racism in the Hispanic community, and among Blacks the feelings toward Latinos only start with *la indiferencia.* By the way, throughout its existence, Jewish Studies has also shown little interest in Latinos and vice versa. Other area studies aren't too different.

All this isn't in the least surprising. On campus, we're as segregated, as envious and self-righteous, as we are on the larger stage. As far as I'm concerned, the purported rivalry between Black Studies and Latino Studies is a mirage. It is a superficial competition based on numbers. At the bottom, there have only been scattered efforts to relate them. Maybe the age of Black America in academia is finally receding. Demographics, no doubt, are always the first sign of a turmoil, be it vociferous or quiet. I'm convinced that the time is near when the attempt to reflect on the Hispanic aspects of the United States—our history, *nuestra historia*—won't be tangential, as it feels today. Browse through the pages of the *New York Review,* the nation's high-brow forum of ideas: when was the last time you encountered a piece on Chicanos? Or else, the *New York Times* itself: why is it that Hispanic-related pieces always pup up as a quota-driven afterthought? Felicia R. Lee's feature is yet another proof—do we need more?—that our national culture is still in black and white, even though our TV sets are as colorful and glitzy as is humanly imaginable.

The university ought to be the place where radical changes begin. What are we in Latino Studies to learn from our shared history with Black Studies and from the "mistakes" made by administrators? When Black Studies reigned supremely because of the guilt society felt toward African Americans, the attempts to embrace Latinos amounted to nothing. Now that Latinos are the main bastion of the lower class, and as they climb the hierarchy in their drive to seize the American Dream, might we avoid a repeat of the solipsism that has prevailed among departments until now? I believe that Latinos will ultimately be far more embracing of Blacks, simply because a percentage of the Hispanic population in the United States—never as large as the *mestizo* component, but present nonetheless—traces its past to Africa. I also think that faculty in Latino Studies, in whatever shape they appear in the wide gamut of institutions nationwide, ought to study the patterns in their respective institutions to bridge the gaps between groups. Hispanics, again, have formed a civilization made of diasporas, an addition and not a subtraction. The anti-Hispanicism in the U.S. is rampant. Latino Studies must fight that battle first. Along the way, though, bridges ought to be built and not burned.

W. G. Sebald

An Obituary

"DYING," MONTAIGNE ONCE STATED, "is without doubt the most note-worthy action in a man's life." The German writer W. G. Sebald, author of the recent, astounding novel *Austerlitz,* would have agreed: he made death—specifically, the void left in German and European history after World War II—the leitmotif of his oeuvre. His characters, seekers eternally pondering the effect of death on us all, live surrounded by silence—the type of silence that comes from the sense that death is always at the door. While Sebald's own death in an automobile accident on December 14 near his house in Norwich, England, came as a shock, it has a noteworthy quality to it, too. At the age of fifty-seven, Sebald (whose initials stand for Wilfried Gerald) was at the prime of his career; his sudden disappearance makes him as sorrowful a figure as any one of his elegiac protagonists.

It is difficult to describe the effect that Sebald's oeuvre had on me. There are parts of it I dislike or have little interest in. What captivates me is the ghost-like nature of his books and the melodic rhythm they distill, which stays with me for months, even years after I've read them. I first read him grudgingly in 1998, two years after *The Emigrants* was first translated by Michael Hulse. I say "grudgingly" because I've grown discontented with the contemporary novel: it has become such a commercial artifact that over the years I've unhappily resigned myself to its platitudes and repetitiveness. I was living in London at the time. Sebald's novel was highly recommended to me, although for a long time I couldn't remember who had recommended it. I bought a copy of the New Directions edition on a trip to the United States and read it in a single night.

Inspired literature is impossible to summarize; I still don't know what *The Emigrants* is about. Among the puzzling ingredients was the inclusion of death photographs every third or fourth page. Sebald, it seems, was a collector of old postcards, magazine ads, anonymous pictures, forgotten diaries he found in antique stores and dumpsters. I was puzzled by the apparent incoherence of these images. I was also puzzled by the refusal to follow a plot and by the centripetal quality of each of the four loosely related biographies of the German exiles that constitute its content: Dr. Henry Selwyn, elementary school teacher Paul Bereyter, painter Max Ferber, and Great Uncle Ambrose Adelwarth. Sebald describes their journeys in staccato prose, making them speak about the Holocaust without uttering much in the way of dialogue. It wasn't until I finished reading that I realized I was in the presence of a masterpiece that offered its secrets slowly and by means of interruptions. I experienced the same reaction that overwhelmed others such as Susan Sontag, Gabriel Josipovici and A. S. Byatt: unconditional admiration.

Sebald was a late bloomer: an academic infatuated with translation who made literature his prime quest only in his late forties. He had been born in Wertach im Allgäu, Germany, as World War II was reaching its nastiest climax. His father was in the army; he never talked about it to his children. That conspiracy of silence, Sebald felt, wasn't exclusively a family affair. It was also to be found in neighborhoods, towns, and, de facto, in the entire nation: the way to reckon with the Holocaust was by silencing its remembrance.

Sebald studied in Freiburg, and in 1966 he took a position at the University of Manchester; in 1970 he made England his permanent residence. Hence, he was, like his protagonists, a displaced person. He married an Austrian and had a daughter who taught primary school. He taught at the University of East Anglia, where he also directed the British Center for Literary Translation. Even though his spoken English, I'm told, had a slight accent, he never renounced the responsibilities of the German language. Language, after all, is a portable homeland: Sebald said he never felt at home in Norwich, but he did feel at home in Goethe's tongue. What effect would his work have had on me had it been delivered in English? The answer is simple: an inconsequential one. For rendered in the language of Heinrich Heine and Paul Celan, the prose has a tone of authenticity that grants it its incantations; as such, it is a meditation on the uses of regret. In Shakespeare's tongue it would have been just a foreigner's tour to hell.

Exile, separation. Norwich wasn't too close to London, but at least it was in the same latitude. After I read *The Emigrants,* I acquired another available book by Sebald—*The Ring of Saturn,* a darker, more elegiac exploration—and I soon mailed him a letter, detailing my experience as "a Mexican expatriate" and stating that I was eager to meet him. I mentioned that I could take a train or drive to him. I'm really not given to tête-à-têtes with people I admire. In fact, in literature I've found it is better not to seek out a favorite author; more often than not, an idealized book is matched by a pedestrian author. Still, I felt the urge to pursue Sebald and talk to him directly. Happily, his response was blunt: a stern guardian of his privacy, he preferred correspondence to an encounter. I was hurt at first, yet quickly learned it was a better answer. Hadn't I learned my lesson? What better way to follow the path of an emigrant than through the route of his shadow?

By chance, the night before Sebald died I went to sleep savoring the labyrinthine plot of *Austerlitz*. Reaching its last page, I came upon a reference to *Heschel's Kingdom* by the London-based South African Dan Jacobson, which was among the first books I read while in England. I suddenly remembered that it had been Jacobson who had first alerted me to Sebald. Jacobson's memoir, I see now, is Sebaldian: a chronicle of his search in Lithuania for the elusive figure of a grandfather.

Sebaldian: perhaps the greatest honor a writer is granted is to have his name turned into an adjective. And what does *Sebaldian* mean? Perhaps elusiveness as a literary strategy and the conviction that memory is a container to be emptied out in life and not the other way around. Cicero said: "I think nothing of being dead; it is the dying that I dislike." It wasn't the ubiquity of death in Nazi Germany that occupied Sebald but the perpetual dying of the post-Holocaust generation.

Xeroxing Shaya Berlin

A COUPLE OF YEARS AGO, while visiting the offices of the *Atlantic Monthly,* I commented on my admiration for Isaiah Berlin to a friend of mine, Cullen Murphy, the magazine's executive editor. Few modern thinkers strike me as being as stimulating, coherent, and lucid as Berlin. His life-long study of freedom as a curtailed human endeavor, his analysis of the roots of the Enlightenment, and his emblematic life as an academic at Oxford all have been continued sources of stimulation. Finally I admitted to Murphy my deep wish to have met Berlin himself. I brought up the famous incident of 1944, in which Winston Churchill confused Isaiah with Irving Berlin—and not, as some have put it, the other way around.

By then, Isaiah Berlin (known in his family as Shaya), having witnessed the Bolshevik Revolution, had worked for the British Embassy in New York and for the British Information Services. His brilliant reports were legendary, and he was known in London and Washington political circles as a shrewd student of diplomacy. Apparently, Churchill, at his wife's request, invited Irving Berlin, composer of "White Christmas," to a small party. Churchill sat next to him, assuming he was the political thinker, and asked: "Mr. Berlin, what's the most important piece of work you've done for us lately, in your opinion? Do you think Roosevelt will be re-elected this year?" Irving Berlin answered: "Well, in the past I've voted for him myself. This year, I'm not sure." Churchill: "Mr. Berlin, when do you think the European War is gong to end?" Berlin: "Sir, I shall never forget this moment. When I go back to my own country, I shall tell my children and my children's children that in the spring of 1944 the prime minister of Great Britain asked me when the European War was going to end."

As it turns out, Murphy told me, Isaiah Berlin had written for the *Atlantic*—specifically, a 1949 review of one of Winston Churchill's books. Murphy proceeded to go to the archives; he dug out a letter and handed me a photocopy of it as a present. I read it right then and there, and immediately recognized Berlin's voice: candid, pungent, well organized. In it, Berlin responded to editorial questions posed to him, and talked about, among other topics, the Cold War, American labor unions, Churchill, and the Irving Berlin misunderstanding.

I knew that Berlin had been a prolific correspondent and that Murphy's present was but a pebble on a long stretch of beach. Henry Hardy, a fellow at Wolfson College in Oxford—which Berlin was instrumental in founding—and the tireless editor of Berlin's papers, now has released *Isaiah Berlin, Letters 1928–1946*, the first of what promises to be a triptych of invaluable epistolary volumes. It commences with Berlin's first letter to G. K. Chesterton, and concludes with a letter from the British Embassy in Washington just as he is about to return to Oxford a year after World War II ended, to become an academic. In between are revelatory letters from London, Oxford, New York, Washington, Moscow, and Leningrad to his parents, friends (including Marion Frankfurter and Stephen Spender), and colleagues (Maurice Bowra), and to admired strangers (Ursula Niebuhr)—all written with enviable acumen. Maybe the age of email has brought us all a bit closer, but a quick glance at this book is all one needs to conclude that it also has made us less careful about style and syntax.

The book includes numerous zesty confessions. "Life is not worth living unless one can be indiscreet to intimate friends," as Berlin once said. The Churchill anecdote is recounted in it, as well as scores of others. The result is a map to Berlin's heart before he reached the age of thirty-nine. Hardy includes, among other items, photographs, chronologies, family trees, glossaries, facsimiles, samples of his dispatches from Washington, some of his essays on freedom and Zionist politics, and book reports that he made for the British publisher Faber & Faber. (The footnotes alone are copious. Indeed, if this collection is said to have a limitation, it is found in the overzealousness of its editor: Hardy believes that everything needs to be annotated and contextualized—to the point of dizziness.)

Without Hardy, Berlin's reputation today would be far smaller. As a trustee of his estate, he has, alone, edited a dozen books of Berlin's work (this one included), and has co-edited a couple more with Aileen Kelly and Roger Hausheer. Yes, Hardy's devotion may verge on the pathological. I've even heard folks ask: has he become Berlin's slave? But the answer is no. He is to Berlin what James Boswell was to Samuel Johnson: at once a keeper and a sharer of the master's legacy.

Anyway, for those us who never had a chance to meet Berlin, *Letters* is a way to summon his ghost. The book opens with a plea by Berlin to those with letters to please forward them to Hardy so that he can include them in the subsequent volumes. Of course, I've already sent him a photocopy of the photocopy that Cullen Murphy gave me.

Becoming a Book at Forty

I'VE BEEN ASKED, TIME AND AGAIN, why I published *On Borrowed Words,* my memoir about language and identity in the Mexico of the 1960s, at the age of forty. Isn't that an unquestionably tender age? Is the author capable of mature reflection when so much of what is being narrated remains so close in time, when so many of the protagonists are still around, ready to scream and shout?

The answer I gave to one interviewer after another, and to inquisitive readers in public forums, might not be altogether satisfying. In all honesty I told them that ever since I was a child I've been haunted—and hunted—by a feeling that death is just around the corner. Where does this feeling come from? Might I be able to pinpoint a specific traumatic event that catapulted the nightmares I've had over the years that the next airplane flight or automobile ride is likely to be the last?

In *On Borrowed Words* I make a haphazard list of the dreams and nightmares that populate my life. None of the ones I convey is directly connected to what I would describe as the "death-isn't-too-far" feeling. Truth is, I can't identify the single sequence that conveys, in my mind, the anxiety I'm inhabited by. The closest I come, in the memoir itself and also in conversations with friends, is a description of my father's career as an actor as an antithesis of my choice to devote my life to literature. My father is the happiest person on stage; otherwise, his existence is marked by a sense of general unhappiness. Those instants in front of the audience are thus precious: he lives, and dies, for them. The writer's path hardly offers a similar compensation. It is mostly a life in solitude, away from the vociferousness of human affairs. It is a life shaped by memory and the imagination, isolated, full of demons. If and when an essay reaches its reader, it does so in equal isolation, in a place and time unknown to the writer.

The pleasure of literature is based precisely on serendipity: encounters happen, and a dialogue is established . . . but when and where remain questions. Whereas my father's fascination with the stage offers an instant reward, a reward that is instantaneous and only happens in the present tense, writing is about postponement, about the procrastination of that reward. Therein, in a nutshell, the clue to my having chosen literature, and not theater: what I write is not for the present only but for the many presents contained in the future. I envy my father's reward, but I prefer to embrace an art whose effect, with any luck, will outlive me.

Or will it? The moment a book of mine is released, and the instant the first copy, the one "hot off the press," as editors like to describe it, reaches my hand, my immediate reaction is ambivalence. I assume it is the same with most writers: I've been impatiently waiting for the moment to arrive, but now that it has, I have strange misgivings. Why did I decide to include an essay that is part of the volume? It is the weakest link. Or else, I browse through the pages and oops, a syntactical uncertainty takes place. Why did I write "nothing works like excess" and not "excess is the rule"? Somehow, I get the sense of being half naked. Is this the way readers will know me? English isn't my first language—it isn't even my second—but couldn't I have done better anyhow?

This is what went through my mind when the early copy of *On Borrowed Words* arrived at the door, though only partially. No other volume I've published has generated in me as much inner turmoil as this one. I suppose the reason has to do with its nature: to embark on an autobiographical quest, I know now, is one of the toughest challenges in a writer's journey. Autobiography is, needless to say, an embattled genre. In recent years, more than one practitioner has claimed to have been "misquoted" in his own autobiography, and the "unauthorized autobiography" has also become a humorous modality. In my case, where the only "ghost" writer is the writer himself, ethereal and not-quite-from-this-earth as he is, all misquotes are my own, obviously.

The publication of *On Borrowed Words* was scheduled for mid-August 2001. My personal copy arrived in the last days of July. My first reaction was to hide it. I've never experienced anything similar: whenever a volume of mine arrives, I go around, happy as a toddler, showing it to my wife, children, and friends. From whom was I hiding? A simple answer: from myself. The cover was exquisite, the design superb, the prose was infused with the smooth, harmonious paste I sought while drafting one version after another. So it wasn't the quality. What bothered me was . . . well, the sheer materiality of the item. It existed because I could touch it. And it was mine, no doubt, because on the inside back jacket my black-and-white photograph was on display.

I stored my copy behind a couple of hefty dictionaries in my library and didn't say a word to anyone. Late that night, when everyone was asleep, I went up and rescued it. I held the book in my hands. A set of questions invaded my consciousness: Is this it? How did you manage to shrink—to simplify, really—forty years of your life into 263 brief pages? And why did you write it in English? Have you betrayed yourself by publishing this narrative the way it is? This is what you chose to leave behind for your children, your relatives, and the readers of today and tomorrow? Haven't you done a disservice to yourself? What about the scores of nightmares you don't list? What about your mother and sister: there are lengthy chapters on your grandmother Bela Stavchansky, your father Abraham, your brother Darián, and on you of course, but where is your mother Ofelia and your sister Liora? And are you certain that using language as leitmotif—your travels from Yiddish to Spanish to Hebrew to English—isn't another falsifying device?

Inauthenticity (*la sensación eterna de inautenticidad*) is a feeling I've lived with since I was little. I was born and raised Jewish in Mexico, but am I truly a *mexicano*? I immigrated to the United States in the mid-1980s and automatically became a Latino, but will I ever be taken for one? And— a crucial query—do I *really* care? I don't, actually. My inauthenticity is a source of strength and even uniqueness. Why be a nondescript insider when everything in you, your skin color, your name, your background, points in the opposite direction?

The origins of *On Borrowed Words* date to 1993, when, at the request of an important quarterly, I wrote an autobiographical essay entitled "Lost in Translation." The piece was published the following year, received favorable notices, and was reprinted in various anthologies. An editor at W. W. Norton read it and believed it was the seed for a more sustained meditation on issues like polyglotism and translation, as well as religion in Latin America. The concrete, and final, title of the autobiography came to me at that stage, when only the essay was available. For decades I've admired authors whose stand in the world isn't promoted by a New York agent. Indeed, agents make me crawl. Somehow, though, I got involved with one, and the book was sold, not to the W. W. Norton editor, but to one at Viking.

At the start, my relationship with the acquisitions editor was productive: we met several times for lunch, and he and his wife came for a visit at Amherst. I agreed with him to a one-year manuscript delivery. In my mind I knew perfectly well what the memoir would contain, the way it would start and end, the fractured narrative skeleton I wanted it to have . . . But every time I made an attempt to write, I simply couldn't. I've never suffered from writer's block. In fact, I just read a not-long-ago-sent email telling me it wouldn't be an altogether harmful idea to endure one: only that way would he have enough time to keep up with my "oeuvre." *Oeuvre* to me sounds posthumous. I answered: who needs time to read posthumous books? Anyway, in a day there are usually more words pouring out of me than I myself can handle . . . but not when I wanted to produce a draft of *On Borrowed Words*.

Voice messages accumulated: Ilan, how is the memoir coming

along? You promised to mail me a chapter several weeks ago. How come I haven't received anything? Frankly, I'm starting to worry. Should I not? Naturally, the answer was yes, you *should* be worried. I too am worried and cannot for the life of me explain what's stopping me from downloading the narrative from my mind to the screen. But the editor took another position: instead of agonizing with the production staff over a delay, he announced that it was time for him to visit me again in my small New England town. He and his wife wanted to enjoy the autumn foliage, so could I book him a room in a local hotel?

It is often said that the devoted editor is an endangered species. The publishing industry is under such pressure to generate income for the huge corporations that have bought one company after another, that no one has time to spend with authors and books anymore. Indeed, it is emphasized that among those involved in the business of making, selling, and enjoying books, the only ones who seldom read are editors. The assessment is accurate, and yet I've been blessed with a number of dutiful, faithful *apasionados,* with whom I've developed more than one solid relationship, of which I'm extremely proud.

During his weekend visit, the editor and I took long, meditative walks on a bicycle path not far from home. On one of these walks, I finally confessed to my writer's block. Not surprisingly, the editor was unfazed: "I knew that much . . ." In a semi-analytic mood, he prompted me to explain, to myself and to him, what was keeping me at bay. After much soul-searching, I finally told him that the act—and art—of writing one's life as if events had been closed and buried was making me uncomfortable: "For the first time in my life, I can't seem to be able to write in the past tense." His reaction was nothing short of enlightening: so why not write the memoir in the present—e.g., as if your life was unfolding before your eyes right now?

In retrospect, it seems like a mundane literary answer. Why didn't I think of it first? Answer: I don't know. What I do know is that, from that weekend on, I stopped fooling around at the desk, looking for subterfuges that would take me away from the computer. Yes, suddenly I began to write . . . As it happens, each of the six chapters in *On Borrowed Words* begins and ends in the present. The bulk of the narrative is told in the past tense, but only after the proximity of events has been established.

But I wasn't finished with the process, and the process wasn't finished with me. Soon after, I received an invitation to deliver three formal lectures. If I accepted, this would force me to put aside other literary responsibilities, including the memoir. After my long struggle, should I agree to it? As is often the case, the invitation was all the more enticing because it came with a generous monetary offer attached. Plus, I was notified around then that I had been awarded a Guggenheim Fellowship. I thought the best way to concentrate on the lectures, and to make use of the money, was to relocate for a year in London, where I would be able to write more freely. I looked forward to the idea of removing myself from my environment, of having a distance from my daily routine, an aspect, needless to say, invariably useful as one explores the inner self. And so with neither agony nor delay, I rang the editor at Viking the next day and told him to officially postpone my delivery date.

The family moved to London in July. Of course, in so enchanting, so stimulating a place, who wants to write? I spent the first several months as far away from any desk as possible, traversing the country, wandering across Spain and Greece . . . I was regularly visited by feelings of remorse. I realized my rendezvous was up when, suddenly, I began to have nightmares. In one, a close friend from my adolescence, Marcos Reznik, who died tragically in his early twenties, showed up unannounced at a party. He looked concerned. In the dream I spotted him from far away. "I haven't seen Marcos in years," I told myself. I began to walk toward him. He too recognized me. When we were face to face, he handed me a locked treasure box made of dark wood. "For you . . ." I thanked him. I then asked him for the key. "It's been lost for ages," he answered. At that point I woke up in despair.

In another nightmare I was in my paternal grandmother's house. When I was a kid I stayed overnight with Bobe Bela several times. At one point, I asked my parents not to take me there anymore. The explanation I gave them is that I had a recurrent dream in her house, in which my sister Liora got decapitated by a car with everyone inside it, my father and mother, my brother and me, and Bobe Bela. In the nightmare I had in London, I returned to Bobe Bela's house after her death, which had taken place several months ago. It was my first visit to the place since I was a kid, and I was scared. Without warning, the floor began to tremble. "An earthquake," I heard someone say. I sought a table under which I could cover myself, but there wasn't enough time. Soon the walls began to crack and crumble, furniture and utensils fell all over. When I woke up my heart was beating fast.

I often dream at night, but the content and persistence of the London nightmares scared me to the core. I realized that these dreams were directly connected with *On Borrowed Words:* somewhere in my subconscious there were messages ready to emerge, emotions and thoughts in need of articulation. I often found myself sitting down in a coffee shop on Finchley Road, scribbling notes on sheets of paper. And as soon as

I finished drafting the lectures, I *literally* forced myself to return to the memoir. This isn't a figure of speech: my discomfort with the nightmares increased. No book I've ever done has generated in me such conflicted sentiments. I'm allergic to literature-cum-therapy, and in no way did I want my autobiography to become a substitute for a couched therapist. On the other hand, the need to turn my family and me into characters in a narrative was an obligation I needed to fulfill.

But again, why do so *en el mezzo del camino* and not toward the end? Until each of the chapters acquired its final shape, my answer was instinctual. My original intention was Quixotic: I wanted to write a polyglotic memoir: the early portion of my life lived in Yiddish (school, my relationship with the immigrant generation in the Jewish community) would be drafted directly in Sholem Aleichem's tongue; the portion lived in Spanish (street life, my discovery of Mexico) would be in Cervantes' tongue—and, as in an engraving by the Dutch painter M. C. Escher, the Hebrew characters in the early part would subtly mutate into the Romanic alphabet without the reader ever noticing it. Then Hebrew (the language of Zionism and Israel, where I spent formative years) would set in, again in a skillful, nondescript way. And the memoir would conclude with a portion written in English, the language I've embraced since I moved to the United States. In short, an autobiographical reflection on language drafted in four different tongues . . . Obviously, neither my Viking editor nor any other one in his right senses would endorse such obtuse idea. A multilingual volume like the one I had in mind would require an equally multilingual reader, versed in the same languages the author is familiar with. How many of these are out there? Not enough to make the project commercially feasible.

I needed to choose a language, sure. Or better, a language needed to choose me. There was never any doubt that English would be the one: it is the only one I've made mine by opting for it freely; my relationship to the other three was more accidental. But my connection to English was undergoing a radical transformation. I had arrived in New York with only rudimentary—*primitive* is a better adjective—skills to speak, read, and write it. Nevertheless, in the last fifteen years I had become more and more Americanized. This meant that I had become more comfortable in and with the English language. My accent, although still palpable (as I hope it will always be), was not an obstacle anymore.

Instead, it had become an asset in my communication with others: yes, I was a foreigner, a non-native speaker, but I had done everything possible to master as indomitable an animal as the tongue of Dr. Johnson. I had studied its historical development and spent hours tracing syntactical roots. In a way, I had become a convert. Everyone knows that a convert to a religion is often better versed in the tradition than those people born into the faith. I was a convert to English: I had sought to be adopted by it, and to achieve my objective, I had immersed myself in the beauties of its past. But this brought along a few degrees of separation from my other tongues: Spanish remained present, but it was second to English, and Yiddish and Hebrew followed behind. I never gave up any one of them, but my attention was focused on improving my English-language skills to the degree possible.

I had an urgent desire to write the memoir *before* most traces of my foreignness disappeared altogether. I wanted *On Borrowed Words* to be a volume about *becoming* an American and not about *having become* one. My practical solution to the idea of a multilingual memoir was to make the book not about language per se—not even about one particular language, such as English—but about translation. That is, it would be written in English, but the reader would experience the prose as if through a veil. The closest image I'm able to come up with is that of a translated manuscript whose original has been lost, as in the case of *Don Quixote of La Mancha*. The authentic author—if "authenticity" is at all possible in literature—is one Cide Hamete Benengeli. Miguel de Cervantes, or else his narrator, comes across the manuscript detailing the adventures of the Knight of the Sad Countenance and his squire in a market in Toledo, which, by the way, used to be Spain's capital. Although *On Borrowed Words* doesn't indulge in devices that suggest the mythical existence of a palimpsest, in my mind as I wrote it I felt the narrative was being translated from some ur-language.

The nightmares I had only increased as the first draft was about to be completed. In order to stop the flux, I decided to write at night and not during the day. The effect of this decision was important: most of the book was composed in a state of tiredness. I discovered that to write while exhausted allowed my defenses to come down and the raw emotions to emerge in a more crystalline form. In retrospect, this method was a revelation: today I still prefer to write at night. It makes me feel closer to the core of my material.

Soon I realized that the nightmares I had were announcements: *On Borrowed Words* was prompting me to revisit my past in a way I had not foreseen, to see long-gone friends and relatives again, to enter places where I had spent my early life. I assume this is typical of the genre. But I wanted more . . . How had the places and faces changed? Would it be an act of cowardliness to physically return to the classrooms of Der Yiddishe Shule and the yards of Universidad Autónoma Metropolitana-Xochimilco? On an impulse, I booked a flight to Mexico. I drove to the old familiar places. I also wandered, incognito, in sites where Mexican Jews gather together, among them the Kehilá Nidje Israel and the Centro Deportivo Israelita. My reaction was one of shock: antiquated buildings were not only falling apart, but had been turned into government offices; and schoolmates were . . . well, yes, as consumed by the passing of time as I was.

In a future trip, when the memoir was already out, I visited, along with my wife Alison and my mother, other sites in downtown Ciudad de México, where the first Ashkenazic immigrants had originally settled: the community center on Calle Tacuba #15; the first Mikvah, where women went for their ritual bath; the apartment complex where my father Abraham went for first grade; the building where the Holy Office of the Inquisition tortured its victims; and the corner of the Alameda Central where *judaizantes,* proselytizing Jews accused by the Inquisition, were burnt at the stake in public autos-da-fé. Some of these places I already knew, others were new to me.

These locations are only indirectly related to me: they were the stage on which the Yiddish-speaking immigrants from Eastern Europe—my ancestors, among them—performed their first acts in this foreign land in the last third of the nineteenth century and during the first third of the twentieth century. During the last decade, a woman under the name of Mónica Unikel, a schoolmate of mine, had come up with the idea of organizing a tour of *el México judío.* As it happens, hers was a response to the increasing demand by American Jewish tourists to trace the roots of the various world Jewish communities. My reaction to Unikel's tour was one of delight and affirmation. I was part of that story, and that story was part of me.

That, unfortunately, wasn't the case with my impromptu visit, on my own terms, to Der Yiddish Shule and other personal locations. Why on earth had I chosen to return? Not for the purposes of research, since most of the information I needed I had acquired through interviews. So then . . . why? I don't have a clear answer. I surely wished I hadn't set foot in them again. The past is suspended in our memory. The moment we return to familiar sites, those memories, as in a kaleidoscope, change their shape. The impact of what we see today revives ghosts long gone; it reinvigorates them by placing them in new settings. But they belong to their place in yesteryear, not in the present. In fact, we're carrying out a transgression of sorts, anachronistically placing figures who belong to different frames in circumstances that don't belong to them.

Upon my return to London, I submerged myself frantically in the memoir. By March it was finished and ready to go to the editor. Except that, unexpectedly, I was informed by my agent that the acquisitions editor had been fired not too long ago. The news shook me. I realized my autobiography was an orphan. I couldn't have known that this was only the beginning of its editorial odyssey. The editor's boss, a respected British businesswoman, quickly took over. She emailed me: "Send me the manuscript right away." When *On Borrowed Words* arrived, she was dissatisfied . . . Why a memoir in translation? You know perfectly well English-language readers dislike translations, don't you? Then her father was suddenly taken ill, and for almost six months there was no communication whatsoever. The cruelest way I know to approach an artist is through silence. I agonized in those months. Why hasn't she called me? Should the volume be taken to another editor? A day after a prominent profile of me was featured in the *New York Times,* a message from the Viking editor was on my voicemail: "Ilan, apologies for my absence but my father passed away not long ago. I finally had enough time to read *On Borrowed Words*. It's simply terrific! You've written a marvelously honest, thought-provoking, powerful book. And blah-blah-blah." From that moment on the process was smooth and unimpeded.

Even though the tale is never told sequentially, the narrative starts in Nove Brudno, Poland, in the 1890s and concludes the moment I become an U.S. citizen in 1994. My initial nervousness hasn't disappeared altogether. Every time I see a copy, every time I think of it, I'm thunderstruck by a feeling of betrayal. So this is me, eh! How did I manage to become a book? Is the reader able to recognize the masks I've built in order to hide behind? It's clear I'm a liar, or is it not?

Of course it is: a liar not to others but to myself.

Keeping a Notebook

❦

KEEPING A NOTEBOOK is a way to trust myself. Over the years I've accumulated a number of them and still see them as chapters of the same endeavor. They are usually Mead Composition books, 100 sheets or 200 pages, 9¾ × 7½ in / 24.7 × 19.0 cm, wide ruled.

I mostly write in long-hand, not cursive. Somehow, I feel this old-fashioned method allows me to be more in touch with certain currents of thought in my mind. A plethora of ideas emerge at any point during my day. The question is, which are worth writing down and which are not? The only way to find out is to stamp them on a notebook page, to see them relate to one another.

I am known for writing all the time: morning, afternoon, and evening. But I only devote the late hours of the night to my notebook. I start writing it when I'm exhausted and all other duties have been completed. It's good to have my defenses down!

In my notebook I use any pencil or pen at my disposal, whatever color. I seldom compose full-fledged paragraphs. Instead, I do all sorts of tricks. I might note the title of a book I want to read, or someone's telephone number on the upper corner of the page, or I might paste in old postcards and photographs (à la W. G. Sebald), as well as newspaper clippings. Or I might draw a doodle.

The technique I use in my notebook writing is through marginalia. I don't write in straightforward fashion but in waves. An idea shows up and becomes a line. I then cross it out and put another one on top, add several below or on the side, and so on. I let myself enjoy non sequiturs.

To others my notebook might appear to be a messy, incoherent affair. Besides, I don't like my notebook to be read by strangers. To me the accretion of material (in Talmudic fashion) distills truth. Truth is what literature is about: the conviction that through words, not just any words but *the right* words, and whatever else accompanies them, I might reach the essence of things.

While browsing through my notebook (and I do it often, at different hours of the day), I realize there are plenty of lists—to-do lists, lists of students' names, lists of archaic words. Here's a list of my books about to be published or those which are on the front burner:

The Norton Anthology of Latino Literature (anthology)
Mr. Spic Goes to Washington (graphic novel, with Roberto Weil)
American Immigrant Writing (anthology)
Gabriel García Márquez: A Biography (2 vols.)
And Thou Shalt Love (book-length Q&A, with Mordecai Drache)
Cesar Chavez: A Pictorial (young adult)
Twentieth-Century Latin American Poetry (anthology)
Borges and the Jews (book-length essay)
Hispanic Anti-Semitism (book-length essay)
Rebellion in the Backlands, by Euclides Da Cunha (introduction)
Remapping La Hispanidad (book-length Q&A, with Iván Jaksic)

Sometimes these lists become an end in and of themselves. I never return to them in the notebook. However, on most occasions, each of the items listed acquires an independent status at a later date.

For the purpose of explaining how I use my notebook in my literary life, I will follow one example. My notebook was essential in shaping my graphic novel *Mr. Spic Goes to Washington.* It was in its pages where I first conceived the project, which eventually evolved into a book. There is an entry that reflects on two words that struck me: Spic and Span: "I could use them as names in a Marx Brothers parody."

I listed some possible titles for this parody: *Spic and Span at the Bullfight* or *Spic and Span Dancing Salsa.*

Next I discarded Span and kept Spic. I wrote: "A graphic novel with Spic as protagonist?" There are lines about a possible plot: Spic is described as a *mestizo,* a gang member with several deaths on his conscience. I began to think of Art Spiegelman's *Maus I and II.* "Nooooo," the notebook argues, "it needs to be more contemporary." Several pages later I imagined Spic's adventure as a cautionary political tale. "Maybe a parody of the 1939 movie *Mr. Smith Goes to Washington,* with Jimmy Stewart." Within a few pages, the novel's title spontaneously came to me.

Some notes on renting the DVD of Frank Capra's movie are then recorded in my notebook. I downloaded the movie poster, printed it, and stapled it on a page. I wrote about a restless night, trying to reconcile sleep while thinking about the plot. "A critique of ethnic politics in twenty-first-century U.S."

In my notebook, I was able to reconcile what came next. I wrote an email to my friend and one-time collaborator, Lalo López Alcaraz, with whom I did a comic book, *Latino USA* (2000). He loved the idea and suggested I approach Spic as S.P.I.C., an acronym for Samuel Patricio Inocencio Cárdenas. A provocative response!

I began to explore some scenarios, such as Spic in East L.A., Spic at the Jefferson Memorial in Washington, D.C., Spic at the Senate. "A comedy?" I wasn't sure where the plot was taking me. I imagined it would be ninety pages. Looking for a cartoonist to collaborate with (at the time, Alcaraz, a top choice, was going through a nasty divorce and struggling with substance dependency) would be a challenge. "Ninety pages: a manageable number," I wrote in my journal.

Now that I am going through my journal, I notice a short list of names of potential cartoonists. Before I contacted anyone, I wrote several pages of content in my notebook. It came to me fast and furiously. In fact, I have a note to myself that I wrote it in two hours. I don't think the verb *to write* is even appropriate. I felt as if the material was dictated to me from above.

In my notebook, I made some doodles (of course, none good enough to become part of the book): a muscular Spic, Spic with mustache and bandana, Spic with a tattoo. Next to one I penciled: "Yes, mucho humor!"

In a brief line, I penciled some thoughts about an email conversation I had around that time with Richard Nash, the editor-in-chief of Soft Skull.

I wrote, "Richard has been recommended to me by Bob Arellano."

Bob Arellano, a Cuban American writer in New Mexico who was educated at Brown, was then doing a graphic novel himself, which he asked me to blurb. I responded positively and suggested I might want to do one myself, and he suggested that I speak to Richard.

Arellano led me to two of the three artists he had worked with. I interviewed them. In the notebook, I detail a conversation I had with one: "He seems difficult. Will something come out of it?" I didn't explain it further, but the connection with that artist (inflexible and snobbish) went nowhere.

Some pages later, I stated that my Boston friend Gerardo Villacres, who is on the editorial board of the newspaper *El Planeta,* as well as his colleague Javier Marin, recommended Roberto Weil, a syndicated cartoonist from Caracas. I printed some of Weil's images from the Web, pasted them into my notebook, and wrote comments around them.

I met Weil via email, not long after I wrote this comment. There is nothing in the notebook about my first encounter with him, nor about the type of relationship we eventually forged. I devoted space to other interests, such as a play called *The Disappearance* based upon my short story and the drafting of my biography about Gabriel García Márquez. I then returned to the content of the graphic novel. I polished the material I had already written, then speculated on its value before sending it to Weil.

Here's one segment from my journal:

Page 15 [three panels]: Panel A: A line at the bottom reads: "Senator Samuel Patricio Inocencio Cárdenas arrives at Ronald Reagan Airport." Spic is carrying suitcases. He has his big crucifix hanging from his chest. His t-shirt has a quote: "I know you're here to kill me. Shoot, coward! You're only going to kill a man—Ernesto 'Che' Guevara." Panel B: seated in a taxi (the Capitol is in background) while talking to the Pakistani cab driver. Spic asks the driver: "Many foreigners in the capital?" The driver responds: "No one is a native in America any more!" Panel C: Spic leaving a grocery store named Easy Mart. Spic thinks, "No hay chiles. Las tortillas son de plástico. Jesús, why have you forsaken me?"

In my notebook I added: "Ask Roberto if the image is too cinematic. Can he make it look as reminiscent? Am I thinking these images in the right way? What's the difference between a graphic novel and a screenplay? And what's the difference between writing a novel and writing a graphic novel? It has to be dramatic. Anyway, wait for his answer."

Here's another segment:

Page 63 [two panels]: Panel A: In his delirium, Spic falls asleep. He is visited by "Ché" Guevara. Ché Guevara says: "I don't care if I fall as long as someone else picks up my gun and keeps on shooting." Then there's apparitions of Abraham Lincoln, who says: "I'm a firm believer in the people. If given the truth, they can be depended upon to meet any national crisis. The great point is to bring them the real facts." And an apparition of Cesar Chavez, who says: "Love is the most important ingredient in nonviolent work." Spic says: "Jijole, is there a way to address Latino issues that isn't through radicalism? I thought I had left that strategy on campus years ago. And is there a significant leader in our community that isn't also a martyr? Death is always lurking in back . . . Those that accept the status quo are ineffective. And those that don't are summarily eliminated in a blinker!" Panel B: Spic wakes up, although he's still in his sleep. He looks around: the Senate is filled with other historical figures: Fray Bartolomé de Las Casas, Thomas Jefferson, Emiliano Zapata, Noam Chomsky, Evita Perón, Fidel Castro, Hugo Chávez. Next to them are still Lincoln and Chavez.

The entry is followed by this line: "This might be too ethereal. Will the reader grasp the fact that Spic, as a character, is going through a crisis?"

Soon after, I seem to have begun emailing portions of the content to Weil because more or less from this point on, *Mr. Spic Goes to Washington* was no longer mentioned in any detail in my notebook. I moved the gestation of the book out from its pages to a one-on-one relationship with Weil and, subsequently, with Nash, who ultimately acquired the graphic novel and published it in August 2008.

My notebook is the perfect space to experiment. Whenever a Mead Composition Book is complete, I store it away in a special place in a room on the third floor of my Amherst house, where I keep my correspondences, manuscripts, and other documents. I make sure to date the first page. The journals which I've quoted here span from May 2005 to March 2008. Oftentimes, I pull out a notebook to see what I thought about an idea. This back-and-forth enables me to see how I conceived an idea.

And I buy another notebook. They are easy to find in any stationery store. Their black-and-white cover looks like a marble stone. (I bought the one I'm describing a while ago. It cost me $1.99 at CVS Pharmacy.)

I don't intend for my notebooks ever to be published. I feel naked in them—comfortably naked, yes, but naked nonetheless.

A Critic's Journey

*To create a place for oneself in criticism means
to recreate the genre altogether.*
—WALTER BENJAMIN

I HAVE REACHED AN AGE at which I am sometimes asked how did I
become a critic. This question is usually followed by a more complicated one: what is it that critics do? I have thought about the matters a
great deal and have some answers to offer. These answers pertain to the
crossroads at which the critic often finds himself today.

I remember the first time I wrote a piece of criticism. I wasn't conscious it was an intellectual path I was embarking on then, though. It
was in the early 1980s. I was still in my early twenties, living my Mexican
days. At the time I was a voracious reader of novels but hardly anything
I would now describe as nonfiction. I also read *Vuelta* devotedly, as well
as other monthly magazines and weekly supplements published or
available in Mexico at the time. I especially enjoyed the sections of critical notices in them. These sections were a window through which I
could see what other readers thought of a book I had read or heard
about.

But the notices invariably left me dissatisfied: they were arbitrary,
impressionistic, without a purpose—even servile; their style was inconsequential, abrupt, immature; if they ever embarked on an argument, in
most cases it was still undeveloped by the time one reached the last line.
It struck me that this was an activity that writers took lightly, without
much commitment. Criticism didn't seem to serve a function in these
notices other than to acknowledge the existence of this or that title
recently released. I smelled nepotism, and *compadrazgo* prevailed in the
field: reviewers wanted to pay tribute to a teacher to whom they owed a
teaching position or some sort of cultural job; or they wanted to eulogize their own friends.

There were exceptions, of course: the reviews of Christopher
Domínguez Michael, for instance: his voice was erudite and enlighten-
ing; it was clear that he had come to criticism by choice. (Domínguez
Michael eventually published a valuable anthology of twentieth-century
Mexican narrative.) But this was an exception in a circle that was ama-
teurish and rather unserious. Then one day I decided to put on paper

my own impressions of a book. I had been reading the Spanish translation of *On Kabbalah and Its Symbolism* by the scholar Gershom Scholem. I had not come across any notice of it, which wasn't surprising, because Jewish topics hardly ever make it to print in the Mexican media.

I was ready to be initiated into the field of book reviewing with a volume I was sure would pass totally unnoticed through the intellectual radar. I took my piece on Monday to the office of the editor of *Sábado*, the literary supplement of *Unomásuno*. It was in Colonial del Valle, I think. In any case, I didn't know the editor personally, nor was there any reason he should have any idea who I was. The editor wasn't there, so I left my telephone number. I returned back home and tried to forget about the affair. But I couldn't. In secret, I waited the entire week for a response, but I never got one. My review was published in the next issue.

I don't know exactly what happened after that. Perhaps I should say, then, that I became a critic by sheer stamina. To see myself in print in *Sábado* was a source of excitement, especially for an apprentice with a short yet solid career as a reader but with little by way of fiction to show to others. I decided to write another review, which I left in the editor's office after I was told he wasn't there. It appeared the following Saturday. Then I wrote a longer essay. Again, the same pattern took place. Slowly, I began to hear from readers who had read my pieces. They appreciated the style and sympathized with this or that view. This in turn stimulated me to write more . . .

Is that really the way I became a critic? I'm not sure. Somehow, the feeling I have now is that I never intended to become one. My dream at the time was to become a writer. And what does a writer do? He invents alternative universes though fiction. I was an admirer then of the minimalist stories by Italo Calvino and Borges, and also enjoyed the novels of Victor Hugo, Milan Kundera, and Mario Vargas Llosa. In retrospect, though, I see that I had a trenchant, reflective mind, and that what I enjoyed in literature was its capacity to formulate thought and to tackle ideas from a variety of perspectives.

It is the life of the mind that mattered to me: How does the mind approach the world? How do we react to stimulation from the environment? To what extent do emotions interfere with our judgment? Indeed, novels attracted me but only as sideboards of the ethical, intellectual, and political dimension of the society they sought to represent. I was convinced that the novel was the conduit through which I, like my idols, would be able to explore the human labyrinth. But time has moved me away from the genre; instead, I've become an addict of the literary essay as a form discovered by Montaigne: the highly individualized meditation on a mundane topic that has the potential to become a kaleidoscope for life itself. I am especially fond of one aspect of the essay that has matured in the last fifty years: its promiscuous nature. By this I mean the temptation to always become something else: a novel, a poem, a folktale, even a comic strip or a video.

Anyway, to say that I became a critic by accident is a simplification; it is, clearly, at the core of the person that I am. Still, there is undoubtedly an element of randomness in this and any other affair. For randomness is the rule of life. This is not what biographers often tell us about a person's route: from birth to the grave, a sense of purpose appears to prevail. But this sense is only clear in retrospect, when life is seen as a straight arrow. At the daily level, it is far messier: choices need to be made, which in turn lead to other choices . . . I made a choice at the age of twenty-four that became a turning point: with few intellectual options in Mexico, I decided to immigrate to the United States. My intellectual journey is chronicled in *On Borrowed Words* (2001). From New York I worked as a cultural correspondent for the dailies *Excélsior* and *La Jornada* and also enlisted my services as a translator in an agency at Columbia University. Plus, I became a graduate student, first in medieval Jewish philosophy, then in Latin American letters.

The job of journalist allowed me to further explore my critical tools: in my dispatches I not only described an exhibit I was asked to report on, but sought to reflect on its significance for my readership back in Mexico. This reflective act was the part I thoroughly enjoyed: my role, as I understood it, was not to inform but to explain. My edition of the *New Oxford American Dictionary* states that *to explain* is to "make (an idea, situation, or problem) clear to someone by describing it in more detail or revealing relevant facts or ideas." It then adds: "to account for (an action or event) by giving a reason as excuse or justification." Indeed, *reason* was what I was after: to apply the intellect to map what was taking place around me and to use language to delineate that map. Soon my reading habits began to change as I gravitated toward thinkers like Edmund Wilson who sought to use an accessible language to explain the intellectual currents of their time.

Other figures became equally important, among them Isaiah Berlin. My experience in graduate school was an unhappy one, yet almost in spite of it I was able to come to terms with the mission of a critic. The work by professors was not only unimpressive but also uninspired; in general, it suffered from an unneeded pretentiousness. In various degrees, each of them saw their role as critic in a narrow fashion: their audience was made of scholars and specialists, even when those specialists addressed manifestations of popular culture; and their oeuvre, in and of itself, was not approached as a source of enjoyment but as a doctrinaire lesson in critical theory and trendy textual analysis. These academics resented the intrusion of students in their routine. They saw those students not as the owners of independent minds but as disciples to train in one or another school of theoretical thinking. The academic climate of the time was infused with obtuse jargon. It was invariably difficult to understand what an academic in vogue then wanted to say by arduously reading an essay of his: one had to infer, to suppose, and thus, to stomach a convolute argument that left the reader puzzled. If the prose wasn't clear, it was the reader's duty to unravel it.

Or was it? My job as a correspondent often put me in tension with them: I wrote too lightly (or, as one would say today, too "lite") in the eyes of some, and for a public that ought not to be taken soberly. My classroom recollections of those years are not exciting ones—with one exception: the lessons I took from Gonzalo Sobejano. He was a Spaniard educated in the traditional school, which places emphasis on the equilibrium between form and content in a text and its relationship with the immediate environment. Superficially, Sobejano gave the impression of being a strict, dispassionate teacher and critic; in truth, he was devoted to his students, trusted their intellectual performance more than those of his colleagues, and believed that a good piece of criticism ought to be, above all things, legible. I took memorable classes from Sobejano on Lope de Vega, Quevedo, and Góngora, and under his tutelage read, with pleasure, novels such as *Misericordia* by Benito Pérez Galdós and *La Regenta* by Leopoldo Alas "Clarín." I remember our honest intellectual exchanges affectionately.

The result is that I became a reactionary in graduate school: almost everything I learned in it I ended up rejecting. To this day I retain my antagonistic attitude toward these pseudo-scientific circles. My impression is that literary studies are intellectually bankrupt. These graduate schools have ceased to do what they should do: train students not to subdue their emotions and blindly apply their talents to subscription to a system of thought; instead, they should be provided with tools to engage in open-minded, independent reflections on literature, politics, and society. The time spent in school should be used to give these untrained minds the shape they need to live up to the challenge of mapping the culture they participate in.

Unfortunately, the accepted belief is that literary criticism is a science: it is a systematic examination of texts, subject to predictable laws that might be reached by careful observation; also, that emotions get in the way of objective criticism, tarnishing any claims of impartiality. But literature is, by its very nature, an expression of individual passion; and so is criticism. A poem either ignites in us a spark, or it doesn't; the same goes for fiction and for essays. It didn't take too long to strike me that what I was taught by these abstruse professors was the polar opposite of what I had come across as a reader of magazines and supplements in Mexico a decade ago: one was pseudo-scientific criticism made for a small elite of initiated followers, whereas the other was a form of criticism that was volatile. Too bad, for criticism is essential to the well-being of society.

It was the Romantics who established the purpose of criticism: literature for them was a transcendent agent that offered an indication of the health of the individuals and society that produced it. Criticism is the mode that serves to evaluate the indicator: it is a bridge that enables us to travel between life at its earthy, mundane level and the imagination that it generates. Thus, literature has a function. The critic is an evaluator: his views are always subjective, but they should not be fortuitous. They should be clearly thought-out and presented, and the target audience ought to be the general reader, for it is that general reader who needs to find the bridge between the concrete and the abstract. Matthew Arnold offered a definition that I've come to embrace: criticism, he said, is "a disinterested endeavor to learn and propagate the best that is known and thought in the word."

Disinterested is the correct term: it means to be evenhanded and unbiased, but not dispassionate to such a degree as to be detached. *Learn* and *propagate* announce a double motion: inward-looking and outward-moving. The critic should attempt to understand what a poem means to him and also the reverberations it has for other people; he should explore its inner message but also place it in historical context. And what does Arnold mean by *the best that is known and thought in the world*? He himself adds in 1869: "How much of current English literature comes into this 'best that is known and thought in the world'? Not very much, I fear." The same ought to be said of today and of any other period: it is left to the critic to discriminate—to distinguish between what matters and what doesn't in the labors of his time. Some periods display an astonishing capacity for intellectual concentration, while lightness and dissipation mark others. This is as it should be, and it is left to the critic to evaluate the movement of perpetual systoles and diastoles.

I said that criticism has a function; it also has a value: to serve as a catalyst for pluralism. For criticism is not, I repeat, a mere catalogue of opinions. For it to have an impact, it ought to remain independent. If it is needed, it might express dissatisfaction with the general state of intellectual affairs in a way that is insightful and also productive; or it might gather force behind an idea or esthetic mood to manifest itself spontaneously. This means that politics are an essential component of it. Every work of art is an expression of a political stand in society. It is up to the critic to reflect on that stand and to understand how it interacts with other political viewpoints. Sometimes this means to make conscious an element in the literature that not even its own author was aware of.

The critic, just like the novelist, ought to speak truth to power and to do so in a persuasive, cathartic fashion. That power is not only represented by the government and the economic interests. It is also the established pattern of affairs in his own time. Yes, democracy and criticism, it strikes me, go hand in hand. The critic's role is not to align himself with this or that political party but to take a step back, to be at once an insider and an outsider in the society in which he happens to live. His voice is most useful when it is non-partisan and unprejudiced. This is not to say, of course, that the critic isn't important in political systems other than democracy. In fact, it is when democracy is absent that his voice is most needed: a reflective, challenging voice, a voice of wisdom though dissent.

I came to luminaries like Arnold and others when I realized the type of mediocre career training I was exposed to. Those years in New York were fruitful as a result of the extra-curricular learning I acquired. I would seclude myself in Buttler Library for long hours, wandering around the stacks, here and there picking books I had heard about but no one had properly introduced me to. Obviously, I realize nowadays that that is how one acquires an education: through curiosity and self-direction. The result of my investigations found its way into pieces I sent to the Mexican newspapers and, in the late 1980s, into the supplement *Diario 16* in Madrid, edited at that time by César Antonio Molina. Those years were of financial expansion in Spain, and Molina used the resources to gather a team of international contributors that was astonishingly diverse.

Becoming one of this stable of contributors was thus rewarding, but it also had its drawbacks. Not long ago, while reading *The Condemned Playground,* by Cyril Connolly, I came across this lamentation: "I wish I had been a better critic, and that I had not written brightly, because I was asked to, about so many bad books." At times I too wished I had not wasted so much ink on lower-than-average literature. But one learns through repetition, and those were years of instruction. And repetition is also the method to find one's own style. In another one of Connolly's collections, called *Previous Convictions,* he adds that "writing for a Sunday paper has tempered my improvidence and widened my knowledge," but he complains that, had he escaped "the weekly stint," he might have written "longer and better." I sympathize with the comments: deadline journalism is an invaluable exercise that, when properly digested, imposes on the critic a succinct style and clarity of mind; but it also predisposes his mind toward condensation, a fact one must react against when seeking to explore ideas in all their fullness.

In the previous paragraph I mentioned the term *style*. What style is, and how one recognizes one's own, are questions often asked of novelists. They are also pertinent questions to ask critics. For any important critic cultivates his style with care and precision, hoping to turning it into a template that is as recognizable as a tombstone's epitaph. The oeuvre of Octavio Paz has a hypnotizing effect on me not only because of what Paz has to say on politics, history, and literature, but also because of how he says it. (I've reflected on this hypnosis in my slim volume *Octavio Paz: A Meditation* [2002]).

The same ought to be said about Walter Benjamin, Lionel Thrilling, Irving Howe, and other critics: their style is a signature. In the case of Flaubert, it is at times present when it is most absent; on other occasions, its deliberate artificiality, its baroqueness—as in the case of Nabokov—is what makes it unique. It will be apparent at this point that for the most part my models have not been from the Spanish-language orbit. The reason for this is complicated. I have attempted to explain it, in part, in *On Borrowed Words,* as well as in the introduction to *The Oxford Book of Latin American Essays* (1997). A summary is pertinent in this piece. I shall divide that summary in two: a personal explanation and a cultural one.

The two are intertwined. I had access in the Mexico of my adolescence to an array of works in translation. In the late 1970s and 1980s the nation's publishing and distribution industry expanded tremendously. Books from all over the Spanish-speaking world could be acquired in bookstores like Gandhi, El Sótano, and El Parnaso. The prices were within the reach of at least the middle class, if not also lower social strata. Mexico became a port of entry for world literature. Unfortunately, as I have already mentioned, the criticism produced in the country was of inferior quality. This is not by chance. Each culture shapes its own critical tradition. The Romantics developed in England, France, Italy, and Germany, countries where the Counter-Reformation had an impact. Spain was not among them: as the rest of Europe embraced the Enlightenment with zest, it buried itself in a prolonged age of obscurantism that didn't disappear until fairly recently. The result is that, although from time to time it has had heroic prophets in the area of criticism who played the role of dissenters, Spain took centuries to apply criticism as a pivotal promoter of change.

The Americas have continued this negligible heritage. Masterful figures like José Enrique Rodó, Fernando Ortíz, Alfonso Reyes, Pedro Henríquez Ureña, Germán Arciniegas, Paz, and Carlos Monsiváis, among others, open a window to debate. But the cultural structure of their society doesn't make their intellectual quest a transforming one: they are read by a minuscule elite, and their impact is limited. Indeed, the critic in Latin America has not been an independent figure. The widespread belief is that criticism is destructive: its function isn't to dissect ideas but to dismantle them. In magazines and supplements, a critique of a novel or a collection of poetry that isn't laudatory is considered to be the work of one's enemy. On occasion novelists and poets have taken upon themselves the role of critics, but the overall effect has not been a productive one. Their mission has been to dissect an artistic movement or to eulogize a masterful work of art. I'm thinking, for instance, of José Lezama Lima's disquisition on the baroque style and Vargas Llosa's explorations of *indigenismo* in the oeuvre of José María Arguedas. The explorations are thought-provoking; at times they even generate controversy.

In the end, though, they are of little consequence because they are not seen by society as conducing a widening of the intellect. These two authors stand as giants because of their fiction, not because of their criticism. On the other hand, some of these figures mentioned have spoken truth to power in a way that goes far beyond what is expected of a critic in Europe. At times their lives have been in jeopardy because of their honesty. The critical tradition south of the Rio Grande is independent and also passionate, but it doesn't serve as an indicator of the health of the individual and society. Or better, the fact that it is inconsequential to the larger state of affairs is an indicator of its value.

I learned to be a critic and pondered what a critic does as a Mexican immigrant in the United States. I quickly realized that by virtue of my mobility and bilingual disposition, I was at the vortex of two parallel traditions: the European one and the Hispanic one. This crossroads has become the quintessential *raison d'être* of my endeavor. To a large extent, in the last decade I have reinvented myself: I have ceased to be a Latin American and have become a Latino. What does that entail?

The answer: I have added English to my Spanish as the language of critical exercise; and I have found inspiration in Paz and also Edmund Wilson, T. S. Eliot, and Sainte-Beuve. My move north of the border at a moment when multiculturalism was in vogue and there were heated debates on bilingual education, affirmative action, and the shaping of the Western canon has sharpened my views. Over the years I stopped sending dispatched to *Diario 16* and instead began to write for the *Nation.* This change brought along a different audience: no longer a Hispanic reader at the periphery of culture but a non-Hispanic one at center stage.

To this I ought to add another ingredient about which I've said little so far: my Jewish ancestry. Inquisitiveness is an essential pedagogical component in it. The rabbis in the Talmud do little else: they dissect a topic from a myriad of perspectives, often giving up on a conclusion that solves the tension between opposing ideologies. Independence of mind is at the core: it is less important for a Talmudist to offer a fresh theory on life than to persuade that this or that idea is of value. Often this act of persuasion takes the argument in various directions. Each of these ramblings is called a *midrash,* and *midrashic* is the adjective I would use to describe the education I received as a child, in Yiddish and Spanish. The Harlem renaissance poet Langston Hughes once talked about the art of "wandering while wondering." It is a suitable image to apply to *midrash* thinking: the aim is to let the mind free, to let it explore undisclosed areas, to allow for it to make untamed connections.

My first experience in New York as a graduate student was at the Jewish Theological Seminary. It was there that I read the Talmud and discussed Maimonides and Spinoza. That was a period of intellectual enlightenment. The experience marked me profoundly. A number of religious and theological personalities had passed through the doors of that institution: Abraham Joshua Heschel, Norman Podhoretz, Moshe Idel, Michael Lerner . . . Reading and sometimes meeting them generated in me an attachment toward the so-called New York Jewish intellectuals, especially Howe, Alfred Kazin, and—a bit older than these two—Trilling.

These authors became idols. I traced their paths, read avidly their oeuvres, and studied the way they sought to balance politics and literature, academic and public life. There was in the late 1980s already a feeling that their legacy was in decline and that their presence was in the process of eclipse by multicultural figures such as Henry Louis Gates Jr. and Cornel West. So I looked for continuity between the Jewish and the Black intellectual traditions. What did they have in common? How did they each respond to the stimuli of their time? What kinds of audience did they have in their own ethnic community and beyond? How did they handle the tension between the particular and the universal, between being Jewish and Black and being American and a member of Western civilization?

Since the 1970s, these intellectuals have been absorbed by academic institutions. This absorption poses positive and negative consequences: it enables them to have a steady income, but it also limits their freedom and, what is worse, institutionalizes their manner of expression. Trilling was the first Jew to be granted tenure in the English Department at Columbia University; Irving Howe taught at CUNY for decades; Kazin had teaching stints in a number of colleges and universities; and Gates and West lead the DuBois Institute at Harvard University. There is in my mind a difference between academics and public intellectuals, though. In a nutshell, the public intellectual is not afraid to antagonize. He sees not only the classroom but also the world as his stage. He is weary of specialization, seeking instead to become a generalist who is able to speak about a multiplicity of topics.

History in the United States is built through dissent; the country is thus fertile territory for intellectuals. But a minuscule portion of it is made of Hispanics (what recently has come to be known as Latinos). Why is this so? Latino letters north of the border date back to the forays by Spanish explorers and missionaries in the sixteenth century and continue through the Mexican-American War and the Spanish-American War. They expand intensely in the twentieth century, especially at the time of the Civil Rights Era, as the Chicano Movement made its impact and the struggle for self-determination by Puerto Ricans outside the island came to the fore.

It wasn't until the late 1980s and 1990s, though, that a pan-Latino category came about, one that became an umbrella under which various national backgrounds (Mexican, Puerto Rican, Cuban, Dominican, Colombian, etc.) coalesced. Since then a young generation of novelists and poets has come about under that rubric and, smaller in number but equal in importance, a cast of intellectual figures whose responsibility it is to articulate the predicament of Latinos today. It is crucial to approach this predicament in an open, democratic, interdisciplinary fashion and with independence of thought, stressing the connections with Latin America, the Caribbean, and Spain, on the one hand, and with other minorities in the United States and with the world at large, on the other. It is the responsibility of these figures to offer a cosmopolitan map of Hispanic civilization.

It is in that juncture where I see myself standing: a Jewish, Mexican, and American critic, whose role it is to discuss not only literature but culture at large for a specialized and also a general audience within and beyond the academy. No area of expertise should become a prison. In an "impure" universe such as ours, where the high- and low-brow intersect, where migration is an endless cross-fertilizer, criticism ought to be understood as an intellectual activity that has no boundaries. Since academia is the take-off and landing platform, it is our obligation to reconfigure graduate schools so that the illness of critical theory that empties any form of passion from the cultural act is overcome.

Careful scholarship is much in need: historical analysis and annotated editions of past and present classics. But students should also be taught to find tools to interact with larger segments of society. The countless -isms that have swept the academic environment since World War II, especially post-modern and post-colonial studies, have championed a sense of relativism that is welcome; but their hoopla has had little impact beyond scholarly circles. The widening abyss that separates academia from society is frightening.

In sum, the critic today must be a polymath: his knowledge should be built through addition and not through subtraction. He should read anything and everything that is of interest, not only the portion that belongs to his field. His learning should be encyclopedic but pedantic. This means that he should not speak to readers as if they were inferior or less knowledgeable than he is, for it is clear by now that knowing more doesn't mean being better than others. In this respect, the connection between culture and ethics, and between culture and politics, should always be kept in mind. The critic isn't superior to anybody; he's a mere observer and his observations are valuable in so far as they serve as a mirror. He will often be the subject of misunderstandings.

A frequent question is: how is it that you are granted the voice to speak about matters you have no authority in? The philistines fail to see that that is precisely the point. Nothing ought to be sacrosanct for the critic, but he should not infer that his authority is more than that of an eyewitness. An observer who is also a participant, whose interest in world affairs isn't different from that of anyone else. If the critic's work is to have any value, it is as a record of what people thought, felt, and dreamed in his age. Cyril Connolly, in *The Condemned Playground,* offered a portrait of himself: "What merits I have," he stated, "are somewhat practical and earthy. I stay very close to the text—no soaring eagle but a low-swung basset who hunts by scent and keeps his nose to the ground. . . . Experience develops in the critic an instinct, which, like the water diviner's, agitates him when near to treasure."

For my part, I am no basset. On the contrary, a reviewer once said that "[he] has acquired eyes that can look everywhere, see everything and, more important, unravel what they have perceived." The comment at once flabbergasted and intimidated me. Over the years I have struggled to make it a mandate: to live up to it, to be an eagle—a believer in reason and dreams and poetic invention as our only salvation. Matthew Arnold said that "to have the sense of creative activity is the great happiness and the great poof of being alive, and it is not denied to criticism to have it." But to do so, he argued, criticism must be sincere, simple, flexible, and passionate above all.

Acknowledgments

The essays in this volume were originally published in the following periodicals to whose editors I owe a share of gratitude:

"Who Owns the English Language?" delivered as the Jackie M. Pitzen Lecture, part of the Five College Fortieth Anniversary Professorship, Amherst College, March 29, 2006.

"The Translators of the *Quixote*," *The Los Angeles Times* (December 14, 2003) and *Humanities* (September–October 2008).

"Teaching Spanish," *The Chronicle of Higher Education* (July 29, 2005).

"How Richard Rodríguez Became Brown," *The Nation* (June 17, 2002).

"Death, Drugs, and Narcocorridos," *The Nation* (January 7, 2002).

"Betraying Latino Students," *The Chronicle of Higher Education* (January 20, 2006).

"Jimmy Santiago Baca: From Bondage," *The Nation* (March 4, 2002).

"A *rebozo* for Sandra Cisneros," *The Nation* (February 10, 2003).

"*Sepharad* Is Nowhere," *The Forward* (January 2, 2004).

"The Holocaust in Latin America," *The Chronicle of Higher Education* (May 5, 2001).

"*Forverts* & I," *The Forward* (August 29, 2007).

"Hispanic Anti-Semitism," *The Chronicle of Higher Education* (November 26, 2007).

"*My Mexican Shivah*," *The Forward* (December 26, 2006).

"Is José Saramago an Anti-Semite?" *The Nation* (June 2, 2003).

"*Don Quixote* at Four Hundred," *The Chronicle of Higher Education* (January 7, 2005) and *The New Republic* (February 10, 2005).

"Javier Marías' Hubris," *The Nation* (March 19, 2001).

"The Jews of Sosúa," *The Forward* (January 5, 2008).

"Delano: John Gregory Dunne," foreword to *Delano: The Story of the California Grape Strike,* by John Gregory Dunne (University of California Press, 2008).

"A Master's Voice: Edmund Wilson," *The San Francisco Chronicle* (December 9, 2007).

"Homage to Ryszard Kapuciski," *The San Francisco Chronicle* (July 13, 2007).

"Language and Colonization," *The Blackwell Companion to Latin American Philosophy,* edited by Susana Nuccetelli (Blackwell Publishers, 2009).

"The Unfathomable César Aira," *The San Francisco Chronicle* (July 16, 2006 and March 6, 2007).

"Renegade Bolaño," *The Washington Post* (October 13, 2007) and *The Chronicle of Higher Education* (December 19, 2008).

"Happy Birthday, Señor Neruda," *The Chronicle of Higher Education* (July 2, 2004) and as the introduction to *I Explain a Few Things: Bilingual Poems of Pablo Neruda* (Farrar, Straus and Giroux, 2007).

"Felisberto Is an Imbecile," *The Nation* (October 7, 2002).

"Macondo Turns Forty," *The Chronicle of Higher Education* (June 15, 2007).

"At the Same Time: Susan Sontag," *The San Francisco Chronicle* (April 7, 2007).

"Black Studies vs. Latino Studies," *The Chronicle of Higher Education* (September 19, 2003).

"W. G. Sebald: An Obituary," *The Forward* (December 21, 2001).

"Xeroxing Shaya Berlin," *The Forward* (October 29, 2004).

"Becoming a Book at Forty," *Creative Nonfiction* (2005) and in *Hurricanes and Carnivals,* edited by Lee Gutkind (University of Arizona Press, 2007).

"Keeping a Notebook," *Writers and Their Notebooks,* edited by Diana Raab (University of South Carolina Press, 2009).

"A Critic's Journey," *The Chronicle of Higher Education* (August 9, 2002).